Lived Experiences of Ideologies in Contextual Islam

An Examination of *Ayyaana* Possession Cult in Marsabit County, Kenya

Judy Wanjiru Wang'ombe

© 2023 Judy Wanjiru Wang'ombe

Published 2023 by Langham Academic
An imprint of Langham Publishing
www.langhampublishing.org

Langham Publishing and its imprints are a ministry of Langham Partnership

Langham Partnership
PO Box 296, Carlisle, Cumbria, CA3 9WZ, UK
www.langham.org

ISBNs:
978-1-83973-232-4 Print
978-1-83973-957-6 ePub
978-1-83973-958-3 PDF

Judy Wanjiru Wang'ombe has asserted her right under the Copyright, Designs and Patents Act, 1988 to be identified as the Author of this work.

All rights reserved. No part of this publication may be reproduced, stored in a retrieval system or transmitted, in any form or by any means, electronic, mechanical, photocopying, recording or otherwise, without the prior written permission of the publisher or the Copyright Licensing Agency.

Requests to reuse content from Langham Publishing are processed through PLSclear. Please visit www.plsclear.com to complete your request.

British Library Cataloguing-in-Publication Data
A catalogue record for this book is available from the British Library

ISBN: 978-1-83973-232-4

Cover & Book Design: projectluz.com

Langham Partnership actively supports theological dialogue and an author's right to publish but does not necessarily endorse the views and opinions set forth here or in works referenced within this publication, nor can we guarantee technical and grammatical correctness. Langham Partnership does not accept any responsibility or liability to persons or property as a consequence of the reading, use or interpretation of its published content.

Now
unto the King eternal,
immortal,
invisible,
the only wise God,
be honour and glory
for ever and ever.
Amen.
(1 Tim 1:17 KJV)

Contents

Abstract xv
Acknowledgments xvii
Arabic Transliteration xix
Chapter 1 1
  Background Information to the Study
    Background and Motivation for the Research 3
    Locating the Marsabit Borana Muslims 4
    Religiocultural Background 6
    Research Rationale 7
    Central Concern 9
    Objectives of the Study 10
    Significance of the Study 10
    Delimitations 11
    Limitations 12
    Operational Definitions 12
    Assumptions 13
    Summary 14
Chapter 2 15
  Scholarly Works on Spirits in Islam
    Reasons for Examining the Concept of Jinn 15
    Studying the Concept of Jinn in Islam 17
      Some Scholarly Works on the Concept of Jinn 17
      Interpreting the Qur'anic Verses on Jinn 20
      Jinn in the Hadiths 21
      Some Aspects of Jinn 22
    Jinn Possession in Islam 26
      Islamic Texts on Jinn Possession 26
      Islamic Official Perspective on Dealing with Jinn Possession 28
      Jinn Possession in Contemporary Islamic Contexts 29
    Spirit Possession in African Muslim Communities 34
      Conceptualizing Spirit Possession 35
      Scholarly Approaches to Possession Cults in African
        Islamic Contexts 36
      The *Ayyaana* Cult among Borana Muslims 49

  Islam and African Possession Cults: Clash or
    Accommodation?..53
  Summary..56

Chapter 3 59
Research Methodology
  Introduction 59
  Research Rationale 60
    Phenomenological Design and Theory of Spirit Possession........60
    Cognitive Anthropological Framework.............................62
    Studying Muslims 65
  Anthropology of Islam: The People Factor 66
  Methods Used for Contextual Study of Jinn and Possession in
    Official Islam 69
    Interviewing Muslim Teachers..69
    Analyzing the Interviews 70
  Anthropological Research on *Ayyaana* among Borana Muslims........71
    Steps in Entering the Field Research Setting..................72
    Ethnographic Sampling...73
    Ethnographic Data Collection Methods.........................74
    Ethnographic Interviews...75
    Recording Ethnographic Data 76
    Collecting Language Data 77
    Participant Observation..78
  Data Management: Coding and Use of NVivo Software......................79
  Data Analysis and Interpretation 81
    Analyzing Ethnographic Data...81
    Analyzing Linguistic Data 82
    Religiocultural Domain Analysis....................................83
  Comparative Analysis 84
  Ethical Issues 85
    Permission from National and Local Administration.............85
    Protection and Sensitivity to Human Subjects 85
  Summary..86

Chapter 4 89
The Islamic Model of the Spirit World
  Introduction 89
  Conceptualization of the Spirit World by Muslim Teachers...............90
    God and the Spirit World 91
    Perception of Angels in the Context of *Al-Ghaib*..........93

    Man in the Context of *Al-Ghaib* 94
    Al-Ghaib as the Imaginal World in Official Islam 95
  The Concept of Jinn in Official Islam as Represented by the
    Muslim Teachers 97
    Categorization of Jinn by Muslim Teachers 97
    Attributes and Abilities of Jinn according to
      Muslim Teachers 104
    Man's Relation with Jinn 107
  Jinn Possession as Perceived by Muslim Teachers in Marsabit
    County 110
    Symptoms of Jinn Possession 111
    Reasons for Possession 112
    Dealing with Jinn in Marsabit County 115
  Perception of *Ayyaana* by Muslim Teachers 119
    Ayyaana as Jinn 119
    Epistemological View of the Muslim Teachers regarding
      Ayyaana 121
    Ontological View of the Muslim Teachers
      regarding *Ayyaana* 122
    Perception of the Muslim Teachers regarding
      Warra Ayyaana 124
  Summary 130

Chapter 5 133
*Religiocultural Model of Ayyaana According to Ordinary Borana
  Muslims in Marsabit County*
  Introduction 133
  Conceptualizing *Ayyaana* among Ordinary Borana Muslims 134
    Ayyaana as a Polysemous Word 135
    Ayyaana as Calendric Days 137
    Ayyaana as Fortune 139
    Ayyaana as Spiritual Beings and Cult 140
  Metaphorical and Domain Analysis of *Ayyaana* as Spirits 141
    Ayyaana as *Qileensa Rabbi / Waaqa* 141
    Ayyaana as a *Jeshi* (an Army) 143
    Conceptual Domain of *Ayyaana* as Spirits 145
    Categorizing *Ayyaana* 148
    Descriptive Features of *Ayyaana* 151
    Articulating a Cultural Model of *Ayyaana* 155
  Ayyaana as a "Possession" Cult 156
    Pacification of *Ayyaana* 157
    Subdomain of Intercessory *Ṣalawāt* Prayer 159

  Analyzing the *Salawat* Prayer Sessions 162
  The Subdomain of Healing: Therapeutic Sessions 163
 Summary 168

Chapter 6 171
 Lived Experiences as Instantiation of Religiocultural Model
 Introduction 171
 Dynamism of the *Ayyaana* Model and Lived Experiences 172
 Ritual Experiences of *Ayyaana* Practitioners 173
  Experiences of Female Practitioners in the *Ayyaana* Cult 173
  Initiation Experiences of Practitioners 176
  Positive Perception: Benefits of Being a Practitioner 177
 Ritual Experiences of Ordinary Participants 180
  Induction into the Cult 181
  Socializing Experience with *Ayyaana* 182
 Religious Experiences with *Ayyaana* 183
  Experiencing *Ayyaana* as Local Muslims 184
  As Muslims with Sufi Tendencies 185
  Offering Sacrifices as Local Muslims 186
  Performing *Salawat* as *Dua* 187
  Making the Pilgrimage as Local Muslims 188
  Revering Prophet Muhammad and Sheikh Hussein 189
 Enhancing the Salience of the *Ayyaana* Model through
  Creativity 191
  Ayyaana Songs during *Hadhara* Sessions 192
  Items of *Ayyaana* 194
 Enhancing the Salience of the *Ayyaana* Model through
  Creative Cognition 197
  Creative Borrowing by *Warra Ayyaana* 197
  Creative Anthropomorphism by *Warra Ayyaana* 198
  The Creative Cognition of *Warra Ayyaana* 199
  The Minimal Counterintuitiveness of the *Ayyaana* Concept ... 200
 Summary 200

Chapter 7 201
 Comparative Interdisciplinary Analysis and Theory Formulation
 Introduction 201
 Congruence of the Islamic and *Ayyaana* Models 202
 Variations: The Islamic Model versus the *Ayyaana* Model 204
  Categorization of *Ayyaana* 204
  Variations in Dealing with Spirits 205

    Saliency of the *Ayyaana* Model vis-à-vis the Islamic Model..............206
        The Salience of the *Ayyaana* Model in Promoting *Nagaa* 207
        Increased Salience through Counterintuitive Properties 209
        Formulating the Theory of Experiential Creative Cognition 211
        The *Ayyaana* Cult as a Creative Product 212
        The Experiential Creative Cognition of *Warra Ayyaana*...................214
        Summary...216

Chapter 8 217
    Summary of Findings and Recommendations
        Introduction 217
        Essence and Findings of the Research 217
        Summary of Findings for Research Questions (RQs)..............218
        The *Ayyaana* Model as a Feature of Borana Islam...................224
        Implications for Islamic Studies..225
        Implications for the Anthropology of Islam 228
        Propositions for Further Studies 229
        Summary...231

Chapter 9 233
    Some Missiological Implications for Christian-Muslim Interactions
        Introduction 233
        No Longer the Excluded Middle 234
        Biblical Intepretation of the Spirit World: Included Middle....235
        Imperative of a Missional Response to the Supernaturalistic
            Worldview in African Islamic Contexts 237
        Dealing with Spirits and Spirit Possession in African Islamic
            Contexts 239
        Final Concluding Remarks..240

Appendix 1 241
    The Borana Calendar

Appendix 2 243
    Excerpt from a Conversation between a Practitioner and Ayyaana

Appendix 3 245
    Ashaka's Experience with Ayyaana

Appendix 4 247
    References to Jinn in the Hadith (Bukhari and Muslim)

Appendix 5 251
    Scholars Who Have Studied or Alluded to Ayyaana *and the Sheikh Hussein Cult*

Glossary of Non-English Words 253

Bibliography 257

List of Tables

Table 1: Some Scholarly Works on Spirit Possession among African Muslims...36
Table 2: Categories of Interviewees in Marsabit County 74
Table 3: List of Muslim Teachers Interviewed 89
Table 4: Attributes and Abilities of Jinn..104
Table 5: Perception of *Ayyaana*'s Existence by Muslim Teachers.....................120
Table 6: Perception of *Ayyaana* as Evil Jinn by Muslim Teachers....................120
Table 7: Usage of the Word *Qileensa* (Wind) 142
Table 8: Nomenclature of *Ayyaana* Spirits 148
Table 9: Religious Features of *Ayyaana*...151
Table 10: Behavioral Features of *Ayyaana* 153
Table 11: Participant Observation Schedules of *Salawat* Sessions...................160
Table 12: Islamic Features in *Salawat* Sessions...162
Table 13: Similarities between the Nature of Jinn and *Ayyaana*......................203

List of Figures

Figure 1: Diagram showing the Synthetic Triangular Approach (STA) 68
Figure 2: Stages in the NVivo analyzing process 80
Figure 3: Plan for comparative analysis of models 84
Figure 4: Allah and the created world 91
Figure 5: Semantic relationship of the exalted beings 98
Figure 6: Categories of jinn according to Muslim teachers 99
Figure 7: Characteristics of jinn 106
Figure 8: Comparison of good jinn and *ayyaana* by the Muslim teachers 122
Figure 9: Weighing the Muslim-ness of the *warra ayyaana* 129
Figure 10: Domain of spirits 146
Figure 11: Diagrammatic representation of the religiocultural model of *Ayyaana* 155
Figure 12: Intersection point between *warra ayyaana* and *warra oblia* 159
Figure 13: Episodic sub-model of healing in the *Ayyaana* cult 165
Figure 14: Dynamic relationship between lived experiences and the *Ayyaana* model 172
Figure 15: The place of music and artifacts to enhance the *Ayyaana* model 191
Figure 16: Creative borrowing of elements 198
Figure 17: Different categorizations of *ayyaana* 204
Figure 18: Increased salience of the *Ayyaana* model 206
Figure 19: Formulating the theory of experiential creative cognition 215
Figure 20: Centrality of *nagaa* in the *Ayyaana* cult 225
Figure 21: Tension between the ideological expression of Islam and the lived experiences of ordinary Muslims 226
Picture 1: Items of a weekly domestic session 183
Picture 2: Picture of *ule* carried by *Ayyaana* practitioners 195

Abstract

This dissertation attempts to study the proclivity of Borana Muslims toward the *Ayyaana* possession cult in Marsabit County. The Borana Muslims who participate actively in this cult claim to be authentic Muslims. This claim raises a pertinent question: do their lived experiences comply with the precepts that are stipulated in the Islamic texts concerning the spirit world? This study seeks to answer this question, which has not been given due attention by most contemporary Islamic scholars. There has been an overly skewedness toward the ideological expression of Islam in the heightened need to demystify Islam in the wake of terrorist activities that have turned the limelight on the religion. Yet such a focus does not provide a comprehensive understanding of the lived experiences of local Muslims vis-à-vis the canonical obligations in Islam.

This study thus seeks to bridge this lacuna by describing the lived experiences of Borana Muslims as they engage with spiritual beings within their religiocultural setting. The beliefs and practices involved in the *Ayyaana* possession cult are examined in light of the official Islamic tenets as understood and taught by Muslim teachers in Marsabit County.

A multidisciplinary approach has been employed that uses a cognitive anthropological, theoretical framework. Specifically, this study uses the cultural model theory as proposed by Giovanni Bennardo and Victor de Munck, and it has also adapted part of their methodological suggestions on discovering cultural models. The study has further used the synthetic triangular approach (STA) guideline, proposed by Caleb Kim, in studying religiocultural phenomena among Muslims from an anthropological perspective. The research methods involved in-depth ethnographic interviews and participant observation. The interviewees included both Muslim teachers and Borana Muslims who participate in the *Ayyaana* possession cult. Participant observation of the different *Ayyaana* cult sessions helped to triangulate what the interviewees said. The theory of minimal counterintuitiveness (MCI) has also been used to analyze the findings.

The findings of this study are discussed in four analytical chapters. Chapter 4 describes the Islamic model of the spirit world as constructed by the Muslim teachers in Marsabit County. Chapters 5 and 6 describe the religiocultural model of *Ayyaana* as construed by the Borana Muslims who participate in the *Ayyaana* cult (they are referred to as *warra ayyaana* – *ayyaana* people).

Chapter 7 offers a comparative analysis that shows how the religiocultural model of *Ayyaana* compares with the Islamic model of jinn. It was realized that the two models have some similarities based on the supernaturalistic worldview espoused in Islam. However, the religiocultural model of *Ayyaana* differs significantly from the Islamic model of jinn. The latter is foregrounded in the cognition of the *warra ayyaana*, while the Islamic model is backgrounded. The religiocultural model of *Ayyaana* is found to be more salient and hence easily transmitted, because it is deemed to offer better explanations to their frustrations with supernatural phenomena.

Acknowledgments

I would like to express my most sincere gratitude to my PhD primary supervisor, Prof. Caleb Kim. You have walked with me since my MTh years, and you did not tire to walk with me through my doctoral journey. From the beginning, you believed in me and inspired me to take up the challenge of doctoral studies. It has been an arduous task, yet you have guided me with a lot of patience and love. When ill health set in, you still found time to read and comment on my chapters. You have truly been my inexhaustible source of inspiration, support, patience, and wisdom.

I am grateful to my associate reader, Prof. Robert Carlson. You not only read my chapters but also opened your house for the Cognitive Study Group where I was acclimatized to the cognitive theories that I have used for my theoretical framework.

My gratitude also goes to Dr. Josephine Mutuku. Words cannot express the appreciation I have for the encouragement and motherly kindness you have accorded me. God bless you. Your motherly heart is felt in ISAR (Institute for the Study of African Realities).

I cannot forget to thank my fellow doctoral students and candidates. We have walked this journey together, amid tears and prayers. God has been faithful as we constantly encouraged each other that "this thing is doable." Thanks, too, to other colleagues who took time to read and comment on my chapters. My special thanks also go to Christine Derungs for editing this work. *Asante sana*.

This dissertation could not have been accomplished without my wonderful Borana friends, both Christians and Muslims. I express my gratitude for all the information they availed through the long hours of observation and interviews. Thank you, *obolean* Baraqo Sales, Wario William, Pastor William

Waqo, Joseph Diba, Halkano (Sololo), and Guyato (mama Gideon) for assisting me in collecting data and for translating the interviews for me. *Galatoma, Waaqi isaan ebisin, obolean.*

My dissertation journey was made possible through scholarship from Langham Partnership and ScholarLeaders International. I cannot cease to say thank you for availing these funds over the years. Thank you for enabling me to travel overseas and access the wealth of resources there. I gained a lot from this study visit. God bless all those who gave through these two organizations. It was not only financial support that was availed. I appreciate the prayers and words of encouragement from both staff and supporters of the two organizations.

My family bore the brunt of the load during my years as a doctoral student. My special gratitude is to my dearest husband (*diris kiyya*), Harun Wang'ombe, and my children, Abraham Baraka, Miriam Nuru, and Emmah Neema for their unconditional love, prayers, and dedicated patience. Thanks to my father, the late Mr. Amon Nduati, and my mothers, Mrs. Emily Nduati and Mrs. Miriam Karuku, for your prayers, too. My siblings, Anton Kimani, Dave Kahura, Alice Nyambura, and Susan Gathoni, have been there for me. Thank you very much.

To God most high: what can I say to you, Abba Father? Were it not for your grace, where would I be? *Abbo Waaqa kiyya, si galatesa, si galatesa! Galatom, galatom si jedda!*

Arabic Transliteration

The Arabic words used in this dissertation have been transliterated using a system offered by Kim[1] and Jones[2] as shown in the table below. All the Arabic words have been italicized except for some nouns that have been anglicized.

Arabic Letter	Arabic Name	Transliteration
ا	Alif	ʾ
ب	Bāʾ	b
ت	Tāʾ	t
ث	Thāʾ	th
ج	Jīm	j
ح	Ḥāʾ	ḥ
خ	Khāʾ	kh
د	dāl	d
ذ	dhāl	dh
ر	Rāʾ	r
ز	Zāy	z
س	Sīn	s
ش	Shīn	sh
ص	Ṣād	ṣ

---

1. Caleb Chul-Soo Kim, *Supernaturalism in Swahili Islam: With Special Reference to the Therapeutic Cults of Jinn Possession* (Ann Arbor, Michigan: UMI Dissertation Services, 2001).
2. Alan Jones, *Arabic Through the Qurʾan* (Cambridge, UK: The Islami Texts Society, 2005).

Arabic Letter	Arabic Name	Transliteration
ض	Ḍād	ḍ
ط	Ṭā'	ṭ
ظ	Ẓā'	ẓ
ع	'ayn	'
غ	Ghayn	gh
ف	Fā'	f
ق	Qāf	q
ك	Kāf	k
ل	Lām	l
م	Mīm	m
ن	Nūn	n
ه	Hā'	h
و	Wāw	w
ي	Yā'	y

Vowel Signs

׳	Fatḥa	a
׳	Ḍamma	u
׳	Kasra	i
׳ا	Alif after fatḥa	ā
׳و	Wāw after ḍamma	ū
׳ي	Yā' after kasra	ī

CHAPTER 1

Background Information to the Study

This study is about Borana Muslims' interactions with *ayyaana* in the northern part of Kenya. *Ayyaana* is a polysemous word in *afan Borana* (the Borana language), but it will be used here to denote spiritual beings that are widespread among Borana Muslims. *Al-ghaib* (the realm of spirits) is real to Muslims. It parallels the human world as spirits interact with human beings in diverse ways. The Islamic texts sanction the existence of these spiritual beings, hence necessitating every Muslim to believe that they exist. They experience these spirits incessantly in their daily lives. This interaction, therefore, becomes an integral aspect of their religiocultural setting. It is definitive in the way they practice their Islamic faith. Therefore, studying the interaction of Muslims with the spirit world within specific religiocultural contexts offers a deeper understanding of these particular Muslims.

Those who have delved into such significant studies have illustrated that beneath the veneer of the ideological expression of Islam is another face of Islam that needs to be explored for a better understanding of Muslims. This face has been designated different rubrics such as "popular Muslim piety," "popular Islam," "low Islam," or "unofficial Islam."[1] Apparently, it has attracted relatively less attention from both Muslim and non-Muslim scholars of Islam. The focus of Islamic studies has majorly been on the ideological face of Islam as many scholars and Muslim leaders prefer to dwell on the institutionalized Islamic laws and theologies.

---

1. Kim, Travis, and Travis, "Relevant Responses," 240. The term "popular Muslim piety" was put forward in this chapter by its authors.

On October 27, 2018, Jamia Mosque, situated in the city of Nairobi's central business area, opened its doors to the public. Muslims and non-Muslims alike intermingled inside the mosque, some for the first time. A guided tour of the mosque excited the non-Muslim audience as they also watched the Islamic prayers live. It was a grandiose display of the official wing of Islam, which aimed at promoting a better understanding of Islam. Such publicity seeks to demystify Islam to non-Muslims. Furthermore, classical studies have produced seminal documentations of Islam, especially with the heightened interest in Islam in response to atrocities like the attack of September 11, 2001. However, with such a focus on the official wing of Islam, a cardinal question is whether such classical approaches can in fact demystify Islam. The essence of such a question is whether the lived experiences of Muslims comply with the official requirements stipulated in the Islamic texts. Clinton Bennett highlights this concern when he poses a question regarding the relationship between "official Islam (precepts) and what people actually believe and practice."[2] Such an interrogation removes the attention from the widespread ideological focus in Islamic studies and instead considers Muslims as people. This concurs with Marranci's suggestion, "We should start from Muslims, rather than Islam."[3] It may also mean taking a "step back from Islam" in order to deal with pertinent issues that enhance a comprehensive understanding of the diversity in Islam and its adherents.[4]

Anthropologists of Islam have continued to realize that "what Islam is depends on how it is interpreted," as Marranci notes.[5] This suggests that Muslims need to be understood first in order to then understand Islam. Such anthropological approaches have revealed the existence of diverse interpretations within Islam that are generally pegged on two broad outlooks. Scholars have employed different terminologies to show the dichotomy: "official"/"folk," "orthodoxy"/"heterodoxy," "great tradition"/"lesser tradition," "textual"/"non-textual," etc.[6] Robert Redfield suggested the concept of the "great traditions"

---

2. Clinton Bennett, *Studying Islam*, 101.
3. Marranci, *Anthropology of Islam*, 7.
4. Lukens-Bull, "Between Text and Practice," 4.
5. Marranci, *Anthropology of Islam*, 29.
6. Whitehouse, *Arguments and Icons*. In cognitive science of religion, Harvey Whitehouse refers to the theory of "modes of religiosity," which has the dual modes, namely, the doctrinal

and "little traditions" in anthropological studies of world religions,[7] and this concept has been carried over to Islamic studies.

The evident heterogeneity (also found in other major religions) arises from the way Muslims in different contexts articulate Islam. It is this contextual dimension that has continued to motivate anthropologists of Islam to study the lived experiences of Muslims. Yet there remains a relative paucity of empirical investigations that focus on Muslims as people who practice Islam, especially in Africa. This has been a motivational drive that has stirred me to understand Borana Muslims as Africans practicing Islam within their religiocultural context.

Background and Motivation for the Research

The motivation to investigate the cognitive dimension underlying the phenomenon of spirit possession arose during my interactions with ordinary Muslims. As a non-Muslim, I sought to understand their belief systems and the ways of life that I saw displayed within different Islamic communities. Their belief in *al-ghaib* was unmistakable. Both young and old spoke about the inhabitants of this trans-empirical realm as an integral part of their worldview. Their daily lives reflected the ardent belief in the spirit world that intersperses their religiocultural space.

Umar Abd-Allah confirms that belief in the unseen world is paramount for all Muslims and that it should be placed within the context of the "absolute oneness of God."[8] It is therefore expected that all Muslims adhere to the stipulations provided in the official texts and thus have a homogenous creed and a pragmatic approach that unifies behavior. Yet, anthropological studies continue to indicate a disparity between the observance of the official tenets and the lived experiences of Muslims as they encounter the spirit world. Furthermore, this interaction with non-human entities is a fundamental aspect of the religiocultural dimension of Muslims' religiosity, especially in

---

mode and the imagistic mode. See also Whitehouse, *Modes of Religiosity*; and Whitehouse, "Modes of Religiosity," 108–12.

7. Redfield, *Peasant Society and Culture*.
8. Umar, "Perceptible and the Unseen," 210.

Africa. Studying such interactions, therefore, essentially paves the way to a greater understanding of particular African Muslims.

The necessity to carry out a descriptive and analytical study of the Borana Muslims in Marsabit County was occasioned by a need to understand them. One area of focus that I deemed would unveil a deeper sense of their identity is in relation to the spirit world. I became fascinated with their frequent reference to the spirit world while I worked among them from 2007 to 2013. I wanted to understand this interaction more as a conduit to knowing them better. Two words featured constantly in their conversations: *nagaa* and *ayyaana*. The centrality of these words is evident in that they form part of the customary greetings. The common inquiry on wellness permeates their daily conversations: *Nageni badada*? (Is everything well?) *Ayyaana kiya dansa.* (My fortune is good.) The polysemous aspect of the word *ayyaana* is herein noted and will be discussed in chapter 5. This study focuses on the meaning of *ayyaana* that is spiritual beings that interact closely with Borana Muslims. A number of scholars have mentioned *ayyaana* in their studies (see chapter 2). However, their focus has not been on the Borana Muslims' participation in the *Ayyaana* cult in Marsabit County. This study seeks to fill that lacuna and to provide significant knowledge about the Borana Muslims located in this county.

Locating the Marsabit Borana Muslims

Borana Muslims are found in the vast county of Marsabit in northern Kenya. The county comprises four subcounties: Moyale, Saku, Laisamis, and North Horr. Different tribal groups inhabit these areas including the Samburu, Turkana, Rendille, Garre, Borana, Gabra, Burji, Watta, and Sakuye. The last six tribal groups in this list speak the Borana language and are found in the North Horr, Moyale, and Saku subcounties.[9]

Marsabit County has two urban centers, namely, the towns of Marsabit and Moyale. These were key research areas for this study since the majority of Borana Muslims are found in these towns and their vicinities. The

---

9. Orma people are also Borana speakers, but they reside in the Tana River and Lamu Counties. The Aweer (formerly the Boni) people in Lamu are also Borana speakers.

county borders Isiolo County to the southeast, which the Waso Borana people inhabit.[10]

I intentionally did not interview the Waso Borana Muslims in Isiolo County. My focus was on the Marsabit Borana Muslims in the subcounties of Moyale and Saku. I went to various villages in the two subcounties, where the Borana "proper" are found.[11] These villages are situated within the Marsabit, Sololo, and Moyale towns.

A majority of Borana speakers trace their origin to Ethiopia, where they are part of the larger Oromo ethnic group.[12] They started migrating southward into the Northern Frontier District (NFD) of present-day Kenya around the sixteenth century.[13] In spite of the geographical distance from Ethiopia, many Borana people still refer to Ethiopia as their homeland. The porous borders in Moyale Subcounty allow for free mobility between the two countries. This enables continuity in traditional Oromic practices, including those concerning *ayyaana*.

The Oromo-speaking people occupy a stretch of land from the Ethiopian province of Tigre to Tana River County in Kenya. All these people speak different dialects of *afan Oromo* (the Oromo language).[14] They have some similar religiocultural concepts that differ, however, in specific ritual performances depending on their geographical location, as is the case of the Waso and Marsabit Borana people in Kenya.[15]

Due to the proximity of the Somali people, the Waso Borana have become predominantly Muslims. The colonial government facilitated their settlement in what was, at the time, the Isiolo District. Schlee posits that before the

---

10. Marsabit town is the seat of the county government and is 270 km north of Isiolo Town. It is situated at a higher altitude of 1500 m above sea level and hence enjoys a favorable climate, unlike most parts of the arid and semi-arid areas that characterize the northern part of Kenya.

11. The Borana "proper" are contrasted with the other Borana-speaking tribal groups. See footnote 13 for further explanation.

12. The Oromo are one of the largest ethnolinguistic people groups in Africa. They are subdivided into several distinct tribal groups. There are more than 20 million Oromo people in Ethiopia, while Kenya has approximately 200,000 Oromo-Borana speakers. See Kelly, "From Gada to Islam." Most Borana speakers are pastoralists, although the changing climatic conditions have forced some of them to practice farming.

13. Leus and Salvadori, *Aadaa Boraanaa*, vii.

14. Gerba, "Typology of Oromo," 18. Gerba mentions that the Oromo people constitute 32.5 % of the Ethiopian population according to the 2007 census.

15. Gerba, "Typology of Oromo," 18.

resettlement, there were Borana people in Wajir County (in the northeastern part of Kenya). In 1932, they had to give up their water wells to avoid conflicts with the Somali people. The British colonial administrators compensated the Borana people by allowing them to settle in Isiolo.[16] They are called Waso Borana because of their proximity to the river Waso Nyiro found in Isiolo County. Wario notes that the Waso Borana people were restricted from accessing their ancestral land or having contact with their Borana kinsmen in Marsabit and Moyale.[17] Consequently, they could not continue with their traditional customs and norms. They interacted with the Somali Muslims in Isiolo, which resulted in the twin process of Islamization and Somalization.[18]

Religiocultural Background

The deliberate minimal interaction with the Somali people in Marsabit ensured that there was little to no cultural exchange between the Somali and Borana people.[19] Thus the Marsabit Borana escaped the process of Somalization, which their Borana counterparts in Isiolo underwent. Nevertheless, the process of Islamization in Marsabit began when a few Arab and Somali Muslims went to the region as traders. They constructed mosques in major town centers like Marsabit and Moyale. The Islamization of the Marsabit Borana was slower compared to that of the Waso Borana. Their nearness to Ethiopia ensured that the Borana people in Marsabit and Moyale towns would sustain a dynamic religiocultural interaction with the Oromo people. They have continued to observe their Borana rituals alongside the Islamic faith, as Aguilar affirms:

> Today, the Boorana consider themselves Muslims, but they continue practicing Boorana rituals, such as Boorana prayers, the sacrifice of coffee-beans (*buna qalla*), and the communication

---

16. Schlee, *Identities on the Move*, 47.

17. Wario, "Networking the Nomads."

18. The term *Somalization* was coined to refer to the process where non-Somali people adapted the Somali religiocultural practices while still retaining their own identity. The Waso Borana, for instance, embraced the Somali cultural practices but still retained their language and identity as Borana. See Braukamper, *Islamic History and Culture*, 132. Baxter also refers to the terms *Somalization* and *Islamization*. See Baxter, "Social Organization."

19. Fugich states that Borana people recalled their suffering at the hands of Somali people during the Ogaden war. See Fugich, "Tradition, Memory, Creativity," 18–34.

with the world of the spirits (*ayyaana*), through a possession cult, known in the area as the *ayyaana* cult.[20]

At that time, Aguilar did ethnographical studies among the Waso Borana people in Garba Tulla, Isiolo District (see the review of his scholarly works in chapter 2 of this study). His conclusion about the integration of traditional Borana rituals with Islam is an aspect of the religiocultural diversity that is evident among the Marsabit Borana Muslims, as the findings of this study demonstrate.[21] Yet there are significant differences between the Waso's and the Marsabit Borana Muslims' expression of their respective religiocultural worlds. An example of such a disparity is the divinatory role of the *risa* (the eagle) as the "voice of God for the Waso Boorana," as illustrated by Aguilar.[22] This gave a cue for the current study as I investigated the place of the eagle in the *Ayyaana* cult in Marsabit. As the findings of this study illustrate, the Marsabit Borana Muslims do not place as much emphasis on the eagle as a direct messenger from Allah through the traditional ritual leader, *Qallu*. Their proximity to Ethiopia, their ancestral land, enables them to access the *Qallu* and hear his words more directly. Hence the divinatory role of the eagle in their religiocultural context, though not altogether absent, is not elaborate compared to that of the Waso Borana.

Research Rationale

Focusing on the "people factor" instead of the ideological dimension of Islam provides a valid impetus for this study.[23] Such a focus paves the way for meaningful comprehension of Muslims' lived experiences. It is on such a premise that this dissertation has been written – to contribute knowledge about the lived experiences of ordinary Muslims in Marsabit County. Few scholars have written about the spirit world as experienced by the Borana Muslims in Kenya. It has been mentioned that most of these scholars have located their research in Isiolo County among the Waso Borana Muslims.

---

20. Aguilar, "Religion as Culture?," 236.

21. For more on how Borana people accepted and rejected aspects of Islam in northern Kenya, see Baxter, "Acceptance and Rejection," 233–40.

22. Aguilar, "Eagle as Messenger," 60.

23. I got the phrase "people factor" from Kim, who uses the term to distinguish this factor from the ideology factor in Islamic studies. See Kim, *Islam among the Swahili*, 3).

There are variations in the beliefs and practices within the *Ayyaana* cult between the Waso Borana, who are closer to Somali Muslims, and the Marsabit Borana, who are closer to Ethiopia. This rationalizes the need to examine the phenomenon among the latter Borana Muslims.

Islam is expanding in Marsabit County. It is expedient to document the kind of Islam practiced for better comprehension of the adherents. A comprehensive account is not attained when only the ideological dimension of Islam is studied. To mitigate such a foreseen deficiency, this study takes a phenomenological perspective that seeks to listen to the Borana Muslims narrate their experiences as Muslims within their religiocultural context. Such a need has been highlighted by Paula Saukko, whose discussion on studying cultures alludes to the necessity of doing justice to the realities of the people under study.[24] Caleb Kim concurs with this as he mentions the need to study Muslims as the "object of studies" instead of concentrating merely on non-human issues, as some classical Islamic studies tend to do.[25]

This study has a multidisciplinary approach to studying the lived experiences of Borana Muslims as they participate in the *Ayyaana* cult of "possession."[26] This approach entails the use of cognitive theories to analyze and interpret the findings. The Borana Muslims have been studied individually and collectively, hence the anthropological framework of this study. A number of scholars have engaged in the area of the anthropology of Islam as they have realized the need to focus on people. I found an appropriate methodological guideline that suited my pursuit to investigate the lived experiences of the Borana Muslims. This guideline is the Synthetic Triangular Approach (STA) initiated by Kim.[27] His aim is to "produce as accurate a phenomenological depiction of Muslim life as possible. This approach aims not only to describe but also to understand cultural experiences of ordinary Muslims."[28] This study is phenomenological, as described in chapter 3 on the methodology and ethnographical tools employed. I have also used a cognitive

---

24. Paula Saukko, *Doing Research*.
25. Kim, *Islam among the Swahili*.
26. The *afan Borana* term for "possession" lacks an equivalent word in English, hence the quotation marks. However, I will not place the marks around subsequent occurrences of the word in this dissertation.
27. Kim, "Considering 'Ordinariness,'" 177–92.
28. Kim, 4.

anthropological framework to examine the cognitive underpinnings of participation in the *Ayyaana* cult. The cultural model theory was particularly relevant in this endeavor.

Central Concern

The aim of this study is to describe the religiocultural model of *Ayyaana* based on the cognition of Borana Muslims who participate in the *Ayyaana* cult of possession, and to examine the model in light of the Islamic model of jinn construed by the Muslim teachers in Marsabit County. This central concern is thereby guided by the following research questions:

1. How can the Islamic model of the spirit world according to the Muslim teachers in Marsabit County be best described?
    i. What knowledge do the Muslim teachers have about the spirit world in Marsabit County?
    ii. What is the official position on jinn and jinn possession as known and taught by the Muslim teachers?
    iii. What is the official Islamic position on dealing with spirits in Marsabit County?
    iv. What is the perception of *ayyaana* and participants of the *Ayyaana* cult by the Muslim teachers?
2. What is the religiocultural model of the *Ayyaana* according to Borana Muslims who participate in the *Ayyaana* cult?
    i. What do the adepts and practitioners of the *Ayyaana* possession cult believe about *ayyaana*?
    ii. What are the rituals involved in the *Ayyaana* possession cult?
    iii. What are the lived experiences and perceptions of Borana Muslims who participate in the *Ayyaana* cult?
3. How does the religiocultural model of *Ayyaana* compare with the Islamic model of spirits in Marsabit County among the Borana Muslims?
    i. What are the similarities between the religiocultural model of *Ayyaana* and the official Islamic model of the spirit world taught by the Muslim teachers in Marsabit County?

ii. What distinctive features of the *Ayyaana* cult tend to make Borana Muslims deviate from the official path concerning spirits and possession?
iii. What suitable theory or theories explain the relationship between the *Ayyaana* and Islamic models?

Objectives of the Study

This study primarily aims at understanding the Borana Muslims by examining their lived experiences as they participate in the *Ayyaana* possession cult. This practical aspect is examined in relation to the Islamic teachings that are espoused by the Muslims teachers in Marsabit County. The intention is to comprehend how their lived experiences resemble or digress from the official Islamic tenets on the spirit world. Such a venture offers a more comprehensive understanding of how Islam is lived out among Borana Muslims as a segment of African Muslims. It has been pointed before that there is scarcity of scholarly works on the lived experiences of African Muslims, especially in terms of their encounter with the spirit world.

To achieve the highlighted objective, the Islamic model of jinn is first examined and described as construed by the Muslim teachers who are the custodians of official Islam in Marsabit County. The religiocultural model of *Ayyaana* is then described and compared with the Islamic model of jinn. The disparities and similarities are explained using a theory that I suggest to describe how I have understood the Borana Muslims in Marsabit County in relation to the spirit world.

Significance of the Study

This study reinforces the need for a balanced perspective in the study of Islam. The amount of effort put in the ideological study of Islam should be congruent with the effort put into studying the lived experiences of Muslims in their contexts. Such a balanced endeavor offers a more comprehensive understanding of Muslims and Islam.

This study is significant in adding knowledge about the Borana Muslims in the academic circles. It provides a database of information for Islamic studies with a specific focus on African Muslims. Anthropologists will also benefit from this descriptive study of the phenomenon of *ayyaana* as understood by ordinary Muslims.

Non-Muslims who aspire to work with Borana Muslims in Marsabit County will also find the information herein useful. Medical practitioners working in the county will benefit from this study as well, as they understand why some Borana Muslims, in the event of illness, prefer to go to the *Ayyaana* practitioners instead of attending the medical facilities available in the county.

Delimitations

This study focuses on the Borana "proper" who are found in Marsabit County and not the other Borana speakers like the Gabra, Sakuye, Orma, Watta, Burji, and Munyoyaya.[29] The reason for choosing the Borana "proper" is that they are the largest in number of all the Borana-speaking groups. I have also interacted more with the Borana "proper" than with other Borana speakers in the recent past.

The *Ayyaana* possession cult is widely practiced in the northern and northeastern regions of Kenya. It also has a larger following in southern Ethiopia. This study has not examined the cultic beliefs and ritual practices in other regions besides northern Kenya. Some historical background of the *Ayyaana* possession cult in southern Ethiopia was considered, even though this study did not delve much into the historicity of *ayyaana* spirits.

As Borana Muslims are primarily Sunni, this study will confine itself to what Sunni Islam teaches about the spirit world. The Sunni sect is divided into four main Islamic *madh'hab* (schools of law): *Hanbali*, *Hanafi*, *Shafi'i*, and *Maliki*. Borana Muslims generally observe the *Shafi'i* school of law. This study was restricted to the *Shafi'i* School's interpretation of the world of spirits and did not delve into the other schools' interpretations.

This study has a multidisciplinary inclination in its framework. However, it has excluded a psycho-medical perspective in spite of having a cognitive angle. This study does not delve into dissociative aspects of spirit possession as a number of anthropologists have done. Neither has ethnomusicology

---

29. Stroomer calls the Borana "proper" the "Borana Oromo." These are part of the Southern Oromo dialects found in Kenya. See Kim, "Considering 'Ordinariness,'" 180. The Borana "proper" are popularly referred to as the "Borana Gutu" to distinguish them from the other Borana speakers. See Wario, "Networking the Nomads," 43).

been indulged in this study, even though the rituals involve a good amount of music and dance.

This research describes the phenomenon of spirit possession. It is basically descriptive and analytical; it is not prescriptive. This is because of the phenomenological perspective that this study has taken, which is deemed useful in gaining a better understanding of the ordinary Muslims interviewed herein.

Limitations

One limitation for this study is language. I am not a native Borana speaker. I have endeavored to learn as much of the Borana language as possible, especially the lexical requirements for this study. The limitation of time prevented me from perfecting my language skills. Since most of the interviews were done in the Borana language, I enlisted the help of Borana research assistants who are proficient in the language.

Participant observation has been a key method of collecting ethnographic data for this study. This entails taking a participatory role in the possession rituals to understand vividly. However, due to the nature of spirit possession rituals, it was not possible to attend the ritual sessions actively and to be possessed by the spirits. I was a passive observer and trusted what the adepts narrated as valid.

Operational Definitions

There are terms that I have used in this dissertation that need to be defined operationally to avoid ambiguity. I define some of them in this section. The meanings of other key terms that I have used are provided in the glossary.

I use the term *ordinary Muslims* instead of *folk Muslims* to indicate the type of Muslim who feels overwhelmed and frustrated when confronted by different calamities in life.[30] Such a Muslim seeks for solutions from different sources of power than Islam in order to deal with these pertinent issues. The term *ordinary Muslims* further distinguishes the Muslim people from their

---

30. Kim, "Considering 'Ordinariness,'" 180. Kim describes "ordinary Muslims" as Muslims who "feel awed and frustrated by various life challenges such as sickness, death, misfortunes, calamities, and the like." Cf. Love, *Muslims, Magic and the Kingdom*, 2. Love describes folk Muslims as people who "confess Allah but worship spirits."

Muslim teachers and leaders who attempt to uphold the canonical precepts of Islam. It does not imply, therefore, that the latter are "extraordinary."

The term *official* is used to express what has been authoritatively sanctioned in Islam. The term is borrowed from Western sources to refer to official or orthodox Islam as opposed to "popular" Islam. Preference is herein given to the term *official* rather than *orthodox*.

The term *Borana* is used in this study to denote the Borana people who live in Marsabit County and not the Waso Borana who reside in Isiolo County. The name *Borana* is preferred instead of other spellings like *Boraanaa*, *Boran*, or *Booran*.

This dissertation examines the *Ayyaana* cult. The term *cult* refers to the system of veneration and devotion directed toward spirits. The people who participate in such a ritualized system, then, constitute a group that is herein referred to as a *cult*.

Various anthropologists have given the definition of culture that suits their perspective. I have used a cognitive definition that includes the mind as an aspect of culture. Hence, I use the cognitive definition of culture as the shared knowledge by a people that enables them to act in a way that is acceptable to them as a group.[31]

This study uses the cognitive theory of cultural models. I refer to cultural models as mental representations of aspects of life that are organized in individual minds of people and are also collectively shared within a group. These models are assumed or taken for granted,[32] but they are useful in helping people understand their world as well as in motivating behavior.

Assumptions

Some earlier interpretations of the phenomenon of spirit possession, like that of James G. Frazer, considered spirit possession to be "faked," as recounted by

---

31. Goodenough, "In Pursuit of Culture," 6. I follow Ward Goodenough's definition of culture, which was formulated in 1957 but is still influential in cognitive anthropology. He introduced cognition into anthropological spheres and defines culture as what one needs "to know to communicate acceptably with one another."

32. Quinn and Holland, "Culture and Cognition," 4.

Schmidt and Huskinson.[33] My position is that spirits do exist, even though they cannot be seen, and that spirit possession is real.

Summary

This chapter has offered background information to the study of Borana Muslims in Marsabit County, Kenya, as they participate in the Ayyanna cult. It has been noted in the chapter that the Borana Muslims in Marsabit County differ in their socio-cultural background from their Waso Borana counterparts who inhabit the neighboring Isiolo County. This study focuses on the Marsabit Borana because of my interaction with them for a couple of years. There are other Borana-speakers in Marsabit County, but I likewise focused on the Borana *Gutu* (proper) in contrast to the other Borana speakers who are not pure Borana, per se.

Studying the Marsabit Borana Muslims is premised on the need to consider the lived experiences of Muslims, which translates to focusing on the "people factor" than solely on the classical issues of Islam. In order to study such lived experiences, an anthropological perspective has been chosen that is based on undertaking a qualitative research approach. This chapter has explained the justifications for carrying out the study, as well as the purpose that underlies it. The delimitations and limitations are also mentioned in order to show the realism of this endeavor.

---

33. Schmidt and Huskinson, *Spirit Possession and Trance*.

CHAPTER 2

Scholarly Works on Spirits in Islam

This chapter reviews what different scholars have written about the supernatural world according to Islam. The aim of this review of precedent literature is twofold. It is first to understand the perspectives or theoretical frameworks as well as the intentions of the authors. Second, it is to evaluate their relevance to this study.[1]

It would be inappropriate to assert that the world of spirits is a confine of "popular Islam."[2] The Islamic texts are rife with allusions to spirits. It is therefore imperative to review scholars who have written on the world of spirits as found in the Qur'an and the Hadith. This is followed by a review of authors who have explored the phenomenon of spirit possession using different approaches. Their methodological perspectives as well as their conclusive theories will be highlighted. The cognitive anthropological approach is of particular interest to this current study.

Reasons for Examining the Concept of Jinn

In her book on jinn, El-Zein poses a relevant question in her introductory remarks: "Why write a book on the jinn?"[3] I commend her for being candid to mention that the question arises from what she deems as the "Arab/Muslim

---

1. Elliston, *Introduction to Missiological Research*, 42.
2. The dualistic terms "orthodox" and "popular" Islam are considered to be "Eurocentric interpretive categories." See Langer and Simon, "Dynamics of Orthodox," 273. I use the terms cautiously as I recognize that they are not Islamic classifications.
3. El-Zein, *Islam, Arabs, and the Intelligent*, ix.

redundancy" and the Western dismissal of the supernatural.[4] It is not easy to study ethereal beings. It involves dealing with a hidden world that is invisible to the human eye. This world cannot be subjected to any empirical or physical measurement, according to Ibraheem Kamaal Adham, as quoted by Ameen.[5] These factors contribute to the paucity of literature on the concept of jinn.

Philips reinforces this claim of scarcity of literature in the Islamic world.[6] Kim, however, asserts that a number of "psychiatrists, ethnopsychologists, and anthropologists have dealt with the jinn phenomenon in numerous Muslim societies"[7] Yet Kim's footnote on this negates his assertion of the number of scholars who have delved into the area of jinn. He gives a list of scholars who have supposedly written on the subject, and yet this list does not include a particular focus on the world of jinn as propagated in classical Islam. Hence El-Zein is justified when she gives the five reasons why she has chosen to study jinn in Islam. Of particular interest is her claim that studying the concept of jinn is "essential to understanding Islam inasmuch as it is a concept at the heart of the religion."[8] This is a pivotal sentence, which is affirmed by other scholars.

Philip's aim in writing his book, *The Exorcist Tradition in Islam*, is to fill a "gap in modern research on the Islamic concept of exorcism and the supernatural world related to it."[9] Drieskens realizes the need to examine the concept of jinn as an "integral, though somewhat controversial, part of religion."[10] Ameen's treatise on jinn seeks to strike a balance on what he refers to as the "superstitious approach of attributing all problems to the jinn and evil eye, and the 'modern, scientific' approach of dismissing belief in the jinn as a kind of fairy tale."[11]

---

4. El-Zein, *Islam, Arabs, and the Intelligent*, x. I inferred that El-Zein is a Muslim based on her writing.
5. Ameen, *Jinn and Human Sickness*, 33.
6. Philips, *Exorcist Tradition in Islaam*, 1.
7. Kim, *Islam among the Swahili*, 96.
8. El-Zein, *Islam, Arabs, and the Intelligent*, x.
9. Philips, *Exorcist Tradition in Islaam*, 1.
10. Drieskens, *Living with Djinns*, 13.
11. Ameen, *Jinn and Human Sickness*, 11.

Studying the Concept of Jinn in Islam

Scholars who have examined the concept of jinn in Islam have used various perspectives and employed different approaches. The common denominator with most of these is that they have based their arguments on the Qur'an, the Hadiths, and precedent literature from leading scholars. A number of contemporary scholars have written in the Arabic language. My rudimentary knowledge of Arabic did not allow me to seek for such treatises. However, a few have been translated into English (for example, Ibn Taymiyyah's treatise translated by Bilal Philips),[12] and other scholars have integrated this Arabic literature into their own writing (for example, El-Zein 2009).[13] This section will examine these works beginning with how various scholars have studied the concept of jinn in Islam and how they have interpreted the Islamic texts that are deemed as official.

Some Scholarly Works on the Concept of Jinn

Both Muslim and non-Muslim scholars have studied jinn in Islam for varying reasons, hence their respective approaches. Muslim scholars desire to inform their fellow Muslims to avoid ignorance of the spirit world and consequently the temptation to delve into the sin of *shirk* (association). Various scholars admit that some Muslims have added their traditional practices in spirit possession cults to the authorized belief in jinn as endorsed in the official tenets of Islam.[14] To ensure "correct" beliefs and practices about jinn, Muslim scholars thus attempt to refer them back to the Islamic texts. They seek to interpret the Qur'anic verses that mention jinn as seen in the section below.[15] They also write in simplified yet academic language for easy readership. An educated Muslim teacher in Marsabit would not find these books difficult to read and teach his followers.

El-Zein's monograph on classical Arabic literature on jinn is quite informative. She seems to target a non-Arabic audience, and she interprets the literature, which would otherwise have been inaccessible to non-Arabic

---

12. Philips, *Ibn Taymiyah's Essay*.
13. El-zein, *Islam, Arabs, and the Intelligent*.
14. These scholars include Ameen, El-zein, Al-Ashqar, and others. See Ameen, *Jinn and Human Sickness*; El-Zein, *Islam, Arabs, and the Intelligent*; and Al-Ashqar, *World of the Jinn*.
15. *Ayah* (or *ayat*) is the Arabic word that literally means "sign" or "clue." It is, however, used to refer to a verse from the Qur'an.

speakers. She asserts that her book contains stories and anecdotes that she has translated from Arabic to English for the first time.[16] Her approach is historical as she traces the concept of jinn in the medieval Islamic writing. This is also clearly seen in her 1995 doctoral dissertation where she examines the evolution of the concept of the jinn from pre-Islam to medieval Islam using an interdisciplinary approach that integrates cultural anthropology, comparative religion, and theoretical research.[17]

In spite of such a multidisciplinary perspective, El-Zein, in her book published in 2009, focuses mainly on studying jinn from a religious perspective. She defines religion as the way human beings participate in the unknown as part of a wider culture.[18] This is an appropriate approach to studying the concept of jinn as it acknowledges the religiocultural dimension. I also examine the Borana Muslims' religiocultural setting as I realize I cannot dichotomize religion from culture. Yet, El-Zein's approach differs from my study in that she does not examine the contemporary beliefs and practices pertaining to jinn as this current study does. She alludes to the fascinating venture of interviewing people to investigate their beliefs in the jinn, yet she does not delve into it. This shows how focused she is in her historical approach in her dissertation, even though she mentions that her book takes a phenomenological outlook.[19] El-Zein's work is also exemplary as she discusses the concept of jinn as found in other non-Islamic traditions across the world, which makes her take pride in her "truly encyclopedic" work.[20]

I have found El-Zein's work quite fascinating and slightly different from others written from an Islamic point of view. Other scholars use the Islamic texts to understand the concept of jinn. El-Zein goes beyond these texts and examines classical literary works like the *Arabian Nights*, which she asserts are an "important part of popular Islam." She also examines texts used in "Gnostic Islam" as written by Sufis and "*ishraqi* (illuminist) philosophy such as Ibn Sina and Ikhwan al-safa."[21] Her eclectic viewpoint is further elucidated

---

16. El-Zein, *Islam, Arabs, and the Intelligent*, xxiii.
17. El-Zein, "Evolution of the Concept," ii.
18. El-Zein, vii.
19. El-Zein, xxii.
20. El-Zein, xxii.
21. El-Zein, viii. Later, in her 2009 book, El-Zein corrects the term "Gnostic Islam" and instead uses "mystical Islam." See El-Zein, *Islam, Arabs and the Intelligent*.

by her reliance on works written by Arab historians, analysts, geographers, and others, together with the official texts, the Qur'an and Hadith. It is easy to see her attempt to justify herself and maintain her stance on the official side.

A few scholars have studied the lived experiences of local Muslims in relation to the concept of jinn.[22] Apart from delving into a philological examination of the concept of jinn in Islamic texts, Kim considers what local Swahili Muslims believe and practice with regards to jinn and how this differs from the official tenets as instructed in the Islamic texts as well as by authoritative Muslim scholars.[23] Kim's scholarly approach thus forms a valid methodology that can be adapted to study the lived experiences of Muslims and compare it with what is required in the official tenets.

Like Kim above, Drieskens seeks to study the lived experiences of Muslims as they encounter jinn.[24] She employs a sociocultural, anthropological perspective using ethnographic tools to elicit information from the lower middle class Egyptians in Cairo as she studies how they experience jinn.[25] She begins her treatise with an interesting sentence: "Despite their amoral and unreliable character, I have tried to be faithful to the djinns as my starting point."[26] She is the first author I have encountered who seeks to "be faithful" to the jinn. Yet, she does not explain further how she tried to be faithful to them. Her discourse is more faithful to the ordinary Cairenes with whom she interacted daily and who gave her stories about jinn. This immersion into the community is very commendable and advisable for me as I seek to examine the experiences and cognition of the Borana Muslims who participate in the *Ayyaana* possession cult. The difference between my study and Drieskens's is that I seek to analyze the experiences of these participants in light of the official Islamic stance. This entails examining the official perspective of the Muslim teachers on the concept of jinn. Drieskens prefers not to focus on the specialists in religious matters in Cairo. She assumes that the Qur'an and Hadith influence the ordinary Cairenes, yet she states the contradictory nature of the way these

---

22. Scholars who have delved into the study of lived experiences of local Muslims include Kim, "Supernaturalism in Swahili Islam"; Kim, *Islam among the Swahili*; Drieskens, *Living with Djinns*; and Lebling, *Legends of the Fire Spirits*, and others.
23. Kim, "Supernaturalism in Swahili Islam"; and Kim, *Islam among the Swahili*.
24. Drieskens, *Living with Djinns*.
25. Drieskins prefers to use the spelling *djinn* rather than *jinn* throughout her book.
26. Drieskens, *Living with Djinns*, 13.

texts present the concept of jinn.²⁷ Her forthright way of referring to some of the conflicting issues on jinn as found in the Islamic texts differs from some scholars who have interpreted the Qur'anic verses seen below.

Interpreting the Qur'anic Verses on Jinn

Several authors have done textual studies of the Qur'anic verses on jinn.²⁸ Most of these scholars have interpreted the Qur'an using the traditional methodology that refers to the authorship of medieval Islamic scholars.²⁹ Delving into such a study indicates the acceptance that the Islamic texts were written within a supernaturalistic worldview that embraced a realm beyond the physical. Scholars have noted the prominence given to the concept of jinn in the Qur'an as compared to other phenomena like the evil eye and black magic. The word *jinn* is mentioned twenty-nine times in the Qur'an.³⁰

The scholars reviewed in this chapter have not attempted an exegetical study of the Qur'anic verses on jinn. They have integrated the verses within their discussions on specific aspects of the concept using various approaches. Kim's textual study of the Qur'an *ayahs* commences after a philological examination of the concept of jinn during pre-Islam and Islamic periods.³¹ El-Zein also traces the historical development of the concept from the pre-Islamic *jahiliyya* period to the inception of Islam.³² These two authors perceive the necessity of a synchronic approach to examine the concept of jinn in Islam. This was deemed necessary since the pre-Islamic supernaturalistic beliefs were foundational in formulating the concept in the Islamic texts.

---

27. Drieskens, 93.

28. Including Taymeeyah, Philips, El-Zein, Al-Ashqar, and others. See Taymeeyah, *Ibn Taymeeyah's Essay*; Philips, *Exorcist Tradition in Islaam*; El-Zein, *Islam, Arabs, and the Intelligent*; and Al-Ashqar, *The World of the Jinn and Devils*.

29. According to Osindo, interpretion of the Qur'an can be divided broadly into two methodologies, namely, traditional and modernist. The former acknowledges the authorship of medieval Islamic scholars. See Osindo, "'Righteousness by Faith,'" 142. Philips, for instance, adheres to the traditional methodology when he refers to the views of the "early Sunnite scholars" in his examination of exorcism in Islam. See Philips, "Exorcism in Islam," vii.

30. Mullick et al., "Beliefs about Jinn," 726. Alim.org, on the other hand, reports that the noun *jinn* is mentioned 22 times in the Qur'an. https://www.alim.org/quran/syntax/.

31. Kim, *Islam among the Swahili*, 80.

32. El-Zein, "Evolution of the Concept," vii.

Kim's textual approach includes a semantic study of the terms for jinn and its derivatives as they appear in the Qur'an.[33] The relatively large number of *ayahs* about jinn and its cognates would excuse Kim and the other scholars from delving into a hermeneutical or historical-critical method of interpretation. Ibn Taymiyah and Philips refer to a number of Qur'anic and Hadith *ayah*,[34] but they still do not delve into a textual study. Nevertheless, I appreciate El-Zein's intent to let the official texts speak for themselves phenomenologically in order to explain the "complexity and subtleness of the jinn's concept."[35] She therefore advocates a close reading of the text in order to decipher the "hidden and invisible" message.[36] Yet, El-Zein still does not apply the hermeneutical approach that is mandatory to decipher this hidden meaning she is referring to. Neither does Al-Ashqar, who presents another non-exegetical document with Qur'anic and Hadith references on the nature of jinn, use a hermeneutical approach.[37]

Jinn in the Hadiths

Scholars consent that the Hadiths have contributed to the perception of the spirit world among Muslims. (See appendix 6 for a list of references on jinn in the Hadiths, mainly Bukhari and Muslim.) It is essential to consider how these different scholars address the concept of jinn as presented in the Hadiths. El-Zein acknowledges the immensity of Hadith collections and that references on jinn thus require a "volume of its own." She therefore confines herself to *Sahih Muslim* and *Sahih Bukhari* and occasionally mentions the Hadiths compiled by others.[38] Other scholars have taken this cue and have desisted from giving a comprehensive account covering all the references to jinn in the Hadith. Kim summarizes the Muslim beliefs in jinn according to popular Hadiths. He indicates that many of the accounts of jinn therein resemble the popular practices in Muslim societies.[39] This is imperative to note for this current study.

---

33. Kim, *Islam among the Swahili*, 82.
34. Philips, *Ibn Taymiyah's Essay*; and Philips, "Exorcism in Islam."
35. El-Zein, *Islam, Arabs, and the Intelligent*, xxii.
36. El-Zein, xxii.
37. Al-Ashqar, *World of the Jinn*.
38. El-Zein, *Islam, Arabs, and the Intelligent*, xx.
39. Kim, *Islam among the Swahili*, 90.

Other scholars who have referred to the Hadiths in their discussion on the concept of jinn do not have separate sessions on jinn in the Hadith as Kim does. Muslim scholars especially use the Hadiths to confirm or explain further what the Qur'an says about an aspect of the jinn under discussion.[40] There is a general consensus among scholars that the Hadiths are in line with Qur'anic depiction of the jinn.[41] From the scholars who refer to the Hadiths, it is noted that the Hadiths have more comprehensive accounts that narrate how Muhammad dealt with jinn and thus what Muslims are supposed to do.

Some Aspects of Jinn

Many scholars who examine the concept of jinn in Islam will naturally discuss various aspects of their existence as portrayed in the official texts. This section will examine only three aspects of jinn that I deem helpful for a better understanding of the spirits in Islam. I will seek to review how the scholars discuss the nature of jinn, Muhammad's encounters with the jinn, and last, the abilities of jinn.

The Nature of Jinn

Most scholars consider it expedient to give an elaborate discussion on the nature of jinn as propagated in the Qur'an and the Hadith. Ibn Taymiyah devotes a whole chapter on this before reverting to his focus on spirit possession and exorcism in Islam.[42] Al-Ashqar's treatise entitled *The World of Jinn and Devils* offers a substantive explanation on what jinn are and their relation to "Satan."[43]

The nature of jinn is further indicated by the way scholars classify them. Philips and Al-Ashqar categorize jinn together with angels and humans. Philips asserts that these three kinds of beings inhabit the spirit world. He elaborates that humans are considered to be one of the species in the spirit world because their souls are invisible.[44] Most scholars agree with this triadic

---

40. Such scholars include El-Zein, Al-Ashqar, Philips, Taymiyya, and others. See El-Zein, *Islam, Arabs, and the Intelligent*; Al-Ashqar, *World of the Jinn*; Philips, *Exorcist Tradition in Islaam*; and Taymiyya, *Ibn Taymiyah's Essay on the Jinn (Demons)*.

41. Kim, *Islam among the Swahili*, 90.

42. Philips, *Ibn Taymiyah's Essay on the Jinn (Demons)*.

43. Al-Ashqar, *World of the Jinn*.

44. Philips, *Exorcist Tradition in Islaam*, 5.

classification of the spirit beings.[45] Thus for this study, it is expedient to explore whether the Borana Muslims in Marsabit place jinn and *ayyaana* in the same category. Classification of these spiritual beings is deemed important since it will determine how they are dealt with.

It is apparent that Muslim scholars do not dispute the fact that jinn are part and parcel of the human world even though they are created differently. There is no dichotomy between the realms of human beings and supernatural beings. Muslim scholars see a close semblance between jinn and human beings in terms of their nature. There is evidently a consensus that jinn are intelligent beings like humans.[46] El-Zein discusses this in more detail than the other scholars referenced. She presents jinn as rational and intelligent like human beings and thus raises the dilemma about a superiority ranking between the two. El-Zein emphasizes the supremacy of human beings over jinn yet acknowledges the supernatural ability of the latter.

Prophet Muhammad and the Jinn

There is a pertinent debate among scholars about Muhammad's encounter with the jinn. According to El-Zein, a majority of Muslim scholars tend to believe that Muhammad never saw jinn.[47] The question of whether the Prophet had a physical encounter with jinn or not is appropriate because Borana Muslims in Marsabit County, like other Muslims, are expected to follow his example.

Ibn Taymiyah and his disciple, Philips, are among Muslim scholars who believe that Muhammad interacted with jinn physically. Both scholars admit that a number of the Prophet's companions testified that jinn were visible to the Prophet. Ibn Taymiyah dismisses one companion, Ibn 'Abbas, who said Muhammad never saw the jinn. Such a dismissal is based on the conjecture

---

45. El-Zein, *Islam, Arabs, and the Intelligent*. El-Zein does not adhere to this classification. She categorizes jinn with angels and demons (see page xi). She therefore differentiates jinn from demons by asserting that jinn should not be "demonized." She also states that Islam differentiates between jinn and demons, putting them in "two distinct categories of beings" (see page 22). This differs from some Muslim scholars who perceive jinn as "demons." Philips considers jinn to be demons when he places the latter in parenthesis after the word "jinn" in his translation of Ibn Taymiyah's essay. See Philips, *Ibn Taymiyah's Essay*.

46. El-Zein, *Islam, Arabs, and the Intelligent*; Al-Ashqar, World of the Jinn; and Philips, *Exorcist Tradition in Islaam*.

47. El-Zein, *Islam, Arabs, and the Intelligent*, 67.

that this companion did not have much knowledge of the Prophet's interaction with the jinn as the other *Sahaba* (Companions) like Ibn Mas'ood and Abu Hurayra did.[48]

Apart from merely following Ibn Taymiyah's position, Philips justifies his stance on the basis of authenticating Muhammad's prophethood. He cites the Hadiths that narrate the Prophet's encounter with jinn that were supposed to be invisible to other human beings.[49] Philips reinforces his avowal by citing respected Muslim scholars like Imam Ash-Shaafi'ee who consented that Muhammad's prophethood was authenticated by this ability to see jinn.[50]

Conversely, El-Zein stands on the side of Muslim scholars who assert that Muhammad did not see jinn physically. In her argument, she first provides a number of narrations given by different people about Muhammad's physical encounters with the jinn. She, however, negates this by asserting that accepting Muhammad's physical encounters with jinn would border on "popular belief" that is used to justify "popular" practices.[51] Two germane questions, thus, would be whether El-Zein would consider Philips, mentioned above, to be advocating "popular" beliefs and practices. Second, would she agree with Philips on the authenticity of Muhammad in his ability to see jinn physically? These questions are left to the discretion of the reader since she does not allude to any of Philips's writings, although the former seems to be an authority on jinn in Islamic circles.

The Abilities of the Jinn

The Qur'an and Hadiths allude to the supernatural abilities of jinn. This forms the basis of what should be taught by Muslim teachers as the official instructions. The purpose for such teachings is to inform ordinary Muslims not to be enchanted by the abilities of jinn and thus be tempted to commit the sin of *shirk* (association). This section reviews what scholars have written about these abilities of jinn as found in the official texts as well as the conclusions they have inferred, which form a basis for their teachings.

---

48. Taymeeyah and Philips, *Ibn Taymeeyah's Essay*, 39.
49. Philips, *Exorcist Tradition in Islaam*, 54.
50. Philips, 55–56.
51. El-Zein, *Islam, Arabs, and the Intelligent*, 66.

Most Muslim scholars agree concerning the anthropomorphous and aerial abilities of jinn. They base their discussion on the accounts described in the Qur'an and the Hadiths. They attest to the ability of jinn to convert to Islam since they are able to listen, hear, and choose.[52] The ability of the jinn to hear or act like human beings does not seem to be a germane question to most of the Muslim scholars reviewed. Only El-Zein poses a rational question regarding the ability of jinn to listen to the Qur'anic recitation and respond positively.[53] She does not answer this question, probably preferring not to critique what the Islamic texts say. This might also be the reason why Muslim scholars will not question the capabilities of jinn as recorded in the texts.

. Many scholars allude to the supernatural ability of jinn to accomplish extraordinary tasks as illustrated in the Islamic texts. Laughlin asserts that the powers and abilities of jinn are what distinguish them from human beings.[54] The general consensus is that it is God who enables them to do such things. This ensures that human beings do not fall prey to worshipping them for their supernatural abilities. This unanimity among Muslim scholars seems to serve a purpose. Pre-Islamic Arabs had a tendency to worship jinn because of their ability to pry into *al-samaa* (the heavens) and take heavenly messages to men, according to Surah 72: 6–9. Hence, Muslim scholars endeavor to restrain anything that would place the jinn on a higher pedestal than Allah and thus avoid the insidious sin of *shirk*. This awareness is important as I strive to understand why Muslim teachers would oppose the *Ayyaana* cult activities among Borana Muslims in Marsabit County. They are the "people of Tawheed" as Ameen calls Muslims, and thus ought to have a "correct" perspective of the abilities of jinn.[55]

---

52. Muslim scholars who consent to the anthropomorphous nature of jinn include Philips, El-Zein, Al-Ashqar, and others. See Phipis, *Exorcist Tradition in Islaam*; El-Zein, *Islam, Arabs, and the Intelligent*; and Al-Ashqar, *World of the Jinn*.

53. El-Zein, *Islam, Arabs, and the Intelligent*, 67.

54. Laughlin, "Brief Overview of al Jinn," 71.

55. Ameen, *Jinn and Human Sickness*, 31.

Jinn Possession in Islam

Most Muslim scholars do not dispute the reality of jinn possession in Islam. A small minority of Muslims does not believe that spirits can possess people.[56] I appreciate the way Philips deals with the disparity of those who do not believe in jinn possession. He reports that those who are skeptical about jinn possession base their argument on both the Qur'an and logical evidence. They do not justify their position by referring to the Hadiths, which makes their stance weak.[57] Philips does well to analyze the converse side of the argument to avoid subjectivity. He concludes that the reality of jinn possession is a position taken by the majority of "orthodox scholars."[58]

Muslim authors use the Arabic term *ṣara'a* to refer to spirit possession.[59] This differs from what El-Zein discovered about the pre-Islamic usage of the term *ṣara'a*, which literally meant "epilepsy." Her philological study reveals that the word *ṣara'a* was later used by the Arabs to refer to the physical love between some jinn and humans that caused madness.[60] This shows that the phenomenon of jinn possession was in existence both during the *jahiliyyah* period and after the advent of Islam, as Kim consents.[61]

Islamic Texts on Jinn Possession

The possibility of jinn permeating human bodies is justified from Islamic texts, as several scholars have noted. Most of these scholars present jinn possession in a negative way. They agree that the Qur'an and the Hadiths associate jinn possession with *shaiṭan* (Loosely translated as Satan). A number of these scholars quote Surah 2:275 as evidence of jinn possession.[62] They assert that the phrase "Satan's touch" refers to possession since the person "touched" by Satan evidently is in a state of insanity.[63] Philips cites Surah 2:275 as evidence of jinn possession in the Qur'an. He cites a number of Muslim commentators

---

56. Some Mu'tazilites were reported to deny the possibility of jinn entering human bodies. See Philips, *Exorcist Tradition in Islaam*, 80.
57. Philips, "Exorcism in Islam," 85–86.
58. Philips, 89.
59. Philips, *Exorcist Tradition in Islaam*, 77.
60. El-Zein, "The Evolution of the Concept of the Jinn from Pre-Islam to Islam", 306.
61. Kim, *Islam among the Swahili*.
62. Surah 2:275 says, "Those who devour interest rise up like one stumbling from Satan's touch."
63. Philips, *Exorcist Tradition in Islaam*, 79; and Kim, *Islam among the Swahili*, 139.

who interpret "Satan's touch" as madness or insanity and hence a state of jinn possession.[64] Dein, Alexander, and Napier also quote Surah 2:275 to state that jinn cause "erratic behavior in one's words, deeds and movements."[65] Kim refers to the Arabic term *yatakhabbaṭ* and mentions that several Muslim commentators interpret this as "the devil's attack that results in madness," implying jinn possession.[66] As I read what scholars have written, however, it raises a pertinent question: does the Qur'an imply that all cases of madness are caused by jinn possession? Evidently, jinn possession is given a negative connotation in the Qur'an as interpreted by various Muslim scholars. Few acknowledge the positive aspect of possession by "good jinn." Laughlin asserts that "Muslims welcome possession of good jinn. Some Muslims who are possessed feel it is a great honor to be chosen and possessed by good jinn."[67] This is useful as I seek to understand the position of Borana Muslims with regard to jinn and *ayyaana* possession. Do they perceive any of this in a positive or negative way?

The evidence for jinn possession in the Hadiths seems to be more explicit since they narrate more incidences than the Qur'an. Scholars refer to the most quoted text that is found in the six books of the Hadiths apart from the Tirmidhi.[68] This text quotes Muhammad as having commented, "Verily, Satan flows in the blood stream of Adam's descendants." Similarly, the interpreters of the Hadiths believe that *shaiṭan* permeates human bodies and thus leads to possession. This interpretation shows that most Muslim scholars associate *shaiṭan* with jinn, and hence a negative connotation of possession is also presented in the Hadiths. The accounts in the Hadiths mentioned by various scholars link possession with "fits" instead of madness. Philips, for instance, gives the Hadith account of a young boy with "fits" and Muhammad commanded the "enemy of Allah," implying the jinn, to "get out."[69]

---

64. Philips, *Exorcist Tradition in Islaam*, 79–80.
65. Dein, Alexander, and Napier, "Jinn, Psychiatry and Contested Notions," 37.
66. Kim, *Islam among the Swahili*, 139.
67. Laughlin, "Brief Overview of al Jinn," 74.
68. Philips, *Exorcist Tradition in Islaam*, 81.
69. Philips, 82.

Islamic Official Perspective on Dealing with Jinn Possession

Muslim scholars have recommended various ways of dealing with jinn possession that they deem authentic. They agree that reciting Qur'anic *ayah* is an excellent way of expelling jinn.[70] The "verse of the throne" (Surah 2:255) is popular and has also been recommended in the Hadiths (al-Bukhari).[71] Ibn Taymiyyah reported that many people affirmed the effectiveness of using this *ayah* in dealing with troublesome spirits.[72] There are other Surahs of the Qur'an that can be used. Ameen lists a number of them, including the first Surah (*al-Fatihah*). He also acknowledges that the practitioners can be "confused" in diagnosing whether a patient has been bewitched or is possessed by jinn. In such a case, reciting the Qur'an is deemed helpful.[73] Apparently, Muslim scholars believe that the Qur'an can also be used to "punish" the jinn.[74] It is not clear how this is achieved. Ameen gives seventeen Surahs that are used for this purpose but does not elaborate on how the *ayahs* are able to achieve this purpose. The reader is thus left questioning whether the Qur'an has inherent power to "punish" the jinn that afflicts the victim of possession.

There are some Muslim scholars who consider drinking concoctions as an authentic way of dealing with jinn in Islam.[75] Ameen says that if the jinn is "stubborn" and does not respond to the punishment from reading the Qur'an, then the use of other remedies, like the nose drops, is allowed.[76] The assumption behind administering these nose drops is that jinn is located in the brain. The drops will thus pass through the nose and go straight to the brain to annoy the jinn, which will be irritated and depart.[77] Ameen's suggestion may appeal more to the popular mind as found in Marsabit County.

Ameen suggests a unique approach that I have not found with other Muslim scholars. He appeals to Muslim doctors to accommodate practitioners

---

70. El-Zein, *Islam, Arabs, and the Intelligent*, 85; Al-Ashqar, *World of the Jinn*, 207; and Dein, Alexander, and Napier, "Jinn, Psychiatry and Contested Notions," 45.

71. Al-Bukhari says, "Whoever reads it [Surah 2:255], Allah will not stop to have a protection for him and Satan will not come close to him until the morning."

72. Quoted by Umar Sulaiman Al-Ashqar. See Al-Ashqar, *World of the Jinn*, 208.

73. Ameen, *Jinn and Human Sickness*, 93.

74. Ameen, 113.

75. Lim, Hoek, and Blom, "Attribution of Psychotic Symptoms," 5.

76. Ameen, *Jinn and Human Sickness*, 128.

77. Ameen, 128.

who use the Qur'an to treat patients.⁷⁸ He writes with such a firm conviction of the effectiveness of these Qur'anic remedies that the reader cannot fail to notice. He also aims at empowering individual Muslims to treat themselves instead of relying on practitioners.⁷⁹ He exposes the dangers of folk practitioners who emphasize rituals like *Zar*, and he encourages Muslims to use *dhikr* and prayers for protection as prescribed by Muhammad.⁸⁰ This indicates there are Muslims who use "un-Islamic" ways to deal with jinn possession as indicated in the section below.

Jinn Possession in Contemporary Islamic Contexts

Empirical research reveals that jinn possession is widespread and not only confined to the Arabian Peninsula, the cradle of Islam, or to Africa. Lebling provides the "geography" of jinn by highlighting different places where the phenomenon of jinn possession is experienced. The Arabian Peninsula is said to be the "heartland of the jinn," and yet it is the birthplace of Islam.⁸¹ Mullick, Khalifa, Nahar, and Walker did a quantitative study in Bangladesh to investigate how the variables of gender and levels of education affected the belief in jinn, magic and the evil eye. They hypothesized that belief in jinn and other supernatural entities was correlated with low education and being female. This was validated by their quantitative research. It is interesting to note further that the Bangladeshi Muslims believed more in the existence of jinn than in black magic and the evil eye.⁸² Khalifa, Hardie, and Mullick did a comparative study of belief in jinn among Muslims in Leicester, UK, and in Dhaka, Bangladesh. They acknowledged that their quantitative study had a number of limitations, like the authenticity of people's responses to the questionnaires. Respondents tended to give answers that were compatible with the official requirements of Islam rather than present what they really believed.⁸³ This illustrates the need to carry out ethnographical research that takes the researcher to meet the interviewees face to face.

---

78. Ameen, 26.
79. Ameen, 24.
80. Ameen, 24.
81. Lebling, *Legends of the Fire*, 115.
82. Mullick et al., "Beliefs about Jinn," 726.
83. Khalifa, Hardie, and Mullick, "Jinn and Psychiatry, 6.

Dein, Alexander, and Napier studied the Bangladeshi Muslims in East London from a socio-anthropological perspective and used ethnographic interviews. Their aim was to investigate the understanding of misfortune in relation to the role of jinn. Their findings can be compared with what Mullick, Khalifa, Nahar, and Walker discovered among Bangladeshi Muslims in Dakha. The two Bangladeshi communities in different socioeconomic contexts depicted similar findings. The socially and economically deprived Bangladeshi are more prone to believe in jinn's role in causing misfortune regardless of their locales.[84]

A review of findings from other empirical studies on the concepts of jinn and possession among Muslims reveals that different groups of people participate in the Jinn cult. Drieskens examined the Cairenes lower-middle class men and women and realized that both educated and non-educated Muslim women and men participate in jinn cults. She did not carry out a quantitative study like Mullick, Khalifa, and Walker did. Yet, she encountered a number of men who not only believed in the existence of jinn but also were or had been possessed.[85] Kim's study of the therapeutic cult of jinn possession among the Waswahili people further affirms that "all levels of Swahili people are found in the therapeutic rituals."[86] There seems to be a consensus among scholars that both male and female participate in possession cults. It is not only women who are prone to possession. This is helpful for this research, as it is not confined to examining women adepts of spirit possession among Borana Muslims.

Apart from the anthropological perspectives employed, scholars have also studied jinn and possession in contemporary contexts from psychological viewpoints.[87] Examining the relationship between mental health and jinn possession among different Islamic content has been popular. Hanley and Brown, for instance, have explored postnatal depression among Arab Muslim women that is usually interpreted as jinn possession.[88] Essentially, studying

---

84. Dein, Alexander, and Napier, "Jinn, Psychiatry and Contested Notions," 35.

85. Drieskens, *Living with Djinns*, 16.

86. Caleb Chul-Soo Kim, "Supernaturalism in Swahili Islam: With Special Reference to the Therapeutic Cults of Jinn Possession" (Ph.D Dissertation, USA, Fuller Graduate School, 2001), 244.

87. Bulbulia and Laher, "Exploring the Role," 52–54.

88. Hanley and Brown, "Cultural Variations in Interpretation," 348.

the phenomenon of possession from different perspectives shows the possibility of using a multidisciplinary approach.

Dealing with Jinn in Contextual Islamic Settings

Studies on jinn possession in different Islamic settings demonstrate that there is an amalgamation of the official beliefs and practices with respective cultural beliefs and rituals in dealing with jinn. This has made some scholars unable to differentiate between jinn and the traditional spirits, and they have examined them as one.[89] *Zar*, for instance, has been termed a "type of jinn possession ceremony" by Lebling, who even asserts that it is not Islamic even though it has some Islamic tendencies.[90] The discussion on whether jinn should be equated to the traditional spirits is relevant to this study. A related question is whether *ayyaana* are classified as jinn or not. This classification determines how to deal with spirits.

Popular approaches include appeasing the jinn by offering sacrifices. Musk, for instance, reports that the Moroccan *jinniya* afflicts victims whose only remedy is to maintain a "give-and-take" relationship.[91] Practitioners who attempt such methods are often termed as non-Muslims even though they insist they are Muslims.[92] Al-Ashqar and other Muslim scholars are against such conciliatory practices. Offering animal sacrifices is seen as an act of polytheism that is prohibited in Islam,[93] and thus it is forbidden, especially by some contemporary Muslims with Wahhabi tendencies.

Hanely and Brown carried out research among married Muslim mothers who were possessed by jinn in an Arabian Gulf nation. They wanted to know about the experiences of these mothers with jinn. The findings of the research demonstrate that the local sheikhs employ Islamic ways like reciting the Qur'anic Surahs and *ayahs*. Yet this is mixed with popular ways like sacrificing a sheep or goat as well as giving expensive items to appease the jinn.[94] Ibn Taymiyyah denounces these as acts of *kufr* and *shirk* which are

---

89. Drieskens, *Living with Djinns*; Lebling, *Legends of the Fire*; and Lim, Hoek, and Blom, "Attribution of Psychotic Symptoms."
90. Lebling, *Legends of the Fire*, 76.
91. Musk, *Unseen Face of Islam*, 40.
92. Dein, Alexander, and Napier, "Jinn, Psychiatry and Contested Notions," 44.
93. Al-Ashqar, World of the Jinn, 212.
94. Hanley and Brown, "Cultural Variations in Interpretation," 351–52.

ḥarām (forbidden) in Islam.⁹⁵ He recommends the use of Qur'anic *ayahs* that can be written, washed, and drunk by the afflicted or possessed person. He justifies this by quoting accounts from the "Companions of Muhammad."⁹⁶ Philips seems to disagree with this idea of drinking Qur'anic verses. He offers a lengthy footnote on the issue and admits it is a *bid'ah* (innovation) since it is neither *sunna* nor Islamic.⁹⁷ Here, then, Philips disagrees with his teacher, Ibn Taymiyyah, yet it is a practice that has taken root in many Muslim communities, like the Borana Muslims in Marsabit County. It was valid to find out if this practice of drinking Qur'anic water is derived from Ibn Taymiyyah's writings in the county.

From the above discussion, it is apparent that there is a dilemma among Muslims. While there is a vehement denunciation of un-Islamic practices, the ordinary Muslim still reverts to such rituals. The main question – the essence of this research – is why they still cling to such practices in spite of the prohibition in the Islamic texts. The Muslim scholars do not seem to offer a substantial explanation. The tendency is to blame the adepts for lack of *taqwa* (piety) and faith in Allah.⁹⁸ Yet it suffices to inquire how much of this piety and faith is instilled in the ordinary Muslims so that they move in the direction required. It is therefore pertinent to this research to investigate how the Muslim teachers attempt to inculcate the correct teachings about spirits as explained in the Islamic texts. This will ensure that people have the expected view of spirits and conversely how to deal with them. Are they entities that one can rightly accommodate within their physical realms, or are they unwanted beings that are to be exorcised? Answering this question entails a review of how scholars have approached the issue of accommodation or exorcism in Islam. This is deemed significant for this research, which adds to the literature on how Muslims deal with spirits.

---

95. Philips, *Ibn Taymiyah's Essay*, 99.

96. Philips, 105.

97. *Sunna* is the term used to refer to a practice that follows the example of the Prophet. For Philips's footnote, see Philips, *Ibn Taymiyah's Essay on the Jinn (Demons)*, 106.

98. Ameen, *Jinn and Human Sickness*, 94.

Exorcism versus Adorcism

Frankfurter asks a germane question: "What does exorcism mean in cultures that live in perpetual relationship with spirits?"[99] He uses a historical approach to examine how Christians dealt with spirit possession in the ancient Mediterranean world.[100] His reference to Greco-Roman literature on spirit possession and exorcism shows that the phenomenon predates Islam. This may reinforce Maarouf's skepticism of using the term *exorcism*. He asserts that it is a Western term that is associated with the history of demonology and uses specific rites and practices employed by the Christian. He prefers to use the term *jinn eviction*, which is the central focus of his study on the Moroccan culture.[101] Maarouf may be right in explaining that jinn are not found in Christian tradition hence his preference for the phrase instead of exorcism. Not many Muslim scholars follow his rationalization. A number of them prefer the term "exorcism" as the authentic way of dealing with jinn and other spirits.[102]

Some scholars have mistakenly referred to appeasement procedures as exorcizing the spirits. Kim critiques Swantz for using the term *exorcism* while referring to the "pacifying rituals" performed by the Wazaramo in Tanzania. Kim bases his criticism on the description of exorcism as the process involved when spirits are "cast out with a vengeance" as they are perceived to be enemies.[103] Bourguignon similarly uses the verb *exorcising* inappropriately to refer to what transpires during the "expensive ceremonies that include lavish gifts to the spirit."[104] Sesi refers to exorcism as "spiritual surgery" in her discussion on the social change among Digo women along the coast of Kenya. She mentions that the "way to appease or exorcise a spirit was mostly through a dance called *kayamba* that was fully controlled by women."[105]

---

99. Frankfurter, "Where the Spirits Dwell," 28.

100. Hilaire Kalendorf also examined the phenomenon of "demonic possession" and exorcism in early modern literature of England and Spain between 1550 and 1700.

101. Maarouf, *Jinn Eviction as a Discourse*, 1.

102. Bilal Philips, *Exorcist Tradition in Islaam*, 1997; Amira El-Zein, *Islam, Arabs, and the Intelligent*, 2009; and Al-Ashqar, *World of the Jinn*, 1998.

103. Kim, *Islam among the Swahili*, 190.

104. Bourguignon, "Suffering and Healing," 560.

105. Sesi, "Social Change among Digo," 109.

A technical word used by scholars to denote pacification of spirits is *adorcism*, coined by sociologist Luc de Heusch to mean "a positive relation between a possessed man and the possessing spirit."[106] Adorcism is basically domesticating the spirits and establishing a "peaceful relationship" with them. This stems from what Kim explains as spirits, which are accepted as "legitimate societal members" and hence are accommodated or domesticated.[107] Instead of using the term *domestication*, Lewis uses *adorcism*, which he explains as being the "accommodation or internalization" in relation to the way people form viable relationships with spirits.[108]

Those who advocate for adorcism therefore imply that jinn are not supposed to be expelled from the human body.[109] But this is strongly refuted as *shirk* by Muslim scholars like Philips.[110] However, Philips and other Muslim scholars who have written on jinn possession have not really dealt with the issue of how to interact with the Muslim jinn, which are considered to be good. Maarouf at least refers to "evil and good spirits." He seems to imply the dilemma of how to deal with these two kinds of jinn. The evil ones are to be evicted while the good ones are to be accommodated since they may be beneficial to people. Jinn eviction is then replaced with "trance dance" in order to appease the jinn in a covenantal relationship with the possessed person.[111] I find Maarouf's approach to the study of the jinn concept more pragmatic as I examine the way Borana Muslims deal with both *ayyaana* and jinn.

Spirit Possession in African Muslim Communities

There are seminal works on the phenomenon of spirit possession that have been written from anthropological, sociological, historical, psychological, and medical perspectives, and also within religious studies discipline. This current review is confined to literature on spirit possession among African Muslim communities. The objective is to grasp the perspectives and approaches employed as well as consequent theories formulated by scholars based on varied

---

106. Heusch, *Sacrifice in Africa*, 216.
107. Kim, *Islam among the Swahili*, 190.
108. Lewis, "Exorcism and Male Control," 26.
109. Lim, Hoek, and Blom, "Attribution of Psychotic Symptoms," 5.
110. Philips, "Exorcism in Islam," 116.
111. Maarouf, *Jinn Eviction as a Discourse*, 2.

empirical procedures. I. M. Lewis's deprivation and centrality theories have been specifically critiqued by a number of scholars. Some of these responses will also be included in this review.

Conceptualizing Spirit Possession

Before reviewing various perspectives of scholars who have examined spirit possession among African Muslims, it is essential to comprehend how they have conceptualized the phenomenon. Scholars have debated over whether to define spirit possession as trance or vice versa. Erika Bourguignon is renowned for dichotomizing possession and trance. Scholars, like Lambek, have criticized this dichotomy.[112] Bourguignon's assumptions are generalized and have overlooked the contextual nature of spirit possession.

Huskinson and Schmidt make a valid claim that spirit possession is a "cultural phenomenon" that is unique to different cultural settings. This makes it defy a single universal definition or interpretation.[113] The call, therefore, is to go beyond preconceived dichotomies and embrace "perspectivism" with an empathetic attitude. According to Huskinson and Schmidt, perspectivism "reveals how no one perspective or interpretation is inherently more valuable or accurate than another, and neither can one perspective be understood by another's terms."[114] The significance of the dimension of "Otherness" in conceptualizing spirit possession needs to be appreciated as explained by Leistle, whose approach I find helpful. Leistle emphasizes the need to include the perspective of the "phenomenology of the Other" in the study of possession as a phenomenon.[115] In this phenomenological study of *ayyaana* and possession among Borana Muslims, I take heed of Leistle's caution that I should not be drawn to a Western structural characterization of possession that considers the phenomenon as irrational.[116] I will discuss Leistle's proposition more – and its appropriateness for my study – in the methodology chapter.

Some scholars have taken the above cue and have preferred to conceptualize possession in terms that closely conform to those of the people under

---

112. Huskinson and Schmidt, "Introduction," 5.
113. Huskinson and Schmidt, 7.
114. Huskinson and Schmidt, 13.
115. Leistle, "From the Alien," 55.
116. Leistle, 57.

study. Constantinides, for instance, defines a possessed person according to the Sudanese perception.[117] Kim also endeavors to describe spirit possession from an *emic* perspective and proceeds to describe the dichotomy between trance-ecstasy and possession based on the terminology used by the Swahili people.[118] He then critiques those who have failed to see this dichotomy, like Sheila Walker as having a Western interpretation that "gives an inaccurate and irrelevant conclusion."[119] The pertinent element I take from this discussion on how different scholar have conceptualized the phenomenon of spirit possession is the need to respect the worldview orientation of the African community under study. It is from such a premise that I now examine how various scholars have studied possession cults among African Muslims.

Scholarly Approaches to Possession Cults in African Islamic Contexts

It has been noted above that the phenomenon of spirit possession has continued to attract an array of scholars. The table below summarizes the theories propounded by various scholars as well as their contributions toward this current study. Notably, functionalism and symbolism are popular perspectives that have been used in trying to explain the phenomenon of possession.

Table 1: Some Scholarly Works on Spirit Possession among African Muslims

Scholar's Name	Research Context	Theoretical Framework/Approach	Theory Advanced	Significance for Current Study
I. M. Lewis[120]	The *Zar* cult among the Somali people	Functional perspective from a sociocultural approach	Deprivation theory	Provides useful variables for the interview guide, for example, women's participation.

---

117. Constantinides, "Sickness and the Spirits," 22.

118. According to Kim, the Swahili people translate both *trance* and *ecstasy* as *jadhba* (or *jazba* or *jaziba*) and it is mainly during the Sufi *dhikri* sessions. It is not the same as what takes place during the *ngoma ya kupunga majini/masheitani* possession cult. See Kim, "Supernaturalism in Swahili Islam," 229.

119. Walker, *Ceremonial Spirit Possession*; and Kim, "Supernaturalism in Swahili Islam," 229.

120. Lewis, *Ecstatic Religion*.

Scholar's Name	Research Context	Theoretical Framework/Approach	Theory Advanced	Significance for Current Study
Linda L. Giles[121]	Swahili coastal spirits in East Africa	Sociocultural approach Considers possession cults as symbolic expressions of culture Addresses the question of meaning rather than function	Cultural symbolism theory (following Clifford Geertz)	Is the *Ayyaana* possession cult culturally symbolic?
Lisa Mackenrodt[122]	Swahili spirit possession in Tanga, Tanzania	Anthropological approach from a functionalistic perspective	The worldview of the Swahili people is shaped by their perception of the spirit world	The use of vernacular language to analyze possession discourse
Kjersti Larsen[123]	*Mashetani* spirits in the town of Zanzibar town	Sociocultural approach from a phenomenological perspective	Theory of "Otherness"	The relationship between spirits and humans
Janice Boddy[124]	*Zar* among the Hofriyati people in northern Sudan	Sociocultural approach	Possession as a "cultural idiom" *Zar* as counterhegemonic and antisociety	Getting a broad cultural perspective within which the *Ayyaana* cult is embraced

---

121. Giles, "Possession Cults"; and Giles, "Spirit Possession."
122. Mackenrodt, *Swahili Spirit Possession*.
123. Larsen, *Where Humans and Spirits*.
124. Boddy, "Spirits and Selves"; and Boddy, *Wombs and Alien Spirits*.

Scholar's Name	Research Context	Theoretical Framework/Approach	Theory Advanced	Significance for Current Study
Caleb Chul-Soo Kim[125]	Jinn among Swahili Muslims in Zanzibar	Anthropological perspective using the STA (Synthetic Triangular Approach) guideline	Spiritual/Psychological perspective Uses worldview theory to analyze data Domain of total synthesis theory	Phenomenological emphasis Employs the STA guideline as a methodology framework
Susan M. Kenyon[126]	The *Zar* cult in Central Sudan	Narrative approach (case study)	Sociological theory	The relationship between the "official"(*zikr*) and "non-official" (*zar*) sanctioned cults
Jean-Paul Colleyn[127]	The *Nya* cult in Mali	Socio-religious approach	Possession is not a peripheral phenomenon	The place of men in the possession cults
Janet McIntosh[128]	The Giriama people along the coast of Kenya	Socio-religious approach	Possession as hegemonic Proposes the idea of a poly-ontological belief system instead of syncretism	Helps to check if Borana Muslims are also polyontological and not syncretic

---

125. Kim, "Considering 'Ordinariness' in Studying"; Kim, *Islam among the Swahili*; and Kim, "Supernaturalism in Swahili Islam."

126. Kenyon, "Case of the Butcher's Wife"; and Kenyon, "'Movable Feast of Signs.'"

127. Colleyn, "Horse, Hunter & Messenger."

128. McIntosh, "Reluctant Muslims"; and McIntosh, "Edge of Islam."

Scholarly Works on Spirits in Islam

Scholar's Name	Research Context	Theoretical Framework/Approach	Theory Advanced	Significance for Current Study
Adeline Masquelier[129]	The *Bori* cult in Niger	Religiocultural approach from a historical and anthropological perspective	Considers the theory of power and resistance Concludes that *bori* is not counter-hegemonic to Islam but upholds the traditions of the Mawri people	Helps to see how power and identity play out in possession cults
Matthias Krings[130]	*Bori* spirits in Kano, Nigeria	Historico-linguistic approach	Possession as mimesis and reconstruction of history	Analyzes the language of the spirits and thus alludes to the importance of the language spoken during *ayyaana* possession
Adeline Masquelier[131]	*Dodo* spirits in Southern Niger	Religo-cultural approach	Considers *dodo* spirits as an anti-traditional aspect of the Mawri people, unlike the *bori* spirits that uphold traditions	Masquelier's comparative study of *dodo* spirits with the *Bori* cult gives an idea of studying *ayyaana* more broadly

---

129. Masquelier, "Bloodstain"; and Masquelier, *Prayer Has Spoiled Everything*.
130. Krings, "On History & Language."
131. Masquelier, "The Invention of Anti-Tradition."

Scholar's Name	Research Context	Theoretical Framework/Approach	Theory Advanced	Significance for Current Study
Adeline Masquelier[132]	*Bori* spirits in an Islamic town of Niger	Socio-religious and historical approach Analyzes *bori* in light of the Muslim discourse	The *Bori* cult functions as a mediating factor between the "traditional" world and contemporary Islam in a paradox	Her ethnographic research procedure and analysis of the interplay between the *Bori* cult and contemporary Islam is helpful for this current study that also examines the interplay between ideological Islam and the lived experiences of Muslims
Susan Rasmussen[133]	Northern Mali	Psycho-social approach in dream analysis	Kaleidoscopic identities and meanings in spirit dreams	Illustrates the place of dream metaphors in construction of cultural models
Anne M. Jennings[134]	Southern Egypt	Religio-sociological approach Examines the *Zikr* ceremony by Nubians as a syncretistic event	Theory of syncretism	Shows the amalgamation of pre-Islamic practices with Islamic ceremony
Lorand J. Matory[135]	Yoruba, Nigeria	Gender, religion, and politics in Yoruba Islam	Disapproves deprivation theory	Significant in showing that it is not always about resistance when there is religious contestation

---

132. Masquelier, "Bloodstain"; and Masquelier, *Prayer Has Spoiled Everything*.
133. Rasmussen, "Ambiguous Spirit Dream."
134. Jennings, "Nubian Zikr."
135. Matory, "Rival Empires."

Scholar's Name	Research Context	Theoretical Framework/Approach	Theory Advanced	Significance for Current Study
P. M. Constantinides[136]	The *Zar* cult in northern Sudan	Sociological approach Discusses the ritual process of the *Zar* cult and employs theories of illness	The *Zar* cult provides symbolic significance of women	Provides an example of how to quantify investigative variables in a qualitative research of possession
Richard C. Jankowsky[137]	The *Stambeli* cult in Tunisia	Ethnomusicology: studying the relation between trance and music	Music and trance are culturally conditioned	Brings out the importance of studying the music involved in possession sessions
Kamal Feriali[138]	Morocco	Music-induced spirit possession: implications for anthropology	Anthropological framework that departs from functionalism and embraces symbolic meaning	Discussion on the tripartite nature of the possession cult is relevant The place of music in inducing trance during possession
Marja Tiilikainen[139]	The *Saar* cult in Somaliland and Finland	Socio-religious perspective	The dynamic nature of the *Saar* possession cult that makes it not disappear	Helps to show the dynamism in spirit possession in revitalizing religiocultural contexts
Richard Natvig[140]	Ethiopia, Eritrea, Djibouti, Somalia, Egypt, and Sudan	Historical perspective that examines the origin and development of the *Zar* cult	Propounds the theory that the *Zar* cult had its origin in Ethiopia	The Ethiopian origin of the *Zar* cult is significant as I note that the *Ayyana* cult in Kenya also has its origin in Ethiopia

---

136. Constantinides, "Sickness and Spirits", and Constantinides, "The History of the Zaar in the Sudan."
137. Jankowsky, "Music, Spirit Possession"; Jankowsky, *Stambeli*.
138. Feriali, "Music-Induced Spirit Possession."
139. Tiilikainen, "Somali Saar."
140. Natvig, "Oromos, Slaves, and the Zar."

From the table above, three things are evident: First, the Swahili people along the East African Coast have drawn the attention of a number of scholars.[141] Second, *zar* and *bori* ceremonies, in the eastern and western parts of Africa respectively, have been studied widely. Boddy, Kenyon, Constantinides, and Natvig, among others, have examined *zar* ceremonies, while Masqualier, Krings, and others have examined *bori*.[142] This reinforces Giles's remarks that the Somali *zar*/Ethiopian *saar* and the Hausa *bori* have been a focus of many scholars who have "tried to bridge anthropological/ sociological and psychiatric theory."[143] Third, the different perspectives and approaches taken by these scholars show the possibility of a multidisciplinary approach in studying the phenomenon of possession in the Muslim world.

The sociocultural approach seems to be popular among scholars.[144] Most of these have employed ethnographic research to elicit information about spirit possession in Islamic communities. Their studies suggest significant clues that I have gleaned for my study of *ayyaana* and possession. The research procedures as well as their analyses of the data collected have provided useful ideas. Basically, there is a need to immerse oneself in the community of study – as Boddy, Larsen, and others did – in order to understand the phenomenon of possession within the cultural setting.

Those who have studied possession from a religious perspective include Colleyn, Masquelier, McIntosh, and others.[145] Some of these scholars, like Kim and Mackenrodt, have examined Muslims' participation in possession cults vis-à-vis the requirements of Islam.[146] Both have examined Swahili Islam as practiced by Swahili Muslims in their encounters with spirits. These authors

---

141. Such scholars include Caleb Chul-Soo Kim, Kjersti Larsen, Linda L. Giles, Esha Faki, E. M. Kasiera, and O. M. J. Nandi. See Kim, "Supernaturalism in Swahili Islam"; Larsen, *Where Humans and Spirits*; Giles, "Possession Cults"; and Faki, Kasiera, and Nandi, "Belief and Practice."

142. Boddy, *Wombs and Alien Spirits*; Kenyon, "Case of the Butcher's Wife"; Constantinides, "Sickness and the Spirits"; "The History of the Zar in the Sudan," Natvig, "Oromos, Slaves, and the Zar"; Masquelier, *Prayer Has Spoiled Everything*; and Krings, "On History & Language."

143. Giles, "Possession Cults," 234.

144. Giles, "Possession Cults"; Giles, "The Dialectic of Spirit Possession"; "Spirit Possession"; Larsen, *Where Humans and Spirits*; Boddy, *Wombs and Alien Spirits*; Masquelier, "The Invention of Anti-Tradition"; and Constantinides, Women Heal Women."

145. Colleyn, "Horse, Hunter & Messenger"; Masquelier, "Lightning, Death and the Avenging"; and McIntosh, "Edge of Islam."

146. Kim, *Islam among the Swahili*; Mackenrodt, Swahili Spirit Possession.

also see the need to begin their treatise by examining the historical background of the Swahili people. Their discussion of the world of spirits follows as they deal with the therapeutic aspects involved in the spirit cults. I have found Kim's work quite useful as he approaches the therapeutic cult of jinn among ordinary Muslims using a methodological guideline that I have adapted appropriately in this study. His textual study of the relevant references to jinn spirits in the Islamic texts enriches my study. Most important is his focus on comparing these Islamic requirements with the lived experiences of ordinary Muslims as they engage with the world of spirits. This is a non-reductionist approach that is not limited to the functionalist perspective that has been popular among scholars of spirit possession.

Functionalism versus Symbolic Meaning in Interpreting the Possession Phenomenon

Scholars who have delved into the functionalism perspective consider possession cults as serving a particular emancipatory function that appeals to the sociological and psychological needs of participants. I. M. Lewis is especially noted for this and has had quite a following. The subsequent section includes some responses to his popular theory emanating from this functional approach.

Lambek and Giles are among the scholars who allude to the reductionist aspect of the functional approach.[147] They support the analysis of spirit possession in terms of the "symbolic medium," which deals with "the question of meaning rather than merely of function," according to Giles.[148] She follows what she refers to as Clifford Geertz's "seminal concept of the 'cultural text' . . . 'written' and 'read' by the society concerned; they are stories that the society tells itself about itself."[149] Boddy also embraces the symbolism approach in her study of the *Zar* cult in northern Sudan. She states that *zar* is a "cultural idiom" that the Hofriyati people use to articulate certain problems and daily experiences.[150] It is from this premise that Boddy's response to the issue of increased participation of women in possession cults becomes relevant. She

---

147. Lambek, *Human Spirits*. Giles, "Possession Cults on the Swahili Coast."
148. Giles, "Spirit Possession," 142.
149. Giles, 142.
150. Boddy, *Wombs and Alien Spirits*, 137.

suggests that the cultural constructs that define particular gender roles should also be considered – not only the motives and intentions of possessed people.

Stoller analyzes Songhay possession as a symbolic medium. He asserts that the possession ceremonies "reflect symbolic themes of Songhay history."[151] Likewise, Feriali departs from functionalism because he has discovered that "possession trance is *not* primarily utilitarian." He perceives possession as a "cultural template with flexible meanings."[152] Leistle further notes that the complexity and multifold nature of spirit possession does not allow it to be restricted to functionalism.[153] Likewise, Larsen examines possession among the Zanzibari people from a non-functionalistic perspective. She uses the theory of embodiment in exploring how the people experience and relate to possession by jinn, which she calls *mashetani* or *majini*.[154]

Responding to Lewis's Deprivation Theory

Lewis's usage of the functionalism approach led him to formulate the periphery theory that has become a "seminal construct in possession theory," as reported by Giles.[155] McIntosh alludes to the fact that Lewis's theory still pervades the theoretical arena explaining possession.[156] Lewis developed this theory from his extensive study of the possession cults among Somali people and others. He asserts that possession cults are peripheral as they are majorly restricted to socially marginalized or subordinated women in religion. Such cults are also amoral since they do not form part of the main morality cult.[157]

Several scholars share the assertion that possession cults cannot be relegated to the periphery in Islamic contexts.[158] Lambek's study of spirits in Madagascar reveals that possession is a "basic aspect of the social structure."[159]

---

151. Stoller, *Fusion of the Worlds*, 19.
152. Feriali, "Music-Induced Spirit Possession," 126.
153. Leistle, "From the Alien," 54.
154. Larsen, *Where Humans and Spirits*, 4.
155. Giles, "Possession Cults," 235.
156. McIntosh, "Reluctant Muslims," 92.
157. Lewis, *Ecstatic Religion*, 26.
158. For example, see Giles, "Spirit Possession"; Lambek, *Human Spirits*; Kim, *Islam Among the Swahili in East Africa*; Boddy, *Wombs and Alien Spirits*, Boddy, "Spirits and Selves"; Wangombe, *Missiological Study*; Colleyn, "Horse, Hunter, & Messeger"; and Masquelier, *Prayer Has Spoiled Everything*.
159. Lambek, Human Spirits, 69.

Boddy has studied the *zar* spirits in northern Sudan, and he concludes that spirit possession is not just a reaction to problems.[160] The Hofriyati women in Sudan do not use *zar* possession as a strategy to redress the issues surrounding their subordinate status.[161] Boddy considers the marginality theory thus an "unhappily androcentric portrayal of women."[162] Similarly, Giles re-examines the theories of marginality and concludes that possession cults form one of the "most illuminating expressions" in the societies in which they are found and thus cannot be relegated to the periphery.[163] Giles's study of Swahili possession along the coast of Kenya shows that female mediums are not marginalized in the society. Her inference is that the interpretation of marginality is based on subjectivity and ideological stances of non-members of the possession cults.[164]

Research carried out in various places further refutes that possession cults are confined to marginalized women. Colleyn discovers that the *Nya* possession cult in Mali involves men who belong to "powerful lineages" in the society.[165] Apart from men, children also participate in possession cults. I observed the *Ayyaana* possession cult among Munyoyaya Muslims in Kenya and showed that, even though women are the majority, men and children also participate as patients and practitioners.[166] This disproportionate abundance of women in possession cults has been an area of empirical studies.

Cohen disputes Lewis's functional approach on the premise that sociological factors of class and power used to explain preponderance of possession are not the only causal factors.[167] She uses an interdisciplinary trajectory that especially tries to bridge psychology with anthropology in examining the phenomenon of spirit possession. Her approach is reviewed in the next section since she uses a theoretical framework akin to the framework of this current study.

---

160. Boddy, "Spirits and Selves," 398.
161. Boddy, *Wombs and Alien Spirits*, 139.
162. Boddy, 140.
163. Giles, "Possession Cults," 234.
164. Giles, 235.
165. Colleyn, "Horse, Hunter & Messenger," 68.
166. Wang'ombe, *Missiological Study*, 109.
167. Cohen, *Mind Possessed*, 94.

Cognitive Anthropological Perspective: A Review of Emma Cohen's Work

The paucity of literature that examines spirit possessions from a cognitive, anthropological perspective indicates the existence of a dichotomy between the mind and culture. However, the last half of the twentieth century saw Claude Levi-Strauss begin the process of bringing the "mind back to culture."[168] Nevertheless, the need to examine spirit possession from a cognitive perspective was not realized immediately. This was until Emma Cohen presented her book, *The Mind Possessed*, based on data collected from an Afro-Brazilian ritual center. It is probably the first "substantial book on spirit possession" written from a cognitive perspective.[169]

Cohen notes that an extensive study has been done on the phenomenon of spirit possession, yet there have been few attempts to assimilate the different theoretical frameworks.[170] She lists the previous approaches used and critiques them for not appreciating the "cognitive component of possession trance as a subject of causal inquiry."[171] She then opts to use an interdisciplinary approach that employs ethnographic methods to elicit data and analyze it from a cognitive science perspective. She suggests that ideas about spirits and possession are primarily fostered and constrained by ordinary cognitive mechanisms and processes. On gender and marginalization, Cohen proposes an empathizing-systematizing theory stating that women are more inclined to possession because of their empathizing skills that are more developed than those of men, who in turn are better in systematizing.[172]

Cohen's persistent appeal to address the phenomenon of possession from a cognitive perspective is also evident in the number of articles she has written and coauthored. Justin Barrett follows Cohen's premise that human cognitive capacities can provide useful explanations of the regularity of cultural phenomena.[173] They coauthored an article that reports on the findings of an

---

168. Shore, *Culture in Mind*, 29.
169. Samuel, "Possession and Self-Possession," 36.
170. Cohen, *Mind Possessed*, 11.
171. Cohen, 14.
172. Cohen, 203.
173. Cohen and Barrett follow Pascal Boyer and Harvey Whitehouse, who delve into the issue of science of cognition in religion from a psychological approach. See Boyer, *Religion Explained*; and Whitehouse, *Modes of Religiosity*.

empirical study, which examined the cognitive foundations of forms of possession belief recurring cross-culturally.[174] In particular, they investigate why the displacement theory of possession was more prevalent than the fusion and oscillatory theories.[175] Cohen and Barrett realized that the two latter theories are more cognitively engaging and require more reinforcement than the displacement theory in ensuring transmission.[176] According to them, prevalent ideas on possession are propagated by the ordinary cognitive abilities that are employed to make sense of the world around people. Hence, cognitive factors facilitate transmission of popular possession beliefs more than the historio-cultural factors. In another coauthored paper, Cohen and Barrett further their claim about the displacement principle in possession and reckon that this can help explain the nature of the inherent mind-body dualism.[177]

Cohen and Barrett's ability to interweave cognitive theory with both ethnographic and experimental research has been commended by a cadre of scholars. Cohen's book has been applauded because of its pioneer nature. These compliments are also coupled with criticisms from various people. Hale admires the clarity with which Cohen presents her cognitive hypothesis. However, he wonders how this hypothesis can be tested in the field for validity.[178]

Cohen responds to three critics who list a number of issues emanating from her book. Espirito Santo states that Cohen needs to revise her questions that form the basis of her book.[179] Santo also considers it paradoxical that Cohen would aim at explaining the phenomena of possession yet pay little attention to the structure and experience of possession. The fact that she does not engage in a phenomenological approach to elicit knowledge

---

174. Cohen and Barrett, "Conceptualizing Spirit Possession." In their study, Cohen and Barrett used both qualitative research (following Cohen's ethnographic research of the Afro-Brazilian cult) and quantitative research.

175. The displacement theory asserts that the mind of the possessed person migrates and is displaced by the spirit, while the fusion and oscillatory theories claim that the mind of the host fuses with the spirit and becomes one (Cohen 2007, 144).

176. The fusion and oscillatory theories are not easily transmitted within a group because it is hard to comprehend how the human mind can fuse and become one with a spirit.

177. Cohen and Barrett, "When Minds Migrate," 26.

178. Hale, "Book Review," 480.

179. Cohen seeks, in her book, to answer some anthropological questions that concern the cultural recurrence, variability, and easy transmission of some ideas and practices more than others.

about the participants' native explanations makes her ethnographic report a "one-sided conversation."[180] This may also be the reason why Leistle prefers to use phenomenology rather than the "perspective grounded in the cognitive sciences like the one recently formulated by Emma Cohen."[181] Lienard "craves for more ethnographic details" as he reads Cohen's book.[182] I concur with Lienard that Cohen should have included a more detailed description of a typical possession session to substantiate her cognitive claims.

Halloy, another critic, points to Cohen's chapter 7, which discusses the displacement versus fusion principles as the "most controversial." Halloy did his research in a similar Afro-Brazilian cult.[183] He does not disapprove of how Cohen classifies possession as a "minimally counterintuitive concept" and hence easily transmittable. Rather, his main criticism is in Cohen's chapter 7 on the principles of fusion versus displacement. He asserts that the displacement principle is the "theologically correct" discourse – and not the fusion principle, as Cohen advocates[184] – hence people are more inclined toward the displacement theory.

Cohen admits that her book does not seek to offer comprehensive answers to questions raised about spirit possession. It only serves as a maiden research program that encourages the use of various methodological tools to investigate and explain the occurrence and spread of (and resistance to) possession.[185] Cohen's further plea is for an interdisciplinary approach, which she says seems to elude anthropological treatises.[186] I take this prompt in this current research as an approach that has not been used by scholars who have previously studied *ayyaana* possession as indicated in the following section.

---

180. Santo et al., "Author Meets Her Critics," 164.
181. "Conceptualizing Spirit Possession," 83.
182. Santo et al., "Author Meets Her Critics," 170.
183. Arnaud Halloy is an associate professor at the University of Nice. He has "special interest in ritual practice and possession phenomenon." See Santo et al., "Author Meets Her Critics," 169.
184. Santo et al., "Author Meets Her Critics," 168.
185. Cohen, *Mind Possessed*, 15.
186. Cohen, 95.

The *Ayyaana* Cult among Borana Muslims

Lewis's study does not only focus on the Somali people of the Horn of Africa. He also mentions the Borana people of Isiolo in Kenya as they participate in the Husseiniyya Sufi order. He still analyzes the cult using his peripheral theory by stating that the members of this cult are basically the poor who have lost their livestock and thus seek for redress.[187] The Husseiniya cult is also referred to as the Sheikh Hussein cult.[188] It forms part of the *Ayyaana* cult that is the focus of this study. It is therefore expedient to review how different scholars have examined it in various contexts.[189]

The Origin and Expansion of the Ayyaana Cult

Scholars in Kenya and Ethiopia have examined *ayyaana* possession. However, in-depth study seems to be consigned to Ethiopian scholarship rather than to its Kenyan counterpart.[190] The reason for this may be related to the origin of the cult, which is traced to Ethiopia. Scholars examining the concept of *ayyaana* in Ethiopia have also gone to greater lengths than Kenyan researchers to give comprehensive and epistemological discourses. Zitelman's discussion on the Oromo religion includes a section on the Arabic-Islamic roots of the word *ayyaana*. He gives six meanings of the word as quoted from Tamene Bitima.[191] For the sake of this current study, it is helpful to note that the Arabic equivalent word *'iyān* can mean "anything that is clear, visible, or public." It can also imply "personal revelation (of God)." The latter meaning was adapted by Sufi leaders in a mystical sense, according to Zitelmann.[192] Thus, the word *ayyaana* is a loan word that was adapted by the Oromo people and later inculcated into Borana customs. Such an understanding is significant

---

187. Lewis, *Religion in Context*, 145.

188. Osindo, "Examination of the Garre." The Garre Muslims in northern Kenya use the name "Husseiniya" to refer to the *Ayyaana* cult. Garre are Somali people who speak the Borana language.

189. See appendix 7 for a table that gives a summary of how various scholars have studied the cult.

190. Examples of Ethiopian authors are Setegn Eshetu, B. Witalis Andrzejewsi, Thomas Zitelmann, Alice L. Morton, and Karl Eric Knutsson. See Eshetu, "Sheikh Hussayn of Bale"; Andrzejewsi, "Sheikh Hussein of Bali"; Zitelmann, "Oromo Religion, Ayyaana"; Morton, "Some Aspects of Spirit"; and Knutsson, *Authority and Change*.

191. Zitelmann, "Oromo Religion, Ayyaana," 41.

192. Zitelmann, 83.

for my study of *ayyaana* and possession among Borana people as it indicates the Islamic influence on the religiocultural context of the people.

Most scholars consent that the *ayyaana* phenomenon came from Ethiopia, where it is linked to the shrine of the founder, Sheikh Hussein. Authors seem to differ on the origin of this founder. Dahl asserts that the Garre people brought it, probably assuming that the founder was from among them.[193] Other scholars trace the origins to Somalia.[194] Leus and Salvadori state that Somali traders introduced the cult to Boranaland around 1944–52.[195] Braumkamper differs slightly with this assertion when he states that Sheikh Hussein's father was from Arabia but went as a Muslim missionary to Somalia and moved to Bale during the thirteenth century.[196] Lewis acknowledges the cult's recent geographical expansion into Kenya, where it takes on a missionary role.[197] Tablino notes that the *Ayyaana* cult is a recent phenomenon among the Gabra people of northern Kenya.[198] Günther Schlee links the concept of *ayyaana* to the Borana twenty-seven-day week calendar where he asserts that each day is associated with an animal.[199]

The Ayyaana Cult among Borana Speakers in Kenya

Dahl and Aguilar examine the *Ayyaana* cult in more detail than other scholars who have studied *ayyaana* in Kenya.[200] The locality of both studies is Isiolo

---

193. Dahl, *Suffering Grass*, 243.

194. Lewis and Jewell, however, state that the *Ayyaana* cult was "exported to the adjoining Somali Republic" from Ethiopia, where the Somali people called it *borana*. See Lewis and Jewell, "Peoples and Cultures," 15.

195. Leus and Salvadori, *Aadaa Boraanaa*, 36.

196. Braukamper, *Islamic History and Culture*. Bale is in the southeastern region of Ethiopia where the shrine of Sheikh Hussein is, and *ayyaana* people go there for their annual pilgrimage. Schlee and Shongolo state that Bale is a "centre of rather unorthodox and heterogeneous practices" that are refuted by orthodox Islam in Ethiopia until today. See Schlee and Shongolo, *Islam and Ethnicity*, 58.

197. Lewis, *Religion in Context*, 145.

198. Tablino, *Gabra*, 258. Gabra are Borana-speaking people who live in the harsh conditions of northern Kenya, including the Chalbi desert. Wood has written an interesting account, found in two works, on the concept of Gabra men who are regarded as women. See Wood, "When Men Are Women"; and Wood, *When Men Are Women*.

199. Schlee, *Identities on the Move*, 107.

200. Dahl, *Suffering Grass*; and Aguilar, "Eagle as Messenger."

District, Kenya, among the Waso Borana Muslims.[201] Some scholars who have mentioned the cult have done so within broader cultural discourses.[202]

Dahl uses a sociocultural perspective and tends to incline toward Lewis's deprivation theory. For Dahl, the socioeconomic situation that befell the Waso Borana in Isiolo District drew them to the cult. It particularly attracts the "destitute ex-pastoralists, men and women" as well as some "widows and wives of wealthy Somali merchants."[203] The latter group of participants shows that the cult attracts non-Borana men and women from wealthy families who are not destitute. This confutes Lewis's theory of deprivation in my assessment. Furthermore, Dahl's closing remarks point to the ambiguity inherent in the theory. She refers to the challenge of analyzing the supposed social bridges that are perceived as the function of possession cults.[204]

Aguilar alludes to *ayyaana* possession within his discussion of the role of the eagle in divinatory procedures among the Waso Borana Muslims. He uses a socio-religious perspective as he traces the importance of the eagle as a messenger from *Waaqa* (God) as well as a mediator in the *Ayyaana* cult.[205] Aguilar's focus on the divinatory process causes him to refer to the ritual person communicating with the possessing spirit as "*abayen*" (a "diviner").[206] These diviners are also supposed to be possessed by the *ayyaana* spirit in order to articulate the voice of *Waaqa* through the eagle in maintaining *nagaa Borana* (the peace of Borana).

Aguilar highlights the importance of the eagle in the *Ayyaana* cult and in the Waso Borana community as a whole. He further advances his discussion of *ayyaana* in one section of his book, *Being Oromo in Kenya*.[207] He classifies the *Ayyaana* cult as a crucial domestic ritual within the religio-political context that has spanned different generations of the Waso Borana people.

---

201. Isiolo District is now referred to as Isiolo County.
202. Tablino, *Gabra*; Leus and Salvadori, *Aadaa Boraanaa*; Wario, "Networking the Nomads."
203. Dahl, "Possession as Cure," 153.
204. Dahl, 164.
205. Aguilar, "Eagle as Messenger," 61.
206. Aguilar, 62.
207. Aguilar, *Being Oromo in Kenya*. This book was Aguilar's 1993 doctoral dissertation published with very slight changes.

Like Dahl above, Aguilar's discussion on the *Ayyaana* cult seems to be influenced by Lewis's deprivation theory. He asserts that participants of the cult are those denied access to ritual activities and also barren women who are perceived as outcasts.[208] Nevertheless, his main proposition is that the *Ayyaana* cult is the most essential part of Waso Borana ritual identity because it integrates the various traditions garnered over different generations. These traditions include Islamic Sufi practices, Borana practices regarding *ayyaana* spirits, and actualization of *aada Borana* (some past Borana customs).[209]

Unlike Aguilar's assessment of the significance of the *Ayyaana* cult to the Waso Borana traditions, Tablino's study of the Gabra people does not allude to any connection between the Borana customs and Islam.[210] This significant difference in how *ayyaana* are integrated into the customs of the people shows the cultural variability of the phenomenon of *ayyaana* possession and the need to study it within a specific cultural setting. It is therefore expected that the analysis of my study of *ayyaana* among the Borana Muslims in Marsabit County would differ from Aguilar's study of *ayyaana* among the Waso Borana Muslims in Isiolo County.

Wario's study on the *tabligh jama'at* movement among Borana Muslims includes a section on the *warra gariba*, the followers of Sheikh Hussein of Bale.[211] It is important to note how he distinguishes this cult of Sheikh Hussein from the *Ayyaana* cult but perceives a symbiotic relationship between the two.[212] Wario states that the Sheikh Hussein cult is basically a *tariqa* while the *Ayyaana* cult is "its constituent possession cult."[213] He does not go into details about the symbiotic relation between the two entities, probably because this is not his main focus. However, it is helpful to note the historical aspect that Wario mentions. The *ayyaana* were given to Sheikh Hussein to enable the

---

208. Aguilar, "Current Religious Practices ," 253.

209. Aguilar, 254.

210. Tablino, *Gabra*, 259. Gabra people are Borana speakers who also reside in Marsabit County and have *ayyaana* cultic beliefs and practices.

211. The *Tabligh jama'at* movement is an Islamic missionary movement founded in India, which has permeated various Islamic communities in Africa including the Borana Muslims in Marsabit County. The phrase *warra gariba* (people of garib) refers to participants the Sheikh Hussein cult. This is a Sufi *tariqa* that still involves *ayyaana*. Sheikh Hussein is the founder, as will be discussed later.

212. Wario, "Networking the Nomads," 67.

213. Trimingham links Sheikh Hussein with *tariqa*, the Ahmadiyya Sufi order. See Trimingham, *Islam in Ethiopia*, 208.

spread of Islam in the region. Wario conversely alludes to the tension that the *Ayyaana* cult creates. As much as it is deemed to facilitate the spread of Islam, it also inhibits the total replacement of traditional rituals by Islamic ones.[214] This is part of the dilemma discussed in the subsequent section of the interface between Islam and African possession cults.

Islam and African Possession Cults: Clash or Accommodation?

Scholars have recognized the coexistence of Islam and African possession cults since the inception of Islam on the continent. A relevant question has been whether that interaction exhibits instances of clash or accommodation. Generally, African Islam has been portrayed as "religiously flexible and accommodating," according to Rosander.[215] Ali Mazrui similarly refers to the accommodating nature of Islam to indigenous African traditions and customs.[216] Yet examining the interaction between Islam and traditional possessive cults throughout Africa gives a different picture – one that negates the theory of accommodation.

McIntoch narrates the clash between "Islam and Giriamaness" in a hegemonic and counterhegemonic complex involving possession cults.[217] The Giriama people had resisted Islam and continued with their traditional divination and healing rituals for a long time until they were forced by "spirits" to become "reluctant" Muslims.[218] This consequently resulted in an imposed socio-religious hierarchy with the Arab Muslims, with which the Giriama have reluctantly lived.[219]

Unlike the Giriama Muslims, some African communities choose to use possession cults as a parody or resistance to Islam. Boddy illustrates how the Hofriyati people have amplified the *Zar* possession cult as a hegemonic response against Islam.[220] Stoller also views the Hauka possession cult in

---

214. Wario, "Networking the Nomads," 70.
215. Rosander, "Islamization of 'Tradition,'" 1.
216. Mazrui as quoted by Abraham A. Akrong and John Azumah. See Akrong and Azumah, "Hermeneutical and Theological Resources," 73.
217. McIntosh, "Reluctant Muslims," 93.
218. Janet McIntosh, "Edge of Islam."
219. McIntosh, "Reluctant Muslims," 93.
220. Boddy, *Wombs and Alien Spirits*, 5.

Songhay as a kind of resistance and antithesis to Islam.[221] On the other hand, revivalist Muslims are repudiating the cults as un-Islamic since they incline toward *shirk* in their assessment. This is the case with *ayyaana* and the Sheikh Hussein cult in northern Kenya where there has been a rise in reformist Islamic ideology since the mid-1980s.[222]

Apart from the counterhegemonic reaction discussed above, scholars have also inferred a syncretistic relation between Islam and traditional African communities.[223] Mutuku's study of the Digo Muslims along the Kenyan Coast is an example. Islam was accommodated into the Digo traditional system and formed a syncretistic dualism.[224] Likewise, Worku Muhammad suggests a similar dualistic tendency among the Wallo Muslims of southern Ethiopia, whose main root is the quest for power.[225]

Feriali interprets the Moroccan possession trance as a "tri-partite syncretic cultural phenomenon" that involves "Islam, ecstatic Sufism, and witchcraft."[226] Yet Feriali is emphatic that the Moroccan possession cannot be simplistically reduced to any of these three components. It is "not Islam" since a high percentage of the participants – he calls them "trancers" – do not observe Islamic duties regularly. It is not Sufi since "it is not centered on communion with the divine although its structural vestiges appear to be Sufi." And neither is it witchcraft. However, Feriali acknowledges that "different trancers tap differently into those three components."[227] Boddy also asserts that Sudanese Islam has similar tendencies of syncretism, where it adapts itself to the local situations while integrating with the indigenous elements. This was the case where the cult of saints' veneration added to its pantheon the belief in jinn as advanced in the Qur'an and Hadith.[228]

---

221. Stoller, *Fusion of the Worlds*, 37.
222. Wario, "Networking the Nomads," 71.
223. Syncretism has been defined as the combination of the elements in different religious structures to form one system. See McIntosh, *The Edge of Islam*.
224. Mutuku, *Prayer among the Digo*, 76.
225. Mohammad, "Folk Islam in Wallo."
226. Feriali, "Music-Induced Spirit Possession," 41.
227. Feriali, 43.
228. Boddy, *Wombs and Alien Spirits*, 27.

Some Muslim scholars tend to reject the syncretism theory formulated to explain the encounter of Islam with traditional African beliefs and practices. Safari states:

> Orthodox Muslims in Africa ... refuse to believe that Islam ever absorbed African religious elements. They assert that Islam was introduced and accepted by Africans in its purity. Hence, syncretism is out of question. It should not be even alluded to. It is an insult to Islam.[229]

Instead of syncretism, Safari prefers to explain the encounter of Islam with African traditions as adaptation. This process includes purification and rejection of unpalatable customs.[230] Another Muslim scholar, Mohamed-Salih, also refutes the syncretism model in explaining why the Zaghawa of Sudan continued to engage in their pre-Islamic rituals.[231]

Kaniki does not accept the process of adaptation in African Islam alone. He perceives an aspect of "stubbornness" and "durability of the (African) traditional culture."[232] Kaniki reports that the ancestral cults in Africa, in particular, have resisted Islamic influence. Adherents of the *Bori* cult have also displayed resilience in the face of opposition from Islamic scholars, according to O'Brien. She does a historical study and criticizes early explanations of Islamization in West Africa in relation to possession cults. One of the views she critiques is Trimingham's, which she says is based on evolutionary terms that envision a gradual decrease of the cultic tendencies as the "purer" form of Islam takes root. Her criticism is based on the fact that Trimingham does not present any specific historical evidence to justify his discussion on cultic development.[233]

Kim perceives a different dimension of adaptability from that proposed by Safari, above. Kim asserts that there is a continued alliance between traditional African worldviews with the local Swahili Islam, as evidenced in the therapeutic cult of possession.[234] For him, there is a synthesis, which he calls

---

229. Safari, *Making of Islam*, 97.
230. Safari, 97.
231. Mohamed-Salih, "Islam, Traditional Beliefs," xv.
232. Kaniki, "Impact of Islam," 1.
233. O'Brien, "Power and Paradox," 13.
234. Kim, "Supernaturalism in Swahili Islam," 71.

the "Domain of Total Synthesis," that entails an integration of *dini* ("official Islam"), *mila* (local traditions), and popular Islamic practices.[235] It is significant to note that Kim identifies the fuzziness of the borderline he sets in describing the overlap within the three aforementioned religiocultural domains.[236] This calls for a deeper consideration of whether the phrase "total synthesis" would thus be appropriate. Yet, he is one of the few scholars who have attempted to comprehensively explain the complex encounter of Islam with African beliefs and practices involving the phenomenon of spirit possession.

Summary

This chapter has shown that there is a corpus of literature on spirit possession. The world of spirits in Islam, however, does not seem to attract a parallel investigation from either Muslims or non-Muslim scholars.. The former have noted this in their writings and shown the importance of seeking to understand the supernatural world as believed and ritualized by Muslims globally. This chapter thus has reviewed some of this landmark literature with the aim of examining how the authors have approached their studies of the spirit world and the conclusive theories that have ensued. The chapter commenced by illustrating how the concepts of jinn and possession have been studied in orthodox Islam. Evidently, the world of jinn is real, as shown in the Qur'an. A perusal of some of the Hadiths on jinn and possession also shows the prominence of the spirit world in the time of the Prophet. The conclusion one draws from such a study concurs with El-Zein's comment that studying the concept of jinn is essential in understanding Islam since it is really at the heart of the religion.

After reviewing what scholars have written about the supernatural world as found in orthodox Islam, this review then investigated how jinn and possession are experienced in contemporary Islamic contexts. It is noted that jinn possession is not a confine of the Arab world as the cradle of Islam. Neither is it restricted to the deprived people of a society, like women. Jinn possession

---

235. I am adopting Kim's usage of the terms *dini* and *mila* as "official Islam" and "local traditions" respectively. See Kim "Supernaturalism in Swahili Islam," 78. Ordinarily, *dini* is translated as "religion."

236. Kim, "Supernaturalism in Swahili Islam," 80.

is a phenomenon that cannot be relegated to the periphery since its traces are also found within the official circles of Islam. This is seen in the way different Islamic communities deal with possession. The officially endorsed methods are used together with the unorthodox ones, hence enlisting the repudiation from the reformists in Islam. In spite of such prohibitions, the phenomenon of possession is still rife in African Muslim communities. It has been shown that the *Ayyaana* possession cult continues to be part of the Borana speakers in northern Kenya in spite of the resurgence of Islamic reformism. The review of different scholars who have written about *ayyaana* possession reveals that there is no substantial work on the cult as practiced by the Borana Muslims in Marsabit County. Much of the research has been done on the Waso Borana of Isiolo County. There is therefore a need to study the phenomenon in Marsabit, which is what this current study is doing.

This chapter has demonstrated that the functional approach is favored by a number of scholars. I. M. Lewis has been influential as he followed this approach and came up with the deprivation theory. Some recent scholars have deduced that this theory is reductionist and have thus preferred cultural symbolism that analyzes possession cults in terms of their meanings instead of their function.

This review has also shown the need for a multidisciplinary approach to studying possession. Cohen is a forerunner of this approach, especially integrating cognitive sciences with anthropology. However, she was not as descriptive as anthropology demands, a fact that elicited criticism from her readers. Yet her book is a vital springboard from which future studies on possession can be launched and which offers a comprehensive dimension that is needed in understanding how participants experience possession.

CHAPTER 3

Research Methodology

Introduction

Studying the lived experiences of Muslims entails a procedure that answers a pertinent question asked by Paula Saukko: "How can one do justice to the lived experience of people, while at the same time, critically analyze discourses?"[1] This chapter discusses the fundamental issues involved in empirical research on the lived experiences of the Borana Muslims. It will elucidate the specific methodology and methods used to examine them as they participate in the phenomenon of *ayyaana* possession.[2] It is vital to "do justice" to them by providing an emic description of their beliefs and practices that will pave the way for an objective etic analysis of the discourses elicited.[3]

This study is framed based on an anthropological perspective. It, therefore, requires an appropriate methodology that specified relevant methods to collect and analyze data within that framework. It is based on a qualitative research design that sought to answer the research questions on which this

---

1. Saukko, *Doing Research*, 4.

2. I follow Pauolo Saukko's distinction of "methods" and "methodology." "Methodology" refers to the philosophical perspectives that a particular research study takes, while "methods" are the practical tools used in the study. See Saukko, *Doing Research*, 8.

3. The terms *emic description* and *etic analysis* are herein used to refer to the different views of a phenomenon. Emic description is based on firsthand accounts from the people being interviewed. Etic analysis is the researcher's view or analysis based on the emic descriptions given. These emic and etic views are essential for this phenomenological study of the phenomenon of *ayyaana* possession among the Borana Muslims. As I endeavor to be as objective as possible in presenting what I was told by my interviewees, I admit that I cannot be perfect in doing so. However, I try my best to be as close as possible to their subjectivity.

study is hinged. The first question seeks to understand the position of the Borana Muslim teachers on jinn and possession as specified in the official Islamic texts: the Qur'an and Hadiths. The second question aims at providing a comprehensive description of the phenomenon of *ayyaana* possession and discovering the religiocultural model of *Ayyaana* from ordinary Borana Muslims. The third research question amalgamates the findings of the first two and provides an analytical explanation of the discoveries.

Research Rationale

The overall aim of this study is to understand the lived experiences of the Borana Muslims. This cannot be accomplished from a distance; hence the research methods employed needed to facilitate proximity to the Borana Muslims. This gives the basis for choosing a qualitative research design instead of a quantitative one. Margaret LeCompte and Jean Schensul concur that qualitative designs are more appropriate for such studies as this because they "allow us to assess and describe what really is happening."[4] This study follows this conduit by examining the Borana Muslims as they participate in the phenomenon of the *Ayyaana* possession cult. Thus, it takes a phenomenological dimension while taking note of the periodic enigmas that have surfaced about its status as a research tool or philosophical theory.

Phenomenological Design and Theory of Spirit Possession

Different authors on qualitative research designs place phenomenology as a research tradition that investigates the experiences of people as they engage in a particular phenomenon. Michael Patton describes phenomenology as a study that focuses on "exploring how human beings make sense of experience and transform experiences into consciousness, both individually and as shared meaning."[5] John Creswell explains that a phenomenological study seeks to describe the "meaning of the lived experiences for several individuals about a concept of the phenomenon."[6] Both Patton and Creswell emphasize the lived experiences of individuals and groups. Creswell's psychological

---

4. LeCompte and Schensul, *Designing & Conducting*, 113.
5. Patton, *Qualitative Research and Evaluation*, 104.
6. Creswell, *Qualitative Inquiry and Design*, 51.

approach to phenomenology, however, gives preference to individual experiences.[7] The fundamental aspect of a phenomenological design according to these authors is the accurate description of a phenomenon from the informants' perspectives. The phenomenological approach to this current study considered both individual and shared behavior of the Borana Muslims. This required listening to each interviewee individually then verifying with group interviews.[8] The overall objective was to discover the religiocultural model of *Ayyaana* possession. This model is then analyzed comparatively with the Islamic model of the spirit world as understood by the Muslim teachers in Marsabit County.[9]

As mentioned above, this is a phenomenological study that employed ethnographic tools to examine the lived experiences of the Borana Muslims as they participated in the phenomenon of *ayyaana* possession.[10] I have used phenomenology as a theoretical framework as suggested by Bernhard Leistle. I find his phenomenological theory of spirit possession relevant and crucial for this anthropological study of possession. He offers an introductory procedure toward formulating a phenomenological theory of possession. His thesis is that the notion of otherness is fundamental and crucial for an anthropological study that seeks to understand the phenomenon of possession.[11] He

---

7. Creswell, 53.

8. I prefer to use the term *interviewee* instead of *informant* because of the connotations involved in the latter term. Furthermore, the group interviews are not focus groups since this study did not employ focus groups as a research tool.

9. Knibbe and Versteeg remind anthropologists who delve into the phenomenological design not to forget that as much as phenomenology is about "things as they are," it is still interpretational. See Knibbe and Versteeg, "Assessing Phenomenology in Anthropology," 60).

10. As Desjarlais and Throop state, the mandate of phenomenology as a research and theoretical framework is to be descriptive, which makes it a "powerful approach." See Desjarlais and Throop, "Phenomenological Approaches in Anthropology," 95. Yet this mandate does not exclude any form of analysis. This study is both descriptive and analytical, as illustrated in chapters 4, 5, 6, and 7. Analysis is deemed necessary since I am examining two cultural models and how they relate with each other. This provides a comprehensive picture of the lived experiences of *warra ayyaana* according to the objective of the study. Compare this with an interpretative or hermeneutic phenomenological approach, which is a developing arm of qualitative research in psychology and is concerned with detailed examination of lived experiences; cf. Smith, Flowers, and Larkin, *Interpretative Phenomenological Analysis*.

11. Leistle, "From the Alien,"55–56. Leistle discusses spirits as the "Other" and shows how different writers have considered them as intruding into the human self.

points to the need for studying spirits and possession from a notion of the Other instead of the alien.[12]

I agree with Leistle's proposition because it respects the African supernaturalistic worldview that does not consider spirits as alien. Studying the Other with that background is significant since it deems the existence of spirits as a reality in a given cultural setting. This allows for one to study the concepts of spirits and the phenomenon of spirit possession as cultural realities and not as alien entities.[13] Failure to consider possession as a cultural reality prompted Leistle to critique Emma Cohen's approach, in her 2008 article, of examining the phenomenon of possession from a cognitive science perspective.[14] His main contention is that Cohen has approached possession as a "process of concept formation and representation and [it] is ultimately understood as a form of thinking."[15] I concur with Leistle's assertion. I have reviewed Cohen's work in the previous chapter because she has studied the phenomenon of possession and used a cognitive approach as I have done. As fascinating as Cohen's study is, I do not agree with her inclination toward human evolution, as it places possession in people's evolutionary thinking and not as an incessant cultural reality.[16] This is significant to note in this methodology chapter because it allows me to reflect on my worldview orientation.

Cognitive Anthropological Framework

Using a cognitive anthropological framework enabled me, as a researcher, to perceive what underlies the practice and beliefs about *ayyaana* possession. A number of cognitive anthropologists have used various theories in their studies. Some are inclined to psychological perspectives of cognition. These perspectives fall in the sphere of cognitive science of religion. Other cognitive anthropologists use the cultural model theory, which has a more cultural orientation. For this study, I integrate the cultural model theory

---

12. I use the notion of "Other" in the same way. My interviewees perceived spirits as part of their socio-religious space and yet different from them, hence the "Other." This notion of Other, then, differs from the Western notion of "alien," since the latter connotes something that is not part of the social space. The concept of Other in a supernaturalistic setting perceives spirits as part and parcel of the society even though these spirits are different from people.
13. Leistle, "From the Alien," 72.
14. Cohen, "Conceptualizing Spirit Possession."
15. Leistle, "From the Alien," 83.
16. Cohen, *Mind Possessed*, 14.

with the minimal counterintuitive theory. The latter belongs to the cognitive science of religion.

The Cultural Model Theory

Several cognitive anthropologists have used the cultural model theory to explain how cultural knowledge is organized and intersubjectively shared among people. These anthropologists include Holland, D'Andrade, Strauss, Shore, Quinn, Bennardo, and de Munck.[17] I follow the line of study that examines the place of mental constructions in motivating behavior.[18]

Bennardo and de Munck suggest a methodological approach, which I have modified and used for this study. Their approach stems from their definition of cultural models as mental representations that are shared by members of a culture. These models are used to make "sense of and interpret sensory input and also to produce and shape purposive and communicative behaviors."[19] I find this relevant to my objective for this study, which seeks to understand the Borana Muslims' participation in the *Ayyaana* cult and be able to discover a cultural model of *Ayyaana* possession. Bennardo and de Munck's approach is sociocultural, while mine is religiocultural. Thus, instead of using the term "cultural model of *Ayyaana*," I use "religiocultural model of *Ayyaana*."[20] Yet there are useful principles that I have gleaned from their methodological guidelines.

Bennardo and de Munck's tripartite methodology rejects the qualitative-quantitative division and combines the two to suggest a comprehensive *qualquant* design. Their tripartite design includes ethnographic data collection and analysis; language data and linguistic analysis; and experimental data

---

17. Holland, *Cultural Models in Language*; D'Andrade and Strauss, *Human Motives and Cultural Models*; D'Andrade, *Development of Cognitive Anthropology*; Shore, *Culture in Mind*; Quinn, "'Commitment' in American Marriage"; Bennardo and de Munck, *Cultural Models*.

18. Holland, D'Andrade, Quinn, Bennardo, and de Munck are among the scholars who view schemas/cultural models as motivational forces that influence behavior.

19. Bennardo and de Munck, *Cultural Models*, 3.

20. I prefer to use the religiocultural approach because I am studying Borana Muslims within the context of Islam. I am aware that religion in the traditional African context is part of the cultural context. Similarly, Islam is holistic in covering all aspects of human life. However, I chose to use the phrase *religiocultural* in order to delimit my study to the religious and cultural aspects of the Borana Muslims. These refer to the way they interact with the supernatural beings within their cultural context.

with statistical analyses.[21] As noted above, I have employed ethnographic data collection methods that will be specified in subsequent sections of this chapter.[22] Language data and linguistic analysis are paramount in discovering the mental organization of knowledge (cultural models) pertaining to *ayyaana* possession among the Borana Muslims.

Cognitive Science of Religion: The Minimal Counterintuitive Theory

The cognitive science of religion (CSR) is a scientific approach that seeks to provide explanations of recurrent phenomena as experienced within religious contexts. The advantage of CSR is its interdisciplinary nature, which allows the interaction between anthropology and psychology. I chose to refer to CSR theories because they explain the predominance of religious phenomena more than others.

I specifically chose to use the minimal counterintuitive (MCI) theory as advocated by Justin Barrett.[23] This theory deals with intuitive human cognition and helps to explain the inclination of *Ayyaana* adepts to the *Ayyaana* model and not to the Islamic model. The theory further deals with "questions of perception, representation, memory, communication, and motivation,"[24] which are relevant in understanding why cognition about *ayyaana* is more prevalent than that about jinn among the Borana Muslims.

The minimal counterintuitive theory postulates that ideas or concepts that are transmitted more readily are the ones that are minimally counterintuitive. Counterintuitive ideas are those that are considered to be beyond the normal cognitive expectations of the human mind.[25] When such ideas are slightly or

---

21. Bennardo and de Munck, *Cultural Models*, 57.

22. Scholars who delve into empirical discovery of cultural models are not restricted to these methodological suggestions by Bennardo and de Munck. Following such a cue, I too did not undertake the experimental/statistical method outlined by Bennardo and de Munck.

23. There are other pioneer scholars who have delved into the minimal counterintuitive theory. They include Pascal Boyer, Harvey Whitehouse, and Emma Cohen. See Boyer, *Religion Explained*; Whitehouse, *Modes of Religiosity*; and Cohen, *Mind Possessed*. I preferred to use Justin Barrett because he has also examined the phenomenon of spirit possession. See Cohen and Barrett, "Conceptualizing Spirit Possession."

24. Cohen and Barrett, "Conceptualizing Spirit Possession," 252.

25. Counterintuitive concepts are those that are not intuitive or normal in the comprehension of the human mind. Those that are minimally counterintuitive are contrasted with the ones that are bizarre. The former are likely to be remembered more easily than the

minimally counterintuitive, they are more likely to be remembered and hence are more easily transmitted than those that are radically counterintuitive or wholly intuitive.[26] Thus, I use the MCI theory to explain why *Ayyaana* adepts are inclined to a certain model. Their shared mental models of *Ayyaana*, as discovered in this study, shows whether there are minimally counterintuitive beliefs that make them remember more about *ayyaana* than jinn.

Studying Muslims

Studying Muslims in their religiocultural context is about examining their "religious experience" that virtually "takes place inside the minds," as Schmidt admits.[27] Schmidt further asserts that many scholars within the academic study of religions tend to be cautious due to the challenge of valorizing or validating subjectivity over objectivity. Such studies have been relegated to anthropologists and psychologists.[28] The appropriateness of these endeavors is supported by the fact that scholars continue to realize the dynamism in Islam. Makris, for instance, alludes to this dynamism and examines how Islamic practices are observed in local settings.[29]

In studying the lived experiences of the Borana Muslims, I heed Nadia Jeldtoft's call to study Muslims on a micro-level in order to understand how they make "sense of Islam."[30] Her sociological approach focuses on the minority and "non-organized" Muslims in Denmark and Germany. Her usage of the everyday lived religion framework to analyze the Muslims is insightful for this study. I agree with her assertion that only a few studies have attempted to examine how Islam is lived out in the daily lives of ordinary Muslims.[31] She further acknowledges the difficulty of examining such non-institutionalized religiosity using the available methodological and theoretical frameworks.[32]

---

latter since they do not expend a lot of cognitive energy for imagination. Anthropomorphism of spirits in possession cults enables the concept to be minimally counterintuitive and hence easily transmitted as explained in the analytical chapters of this dissertation.

26. Barrett, *Cognitive Science, Religion, and Theology*, 67.
27. Schmidt, "Varieties of Non-Ordinary Experiences," 105.
28. Schmidt, 105.
29. Makris, *Islam in the Middle East*.
30. Jeldtoft, "Lived Islam," 1134.
31. Jeldtoft, 1135.
32. Jeldtoft, 1137.

It is for this reason that scholars have come up with the anthropology of Islam theory.[33]

Anthropology of Islam: The People Factor

Popular anthropologists of Islam like Clifford Geertz recommend qualitative research in examining the everyday life of Muslims, according to Abdullah Drury's review of the book, *The Anthropology of Islam Reader*.[34] Bowen states that ethnographic studies are attracting new scholars of Islam in contemporary times. This inclination ensures that the "voices of the subjects" are included and allowed to "represent themselves" without any biases or prejudice by the researcher.[35] Geertz translates this as the "native's point of view." The essence of his presentation, when he was being awarded the Social Science Prize in 1974, called for *verstehen*, the empathic understanding of human behavior.[36] He studied the Muslim communities in Indonesia and Morocco with an aim to understand how the people perceive themselves. He did this by "analyzing their symbolic forms: words, images, institutions, behaviors."[37] I take a methodological hint from Geertz and other scholars of the anthropology of Islam.[38] They focus on Muslims as people who live within a localized

---

33. Some of the main scholars who have debated the issues around the anthropology of Islam include Ernest Gellner, Clifford Geertz, Talal Asad, Michael Gilsenan, Abdul Hamid El-Zein, Dale Eickelman, and Jens Kreinath. See Gellner, *Muslim Society*; Geertz, *Islam Observed*; Asad, "Idea of an Anthropology"; Gilsenan, *Recognizing Islam*; El-Zein "Beyond Ideology and Theology"; Eickelman, *Middle East*; and Kreinath, *Anthropology of Islam Reader*. Those who have delved into the anthropology of everyday Islam include Nadia Fadil, Mayanthi Fernando, Samuli Schielke, Liza Debevec, Nadia Jeldtoft, and Ronald A. Lukens-Bull. See Fadil and Fernando, "Rediscovering the 'Everyday' Muslim"; Schielke and Debevec, *Introduction*; Jeldtoft, *Lived Islam*; and Lukens-Bull, "Between Text and Practice."

34. Drury, "Review of 'The Anthropology,'" 266.

35. Drury, 266.

36. Geertz, "'From the Native's Point,'" 26.

37. Geertz, 30. I mention Geertz here because he is believed to have paved the way for an anthropological focus on Muslim societies. His seminal work, *Islam Observed*, has been critiqued extensively, especially because of a seeming lack of Muslim voices, even though he examined their societies. See Marranci, *Anthropology of Islam*, 37. I consent with this assertion that is evident right from the title of Geertz's book. How can Islam be observed? Islam is an abstract entity; it is the Muslims who act, and thus they are the ones to be observed. Hence, the title would be appropriately, *Muslims Observed*, in my opinion. However, I appreciate Geertz's inaugural attempt to write about Muslims.

38. Marranci, *Anthropology of Islam*, 10. Marranci mentions that the three main works that have been cited on the anthropology of Islam are *Islam Observed*, by Geertz; *Muslim Society*

setting. My current study will thus contribute to this growing number of scholars who examine African Muslims as people. I particularly avoid any inclinations to examining African Muslims from an Orientalist approach,[39] and I instead examine them with a sole purpose of understanding Muslims from a cognitive and affective disposition.

Marranci adds the dimension of emotions and feelings to the anthropological study of Muslims, which I appreciate.[40] The "feeling" of being a Muslim is more authentic in understanding Muslims and their lived experiences. The African Muslim has feelings and emotions that need to be included in an empirical examination of their lived experiences.

As I read about contemporary methodologies and methods that can be used in the anthropology of African Islam, I found Kim's suggestion quite comprehensive and appropriate. Kim does not allude to the anthropology of Islam in his study of the Swahili Muslim community and its participation in the Jinn cult. Yet I find his emphasis on the "people factor" in studying Muslims closely related to the aspect of the anthropology of Islam. Furthermore, a good part of his study is anthropological. His STA methodological guideline mentioned before is relevant for this current study, which also has an anthropological framework.

The STA guideline is useful in studying Islamic religiocultural contexts. Its key objective is to "produce as accurate a phenomenological depiction of Muslim life as possible."[41] As I study the phenomenology of *ayyaana* and possession among Borana Muslims, I seek to avoid any biased preconceptions, hence my appreciation for the STA. Its multidisciplinary outlook is perceived in its three research components: a textual study of the phenomenon, an

---

by Gellner; and *Recognizing Islam* by Gilsenan. These studies focus on North African and Middle Eastern contexts. Upcoming anthropologists of Islam have continued to critique these works in a bid to offer a more comprehensive understanding of what the anthropology of Islam is and how to examine Muslims empirically. Varisco also provides a critical analysis of how four anthropologists have examined Islam. See Varisco *Islam Obscured*. These four anthropologists are Geertz, Ahmed, Mernissi, and Ahmed. See Geertz, *Islam Observed*; Ahmed, *Discovering Islam*; Mernissi, *Beyond the Veil*; and Gellner, *Muslim Society*,

39. Scholars like Edward Said have critiqued Orientalism as a theoretical disposition that examines the Orient, and especially Islam, based on some power differences between one group that perceives themselves as superior to a lesser group of subjects. See Lukens-Bull, "Between Text and Practice," 2.

40. Marranci, *Anthropology of Islam*, 11.

41. Kim, "Considering 'Ordinariness' in Studying," 4.

anthropological study of the phenomenon, and an interdisciplinary analysis of the data collected from the textual and anthropological studies.[42] The figure below depicts the STA guideline.

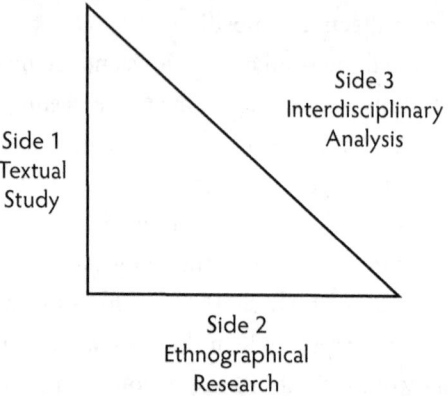

Figure 1: Diagram showing the Synthetic Triangular Approach (STA)[43]

Figure 1 shows the three research components of the STA guideline. They are labeled as sides 1–3 respectively. Side 1 comprises a textual study of the phenomenon as stipulated in the Islamic official texts – the Qur'an and Hadiths.[44] Side 2 is the anthropological study component that examines the cultural phenomenon within the Muslim society using ethnographic research tools. Side 3 integrates the data collected on sides 1 and 2 and uses an interdisciplinary analytical framework to explain any discrepancy or similarities observed in findings of sides 1 and 2. The following section discusses how I used these components as I studied *ayyaana* and possession among Borana Muslims in Marsabit County. Each component addresses the three research questions that are the essence of this study.

---

42. The interdisciplinary nature of analysis will be discussed more in chapter 7 of this dissertation. Basically, it involves a cognitive anthropological approach that is integrative and includes anthropology, psychology, linguistics, and cognitive science-of-religion theories.

43. Diagram adapted from Kim's work. See Kim, "Considering 'Ordinariness' in Studying."

44. Kim prefers to use cognitive-philological study in lieu of textual study since the latter seeks to understand the "mind that underlies written texts" (2014, 5). Reference to "textual study" in this dissertation means the Islamic texts that the Muslim teachers in Marsabit referred to during the interview sessions that I carried out.

Methods Used for Contextual Study of Jinn and Possession in Official Islam

The first research component of the STA guideline comprises a textual study on the topic being examined. As the researcher, I need to know what the canonical Islamic texts say about jinn and possession. Studies have been conducted previously on this topic by various Muslim and non-Muslim scholars.[45] Most have examined the phenomenon of jinn and possession from a general outlook and not a contextual one. I was inclined to do a contextual study that examined what Muslim teachers, as the gatekeepers of official Islam in Marsabit County, know and teach about jinn and possession.

Interviewing Muslim Teachers

Essentially, the gatekeepers of official Islam are the *madrassa* teachers and sheikhs. They all have religious inclinations that are defined by their different Islamic dispositions. Purposeful sampling was carried out to determine which of these teachers to interview. Snowballing sampling was also used since I did not know all the teachers within Marsabit County. I relied on ordinary Muslims to inform me of who their teachers were. The criteria for selecting whom to interview were based on the practice and knowledge of the teachers. Preference was also given to the local teachers who had served for more than five years in a place.

After identifying the Islamic teachers by purposeful sampling methods described above,[46] appointments were made by word of mouth or telephone conversation. The venue for interviews was preferably within the mosque setting but the Islamic teachers were given the opportunity to choose. An interview guide was used for semi-structured interviews with open-ended questions. To ensure good interview questions, I followed Stephen L. Schensul, Jean J. Schensul, and Margaret Diane LeCompte's guidelines provided in their book *Essential Ethnographic Methods*. They suggest a list of eleven guidelines,[47] which I found useful as I interviewed the Muslim teachers.

---

45. Taymeeyah and Philips, *Ibn Taymeeyah's Essay*; Philips, *Exorcist Tradition in Islaam*; Al-Ashqar, *World of the Jinn*; Kim, "Supernaturalism in Swahili Islam"; El-Zein, *Islam, Arabs, and the Intelligent*; and others.

46. I interviewed nine Muslim teachers.

47. Schensul, Schensul, and LeCompte, *Essential Ethnographic Methods*, 154.

The interviews were conducted in Kiswahili as the preferred language since the teachers were expected to be literate and refer to Qur'anic verses in the Arabic language. Their consent was sought to record the conversation. As a woman, I had to seek the company of a man in order not to jeopardize the interview process.[48]

The essence of interviewing the Islamic teachers was to understand what they know and teach about the concept of jinn and the phenomenon of *ayyaana* possession. I asked them, as the gatekeepers of official Islam, to refer to the verses from the Qur'an and the Hadiths as the authentic basis for belief and practices on spirits and possession in Islam.

Apart from knowing what the Islamic texts say about jinn and possession, the Islamic teachers were asked how they practice these teachings as they dealt with the daily encounters of ordinary Borana Muslims with the spirits. I asked the teachers to give their opinion on *ayyaana* and possession, which would be considered the official position.

Analyzing the Interviews

Transcription of the interviews was performed, and the contents were divided into different themes. The aim of these interviews was to understand the mind of the Islamic teachers concerning the spirit world. The interviews reveal the sources of knowledge on jinn and spirit possession. As the representatives of official Islam in Marsabit County, the interviewees disclosed the awareness they have of the Qur'an and Hadiths.

Apart from this awareness, the interviews also sought to find what main Islamic scholars inform the local Muslim leaders. It is paramount to investigate the different Islamic dispositions that these scholars adhere to. Therefore, library research was carried out to further understand the different positions of the scholars.

---

48. It is not appropriate, in Islam, to converse with the opposite sex. I took this seriously and had my research assistant (and my husband) together with me during all the interview sessions.

Anthropological Research on *Ayyaana* among Borana Muslims

This section gives a description of the anthropological research I carried out in Marsabit County among Borana Muslims. This is the second research component (side 2) in the STA guideline that forms the baseline for this research. The objective of this section is to understand the lived experiences of Borana Muslims as they participate in the *Ayyaana* cult. This complies with what Kim expounds concerning side 2 of the STA research guidelines:

> The next step to take is an anthropological research, with ethnographic fieldwork, into the religiocultural issue in question. This is to understand how ordinary Muslims actually think and conduct in a particular cultural situation that is under investigation ... This is where the researcher attempts to grasp how human ordinariness operates in a particular religious context. Based on adequate understanding of official Islamic views of the particular issue, the researcher can delve into how human ordinariness interacts with Islamic ideologies at its practical level.[49]

In a bid to understand how the Borana Muslims think and behave as they participate in the *Ayyaana* possession cult, I looked for research tools that would be comprehensive to gather the data I needed. I found James Spradley's DRS (Developmental Research Sequence) and Giovanni Bennardo and Victor de Munck's tripartite methodologies and methods quite relevant, although I used their steps selectively to suit my own research. The following section describes the specific data collection methods I used while integrating Spradley's Bennardo and de Munck's suggestions.[50] I also found LeCompte and Schensul's books on ethnographic research quite helpful,[51] and I will refer to them occasionally as I describe the ethnographic data collection and analysis methods I used. I begin by mentioning the field entry procedures and the sampling design I used as initial elements that precede data collection.

---

49. Kim, "Considering 'Ordinariness' in Studying," 5.

50. Spradley, *Ethnographic Interview*; Spradley, *Participant Observations*; Bennardo and de Munck, *Cultural Models*.

51. Schensul, Stephen, Jean J. Schensul, and Margaret Diane LeCompte have collaborated to write a series of seven books on ethnographic research. See: *Ethnographer's Toolkit*.

Steps in Entering the Field Research Setting

Schensul, Schensul, and LeCompte suggest six steps for entering a research setting.[52] I used three of them because, even though I had worked in the county since 2007, I was still an "outsider" and needed appropriate steps for considering the place of work as a research site.

Step One: Obtaining Official Permission

I obtained a one-year research permit from NACOSTI (National Commision for Science, Technology, and Innovation), a government institution in Kenya. I took this to the government officials in Marsabit County as well as to the administrative personnel in the county education department. I was given an authorization letter, which I took to the local chiefs of the various villages in which I carried out my study.[53]

Step Two: Establishing Contact with Knowledgeable People

Since I had lived in the area for some time, I already had useful local Borana contact persons who spoke *afan Borana* and Kiswahili fluently. I chose five of them as my research assistants: one woman and four men.

I took time to explain to my research assistants the objectives of my study. I also expounded on the ethical and procedural issues involved in an ethnographical study. Four of them had never engaged in such a study, and I had to patiently explain the steps involved in interviewing and recording. They also helped in transcription since all the interviews were conducted in *afan Borana*.

Step Three: Locating the Gatekeepers

Local gatekeepers are the people who "control access to resources or information researchers need."[54] These were the local administration chiefs as well as the village elders. When I took the authorization letter to the local chiefs,

---

52. Schensul, Schensul, and LeCompte, *Essential Ethnographic Methods*, 77.

53. I began the process of getting certification for my research proposal from the IRB (Institute of Review Board) at Strathmore University since the one at Africa International University (AIU) had not yet been established. I did the online training as required and obtained a certificate of completion. This training helped me to be cautious about how to treat my research interviewees as human subjects.

54. Schensul, Schensul, and LeCompte, *Essential Ethnographic Methods*, 81.

they gave me permission to interview people within their localities. Some of the chiefs also directed me to the practitioners of *Ayyaana* in their villages.

I did not record the conversations with these gatekeepers[55] since they did not fall within the criterion for selecting my interviewees. Their contact was also useful in providing security measures when I told my interviewees that their local chiefs had given their consent for the research.

Ethnographic Sampling

Before implementing any data collection methods, it was expedient to consider an appropriate sampling design. This should be able to check the "sharedness" of the cultural phenomenon under study.[56] This research involves Borana Muslims who participate in the *Ayyaana* possession cult in Marsabit County. It was not realistic to seek to interview all these people.[57] Hence, it was necessary to use an appropriate sampling method that ensured I had a manageable group to study.

I chose to use purposive sampling design. Russell Bernard explains that purposive sampling is used to study "hard-to-find populations."[58] The Borana Muslims who participate in the *Ayyaana* possession cult fall under this category because they do not publicly confess their participation. They may not welcome anyone who seeks to ask too many questions. Fortunately, I had stayed and worked in Marsabit town and its environs and hence had gained a number of reliable friends who led me to participants of the *Ayyaana* possession cult.

The criterion I used to select my interviewees was active participation in the *Ayyaana* possession cult for at least five years. I chose people who participated actively either as practitioners or as ordinary participants who had been initiated into the cult after an initial ailment caused by *ayyaana*. I also interviewed other Borana Muslims who were neither practitioners nor ordinary participants but who had attended the séances for entertainment or because their relatives were involved directly in the cult. A fourth category of interviewees was cultural specialists. These were not active participants

---

55. Only one of the chiefs became an interviewee under the category of indirect participants.
56. Bennardo and de Munck, *Cultural Models*, 59.
57. Schensul, Schensul, and LeCompte, *Essential Ethnographic*, 231.
58. Bernard, *Research Methods in Anthropology*, 145.

in the *Ayyaana* cult. I needed to interview them in order to understand the traditional Borana customs since a number of the customs were integrated into the cultic rituals. The following table shows these different categories of interviewees from both Saku and Moyale sub-counties.

Table 2: Categories of Interviewees in Marsabit County

Interviewees	Male	Female	Total
Practitioners	9	6	15
Ordinary Participants	1	12	13
Non-Patients / Eye Witnesses	3	5	8
Culture Specialists	4	-	4

Locating an interviewee is the first step of Spradley's DRS research procedure. He asserts that the most persistent problems in the relationship between a researcher and interviewees stem from *"failure to locate a good informant."*[59] I found this pertinent, and I sought to take his advice to overcome the challenge. Hence, I looked for interviewees who were "thoroughly" enculturated and were currently involved in the *Ayyaana* possession cult or had close relatives who were directly involved. These interviewees also had adequate time for the interviews because I first made prior appointments. Some of the practitioners were busy but afforded me time for my interviews.

Apart from selecting key interviewees for this study, I also had to select key places where I could observe the activities involved in the *Ayyaana* possession cult. The following section describes how I was able to interact with the key interviewees and also observe what they do.

Ethnographic Data Collection Methods

In this study, I employ ethnographic data collection procedures to elicit information that leads to an ethnographic description of the *ayyaana* and possession phenomenon among Borana Muslims. I have already discussed the preliminary steps in entering the field and the criterion I used in identifying key interviewees.

---

59. Spradley, *Ethnographic Interview*, 46. Italics are the author's.

The phenomenological approach that this study takes is grounded in an anthropological perspective. This emphasizes the "people factor" in studying the lived experiences of Muslims within their local cultural settings. To attain such an objective, I chose to use two main ethnographic tools that enabled me to hear the Borana Muslims recount their experiences as they participate in the *Ayyaana* possession cult. These tools are ethnographic interviews and participant observation. James Spradley suggests the DRS as systematic procedures for both tools. I used some steps in this sequence that I deemed applicable. I also adapted Bennardo and de Munck's tripartite methodology that has a cognitive anthropological dimension.

Ethnographic Interviews

The second step of Spradley's DRS guidelines is interviewing the people. I found some of his suggestions quite useful as I interviewed Borana Muslims. As an outsider, I had to be cautious in the way I approached them. I also had to guide my research assistants regarding appropriate interviewing procedures, even though they were local Borana people. Most of the interviews were conducted in *afan Borana* especially with the interviewees involved in the *Ayyaana* possession cult.[60]

I employed an interviewing structure that involved three steps: building rapport, asking unstructured questions, and then conducting semi-structured interviews. The rapport process was critical to establish a "basic sense of trust."[61] Involvement in the *Ayyaana* possession cult is becoming more stigmatized in Marsabit County with the rise of radical tendencies among Muslims. The participants were consequently cautious to divulge information to anybody. That is the reason that the rapport process was crucial to building trust with the interviewees.

After building rapport with the interviewees, the next step was to ask unstructured questions. These are synonymous with what Spradley calls "grand tour questions," of which the final outcome is a "verbal description of significant features of the cultural scene."[62] This entailed informal conversations

---

60. I have some rudimentary knowledge of the language. I got someone more eloquent in *afan Borana* to ensure that the Borana research assistants adhered to the guidelines of conducting interviews in their language.

61. Spradley, *Ethnographic Interview*, 78.

62. Spradley, 87.

about Borana cultural aspects to begin to understand the religiocultural world as they experience it within the cultic context. Such conversations ranged from "chaotic to reasonably controlled interchanges" as Handwerker also explains about informal interviews.[63] The informal conversations enabled me to formulate guiding questions that I used for semi-structured interviews. According to Handwerker,

> The "structure" in semi-structured interviews comes from asking people the same questions. Don't confuse semi-structured interviews with structured interviews. Structured interviews aim to elicit a specific set of information from everyone interviewed. Semi-structured interviews aim to elicit specific forms of information for many people, just not the same information from everyone interviewed.[64]

I found Handwerker's assertion above quite useful as I needed to understand the difference between structured and unstructured interviews. The latter was more appropriate for my study of the Borana Muslims who were involved in the *Ayyaana* possession cult since I wanted to hear their individual experiences first and then get a general consensus. Handwerker further points out that semi-structured interviews enable a wider "variation in perceptions, feelings, and understandings about experiences of various kinds."[65]

Bennardo and de Munck also emphasize the use of semi-structured interviews to discover cultural models.[66] Interviewees were interviewed on what they knew about *ayyaana*. They were then asked to recount how they were inducted into the possession cult and their experience as participants.

Recording Ethnographic Data

The third step of the DRS guideline is to record the data collected from the ethnographic interviews. I agree with Spradley's avowal that "many weeks or months may pass before systematic interviews with informants occur."[67] That was the case in Marsabit County as I ventured out to collect data. I was

---

63. Handwerker, "How to Collect Data," 120.
64. Handwerker, 121.
65. Handwerker, 121.
66. Bennardo and de Munck, *Cultural Models*, 64.
67. Spradley, *Ethnographic Interview*, 69.

able to begin writing what I heard or saw from various sociocultural settings within and around Marsabit town, where I was located.

After gaining substantial rapport with the interviewees I sought their consent to record the interviews. I used a digital recorder and also wrote down what I observed during the interviews and parts of the conversations that I could understand. Apart from the field notes that were related directly to what I was observing and hearing during the interviews, I also kept a field journal. I wrote my "experiences, ideas, fears, mistakes, confusions,"[68] and I wrote the challenges that I encountered during the interviewing and observation process.[69]

Collecting Language Data

The cognitive anthropological dimension that this study takes necessitated a study of the "content of thought, or knowledge, as distributed through communities of individuals and observed in natural settings," according to James Boster.[70] In the context of this study, the "content of thought or knowledge" relates to what the Borana Muslims believe about *ayyaana* and possession that inclines them toward participation in the cult. The knowledge about *ayyaana* is first found in individual minds. This knowledge is found to be common among the ordinary Borana Muslims who participate actively in the *Ayyaana* cult. Such collective knowledge that is shared is referred to as cultural models.[71] Thus, part of the intention of this study is to discover the cultural models of *Ayyaana* possession among Borana Muslims. Bennardo and de Munck further clarify that a fundamental aspect of discovering cultural models is reliance on linguistic data and analysis.[72] As mental representations, cultural models are discovered from what people say, hence the significance of linguistic data for this research.

Carol McKinney explains that data collection in a cognitive study involves examining the "categorization of folk knowledge and folk inquiry and the

---

68. Spradley, 76.
69. I found this helpful because there were times that I would be quite frustrated and need to pour out my feelings about the research process.
70. Boster, "Data, Method, and Interpretation," 131.
71. Bennardo and de Munck, *Cultural Models*, 3.
72. Bennardo and de Munck, 53.

content of those categories."⁷³ The methods she gives that are used in cognitive studies resemble the ones suggested by Bennardo and de Munck. I used the latter because their approach corresponds to the theoretical framework I have based this study on.

I followed Bennardo and de Munck's recommendation that interviewees should be allowed to freely answer the guiding questions during the semi-structured interview sessions.⁷⁴ I allowed the sessions to flow in *afan Borana* and recorded appropriately. I used the same set of questions for the different categories of participants in the *Ayyaana* cult. These questions were formulated around three main areas: beliefs about *ayyaana*, ritual practices, and individual possession experiences.

Participant Observation

Bennardo and de Munck are precise in stating, "Mental organizations of knowledge are not directly observable . . . What can be observed is the output of that knowledge; that is, human behavior."⁷⁵ This indicates the fundamental role played by participant observation to gain more information that contributes to a comprehensive description of cultural models. Bernard agrees with this when he states the significance of participant observation in cultural anthropology. He argues that the ability of a researcher to get close to the people makes them feel comfortable to divulge information.⁷⁶

I observed several sessions that involved *ayyaana* and possession. Participation was, however, limited due to the nature of the activities involved. Participant observation entails a complete immersion in the culture and then later disengagement from that immersion in order to rationalize what was observed empirically.⁷⁷ I could not immerse myself into the *ayyaana* possession activities.⁷⁸ Spradley helped me to realize there are degrees of participation and that I was not obliged to be a full participant.⁷⁹ I was a

---

73. McKinney, *Globe-Trotting in Sandals*, 197.
74. Bennardo and de Munck, *Cultural Models*, 64.
75. Bennardo and de Munck, 59.
76. Bernard, *Research Methods in Anthropology*, 256.
77. Bernard, 258.
78. A number of anthropologists studying the phenomenon of spirit possession have immersed themselves into the cultic activities until the spirits possessed them.
79. Spradley, *Participant Observations*, 59.

passive participant since I was present at the sessions but still interacted with the adepts after they normalized. However, I did not allow myself to enter into a trance by clapping and singing to invoke *ayyaana* while I attended the sessions. As I observed the activities during the *Ayyaana* sessions, I had three basic questions that guided me: Who are the main participants? What is going on? And what is the purpose of the sessions? I also enquired about the different artifacts used during the sessions or carried around by the practitioners.

I recorded some of the sessions where the leader gave consent.[80] I used both video and audio recorders, although using the former was a challenge during the night sessions. For the sessions where permission was prohibited, I hurried back home and tried to remember and write what I had heard and observed.

Data Management: Coding and Use of NVivo Software

Ethnographic data tends to be immense and can be quite overwhelming, as I realized with my raw data. I needed a guideline that would help me manage the data in an organized way before I could analyze. LeCompte and Schensul offer suggestions that I used selectively. First, I considered the units (variables) to use according to my research questions.[81] I discovered that I could derive some units from the raw data as I checked through. LeCompte and Schensul also concur that the "analyst is constantly transforming these variables for purposes of data reduction, analysis, and more effective representation."[82]

Next, I put all the transcribed data into one document. Then I coded it as I checked for the various units of analysis. I used a simple coding system that I kept refining as I continued to check through the data for the units of analysis. I took LeCompte and Schensul's advice to have a codebook as part of managing the data. They explain that a codebook is a "list of all the codes used for the analysis of a particular collection of data, the names of the

---

80. I was not allowed to record some of the sessions because I was told the *ayyaana* would be annoyed.

81. LeCompte and Schensul, *Analyzing & Interpreting Ethnographic Data*, 114. LeCompte and Schensul use the terms *variables* and *units* interchangeably. I prefer to use *units* as the "basic blocks of theoretical or explanatory development." See p. 115.

82. LeCompte and Schensul, 124.

variables that the codes represent, and a list of the kinds of items that are to be coded for each variable."[83]

For more efficient management of data, I used NVivo software for analyzing qualitative data. It is from QRS International (2001) and has been used widely, even in research that examines cultural models.[84] It can be used for several functions, including storage of data by creating a database from different sources such as interviews, videos, websites, etc. It can also identify commonly recurring words as well as collate data that are related to a particular theme.

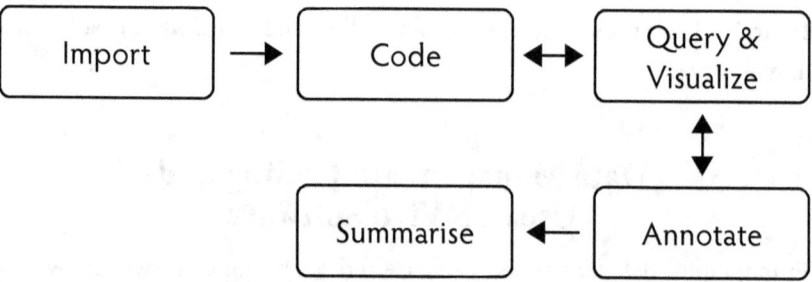

Figure 2: Stages in the NVivo analyzing process[85]

Figure 2 summarizes the main steps I have used to analyze data using NVivo. After I gathered the data into one document, I imported the transcribed interviews and field notes into the system and project for coding. I then did a basic text search across the combined document to look for Borana key words and their frequency (the "Query and Visualize" stage). I proceeded to search for similar themes within the document ("Annotate"), and then I summarized my findings. These procedures are elaborated below for my analysis and interpretation of the data.

---

83. LeCompte and Jean Schensul, 85.

84. Dana Robert Cooley, under the supervision of Benjamin Blount, examined cultural models of fishing and the fishing knowledge among blue crab fishermen in Georgia, USA, and used NVivo analysis software. See Cooley, "Cultural Models and Fishing."

85. Adapted from seminar notes on a presentation at the seminar (Anthropological Research Methods. See, Ruto, "Qualitative Data Analysis Using NVivo."

Data Analysis and Interpretation

The ethnographic and linguistic data was transcribed and translated from the *afan Borana* to English. I continued to enlist the assistance of two of the research assistants since they were Borana speakers. I had to constantly countercheck with them the translation provided in order to get as accurate a paraphrase as possible. It was also necessary to consult another Borana speaker who was more versed in linguistic issues.

Some words had variant spellings given by the different Borana speakers. I also realized that various scholars who have written about Borana culture also spelt some words differently. I chose to use Leus and Salvadori's spellings for consistency.[86] I counterchecked these with Stroomer's comparative dictionary of the Borana in Kenya, which is written from a linguistics perspective.[87]

Analyzing Ethnographic Data

Bennardo and de Munck suggest three modes of analyzing ethnographic data elicited from participant observation: selection, focus, and synthesis.[88] I first selected what was relevant to the objectives of this study. The selected data is derived from what I wrote down after attending and observing the *Ayyaana* possession sessions. I also went through the video clips I took during the sessions to select the relevant data that would answer my research questions.

After selecting the relevant data, I then focused on the *emic* statements of my interviewees as they communicated during the sessions that I observed. I enlisted the help of my research assistants to clarify what was spoken. We watched the video clips together and wrote down the relevant statements in *afan Borana* and translated into English.

Last, I synthesized my observations of the *Ayyaana* possession sessions and the emic data that I had written down. This enabled me to clarify anything I may have written down that was not correct or valid. It also enabled me to ask for more clarity in places where I did not understand what was going on.

---

86. Leus and Salvadori, *Aadaa Boraanaa*.
87. Stroomer, *Grammar of Boraana Oromo*.
88. Bennardo and de Munck, *Cultural Models*, 63.

Analyzing Linguistic Data

Bennardo and de Munck discuss analysis of linguistic data using three levels: word level, sentence level, and discourse level.[89] Analysis at the word level comprises what is commonly called key-word analysis. Key words are the "focal points through which internalized knowledge in the forms of schemas, models, and encyclopedic knowledge are externalized," according to Benjamin Blount.[90] In line with this, I started the process of analyzing linguistic data by first checking for the key words in *afan Borana* that were commonly used by my interviewees as they narrated their beliefs and practices in the *Ayyaana* possession cult. The NVivo software helped me to list the words according to their frequency of appearance.

After listing the key words, I proceeded to find the context surrounding the usage of these words. I searched for the sentences in which the words were used and tried to understand the meanings of the words within the sentences. I also looked for metaphors[91] that may have been used within the "*ayyaana* language."[92] Bennardo and de Munck mention the significance of metaphors since they "represent one of the most common ways in which knowledge is organized mentally."[93] Metaphorical analysis is significant in discovering the content and structures of cultural models. This analysis will involve metaphorical mappings in order to find the systematic correspondences between the source and target domains of the metaphors derived from the interviews.[94]

The third level of analyzing linguistic data is the discourse analysis. Bennardo and de Munck state that discourse analysis is a "primary analytical tool" that has been used to discover cultural models.[95] As I focused on

---

89. Bennardo and de Munck, 65.
90. Blount, "Situating Cultural Models."
91. According to Bennardo and de Munck, metaphor analysis is also a type of sentence level analysis. See Bennardo and de Munck, *Cultural Models*, 66.
92. The adepts used some non-Borana words that were unfamiliar to my Borana research assistants. I was informed that the *warra ayyaana* use some words that are unique to them, hence this reference to the "*ayyaana* language."
93. Bennardo and de Munck, *Cultural Models*, 66.
94. Lakoff and Johnson, *Metaphors We Live By*, 246. Source and target domains are components of metaphors that are used by cognitive linguists to analyze metaphors. See Lakoff and Johnson, *Metaphors We Live By*; and Kövecses, *Metaphor in Culture*. The source domain is more physical and tangible, while the target domain is abstract. Mapping is the systematic correspondence between the source and target domains, according to Lakoff and Johnson.
95. Bennardo and de Munck, *Cultural Models*, 9.

understanding the lived experiences of Borana Muslims, I allowed them to narrate their experiences with *ayyaana*. I analyzed these narratives as discourses by going through the transcribed interviews and also replaying the recorded interviews where I needed more clarity. I also needed to find out the enthusiasm – or lack thereof – of the interviewees as they narrated their experiences. As I went through the discourses, I noticed some structural similarities that became major variables for discussion. For instance, interviewees maintained a similar narrative about how they were inducted into the *Ayyaana* cult.

The fourth level in analyzing linguistic data is the songs analysis. I realized that the *Ayyaana* cult sessions were replete with songs used to praise the Sheikh Hussein, whom they esteemed highly. The songs were in *afan Borana* and were transcribed like the rest of the data for a clearer understanding.

Religiocultural Domain Analysis

Cultural domains are deciphered from the cultural knowledge embedded in "words, in stories, and artifacts, and which is learned from and shared with other humans."[96] The significance of analyzing such cultural domains is that it enables the researcher to discover the various categories used by the people. Spradley states that cultural domains "will not jump out at you from your field notes. They are embedded in what you have already recorded."[97] My task, therefore, was to go through my transcribed data and search for the descriptions for cover terms, included terms, and semantic relationships.[98] These terms are helpful in realizing the different categorization of spirits by the Borana Muslims.

Spradley warns that a researcher's presuppositions can hinder a valid representation of the domains that is true to the cognition of the people being examined.[99] This was a particular caution for me since I have some prior knowledge of the *Ayyaana* possession cult. It would have been easy to examine

---

96. D'Andrade, *Development of Cognitive Anthropology*, xiv.
97. Spradley, *Participant Observations*, 91.
98. I adapted Spradley's procedure for domain analysis in part since I found it helpful. According to him, the cover terms are the names given to a larger category of things or people in a cultural setting. The included terms are the smaller categories that fall under the cover term. The relationship that links the cover terms with all the included terms of a set is what Spradley calls semantic relationship. See Spradley, *Ethnographic Interview*, 100.
99. Spradley, 100.

the cultural domains of Borana Muslims with a "large repertoire of analytic categories" that are irrelevant to them. In spite of the complexity of categories as identified in the field of cognitive psychology, categorization is a significant undertaking that reveals how the mind thinks.[100] Thus, categorization by the Muslim teachers vis-à-vis the ordinary Borana Muslims revealed the different models they have of jinn and *ayyaana* respectively.

Comparative Analysis

The STA's third side entails an interdisciplinary analysis that seeks to "understand the dynamics that lie between Islamic ideology and human ordinariness."[101] Essentially, the aim of this side is to comprehend the relationship between (a) the Islamic model of the spirit world according to the Muslim teachers' knowledge and (b) the religiocultural model of *Ayyaana* as elicited from ethnographic research carried out on the ordinary Borana Muslims' participation in the *Ayyaana* cult. This section thus describes how this integrated analysis was done. I first represent the essence of the integrated analysis diagrammatically below.

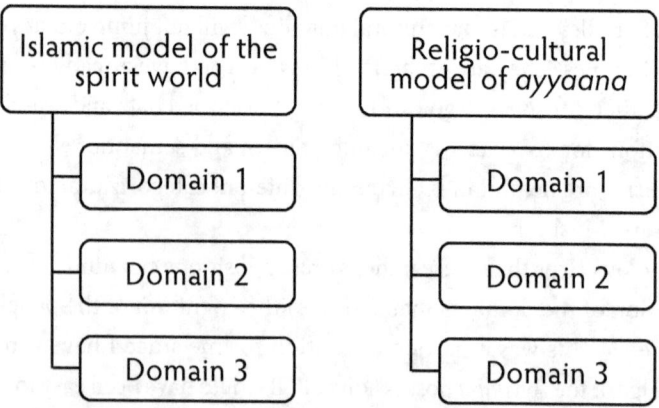

Figure 3: Plan for comparative analysis of models

---

100. Lakoff, *Women, Fire and Dangerous Things*, 5.

101. Kim explains "ordinariness" as the "human condition that represents a general tendency of human mind before it is formulated or empowered by any ideology or theology through a deep and long intentional thinking process." See Kim, "Considering 'Ordinariness,'" 2.

From figure 3 above, the integrated analysis compares different domains from the Islamic model of the spirit world with the domains from the *Ayyaana* model. The items from the Islamic model are those elicited from the Muslim teachers, while those of the *Ayyaana* model were from the ethnographic interviews and observations of what the ordinary Borana Muslims said and did pertaining to the *Ayyaana* cult. The specific details of this comparative analysis are the subject of discussion for chapter 7 of this dissertation.

It is from this comparative analysis that I develop a theory that explains the discrepancies and similarities between the *Ayyaana* model and the Islamic model of the spirit world. I employ some existing theoretical lenses from cognitive anthropology to offer an interdisciplinary explanation.

Ethical Issues

The contemporary world of research is now becoming more cautious, and more ethical measures are being highlighted.[102] Research textbooks are replete with these measures that have become universal. I will discuss two ethical issues that I found relevant for this study.

Permission from National and Local Administration

Apart from gaining the permission of local gatekeepers (administrative chiefs) in Marsabit County as mentioned earlier, I was required to obtain an official research permit from the Kenyan government through NACOSTI. I downloaded the guidelines online and was able to make the application for a research permit, which I eventually received. I used this permit to obtain authorization from the local chiefs to carry out research in the villages.

Protection and Sensitivity to Human Subjects

I concur with LeCompte and Schensul as they narrate that ethical issues in research were established because of the barbaric ways used to conduct experimental research in the Nazi concentration camps during the World War II.[103] Contemporary times are not exempted from such exploitation, and it

---

102. Contemporary researchers in Kenya have to comply more with ethical issues presently than before. Ethical issues in research have been a global concern, especially in the West.

103. LeCompte and Schensul, *Designing & Conducting*, 286.

is therefore fundamental to set guidelines that will ensure the protection of human subjects in empirical studies.

This study deals with people who participate in the *Ayyaana* possession cult. Those who become possessed by *ayyaana* presumably go through some psychological distress and may not want their experiences to be publicized. It is thus necessary to protect their privacy by using pseudonyms to conceal their identity.

One major requirement by IRB was that the interviewees sign a consent form to indicate that they have freely chosen to participate or not in the research process of data collection. I was able to get the Muslim teachers who were literate to sign the consent form. (See a copy of the form in appendix 1.) However, most of my Borana Muslim interviewees who participated in the *Ayyaana* possession cult were illiterate, and I did not give them the form to sign. I got their consent verbally.

As I carried out data collection, I had to remember that I was an outsider in spite of having stayed in Marsabit County for several years. I sought advice on how to approach the elderly Borana people lest I made cultural mistakes that would jeopardize the data collection process. I similarly needed to be cautious when interviewing Borana Muslim men. I made sure I was accompanied by at least one of my male research assistants during the interview sessions.

Summary

This chapter considered Saukko's pertinent theme of studying the lived experiences of people while critically analyzing their discourses.[104] The objective of the chapter was to describe the specific methodology and methods employed to elicit these discourses among Borana Muslims in Marsabit County as they participated in the *Ayyaana* possession cult. The methodology chosen was multidisciplinary and was framed in a cognitive anthropological perspective. This was deemed necessary as it helped me understand the cognitive dimension of their inclination to the *Ayyaana* cult as opposed to what the Muslim teachers taught them. To enhance this understanding, I chose a phenomenological research design that gives preference first to the Borana Muslims' experiences before making any analytical inferences. I used ethnographic

---

104. Saukko, *Doing Research*, 4.

interviews and participant observations as tools to obtain information from the people.

The methodology and methods of data collection and analysis employed in this study were selectively borrowed from other researchers. I was enlightened by Bernhard Leistle's phenomenological theory,[105] which made me approach the experience of the Borana Muslims with *ayyaana* (Other) in an unprejudiced way. I appreciated Bennardo and de Munck's guidelines for discovering cultural models in cognitive anthropological research. I borrowed extensively from their ethnographic and linguistic data collection and analysis procedures. I also used Spradley's DRS steps selectively to refine the ethnographic tools to finer details. Schensul and LeCompte further offered relevant suggestions, which I integrated with the other suggested procedures. Analysis of data was done using the NVivo software.

This study examines Muslims essentially. Ongoing debates on the anthropology of Islam indicate how pertinent the issue is to anthropologists like Clifford Geertz, Talal Asad, and others, as they divert people's attention from studying Islam abstractly. The STA guideline has been described in this chapter as a guideline that I have adapted and modified to suit my research concern. It has been shown that the tripartite elements of the STA guideline correspond to the three research questions of this dissertation.

---

105. Leistle, "From the Alien."

CHAPTER 4

The Islamic Model of the Spirit World

Introduction

This chapter commences the analytical part of this study. It addresses the first research question, which seeks to discover the official Islamic model of the spirit world as propagated by Muslim teachers in Marsabit County. The information herein is derived from interviews conducted with nine teachers in Saku and Moyale Subcounties of Marsabit, as shown in the table below. Their names are given as pseudonyms to conceal identity.

Table 3: List of Muslim Teachers Interviewed

Name	Place
Sheikh Amr	Saku
Maalim Haro	Saku
Sheikh Abdi	Moyale
Sheikh Alisa	Saku
Sheikh Gayo	Saku
Sheikh Ibra	Moyale
Sheikh Khadi	Moyale
Sheikh Munur	Saku
Sheikh Umir	Saku

From the table above, six of the nine Muslim teachers were from Saku Subcounty. I have lived in Saku and thus was able to locate more Muslim teachers there. Nevertheless, there is some similitude between the information derived from the teachers in either place concerning spirits and their involvement in human life.

Based on the findings of these interviews, this chapter will address various themes that emerged consistently. The aim is to provide a descriptive portrait of the mental representations of the spirit world, and consequently the Islamic model as conceptualized by the Muslim teachers. These are essentially the custodians of official Islam. Their view of the spirit world is germane in evaluating the religiocultural model of *Ayyaana* as perceived by ordinary Borana Muslims who participate in the *Ayyaana* cult in Marsabit County. This model will be described in the subsequent chapter as I examine the relation between the two respective models of the spirit world among Borana Muslims.

Conceptualization of the Spirit World by Muslim Teachers

Muslims acknowledge the existence of another world apart from the one they inhabit. This is evident from the words used in their *salāt* (daily prayers), which include the first part of *al-fatiha* (Surah 1): "Praise belongs to God, the Lord of the worlds [*rabb al-'alamin*]." Pluralizing *worlds* indicates a belief in an extraterrestrial world that is accepted officially in Islam. This non-human world consists of spiritual entities that are a major concern among Muslims in Marsabit County as well as globally.

The official conceptualization of the spirit world in the Islamic context of Marsabit County is represented by what the Muslim teachers know and teach.[1] They not only acknowledge the reality of its existence but also admit its interaction with the human world. This section examines this conceptualization as well as the categorization of the spirit world by the Muslim teachers. I begin by discussing how they perceive God in relation to the spirit world. I then proceed to illustrate the place of human beings in the context of the

---

1. The term "spirit" is herein translated from the Kiswahili word *pepo*, which was frequently used by the interviewees. The Arabic word for "spirit" as used in the Qur'an is *ruh*. The "Holy Spirit" is *Ruh al Qudus* (Surah 2:87; 16:102). The "spirit" is also mentioned as parallel to angels in the Qur'an (Surah 78:38; 7:4; 97:4). Essentially, the Qur'an does not refer to false spirits as *ruh*.

spirit world. This is followed by a brief discussion on what the Muslim teachers said about the unseen world, *al-ghaib*.

God and the Spirit World

A discourse on God in Islam is generally broad and beyond the scope of this study. However, it is expedient to acknowledge what the Muslim teachers perceived as his relation to the spirit world. Apparently, they discussed his involvement in the spirit world jointly with the human world. God created both the spirit and human worlds, and their inhabitants exist to serve him. Hierarchically, God is in the topmost position above both worlds and their occupants, as seen from figure 4 below. Such a comparison is arbitrary because he cannot be placed on the same platform of appraisal with the created beings of both worlds.

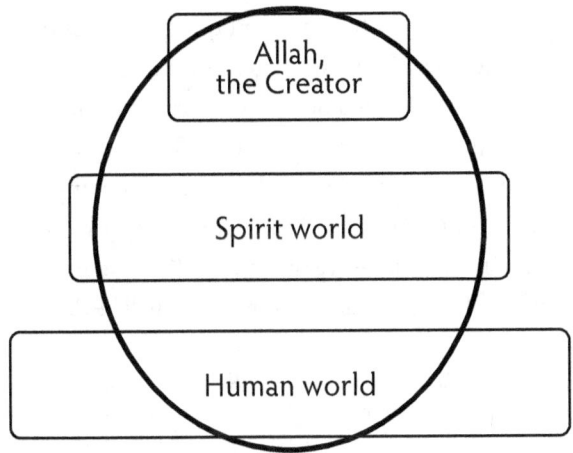

Figure 4: Allah and the created world

I particularly noted the word they used whenever they referred to him. The name *Allāh* was only mentioned when they recited *ayah* that referred to God in Arabic.[2] They preferred to use the Kiswahili word for God, *Mwenyezi*

---

2. The Arabic word *Allāh* means "the God." It is derived from the word *al-ilāh* (God), which is a combination of the definite Arabic article *al-* and *ilāhun* (the god). Henceforth, I will use the anglicized form, Allah, and thus will not italicize it.

Mungu (Almighty God).³ By continually referring to God as *Almighty*, the teachers acknowledged the superiority of God over all his created beings including jinn and other spirits. Furthermore, the Islamic concept of *tauḥīd* (oneness of God) is closely connected with this supremacy of God that is apparent in the universe he created.

According to the Muslim teachers, the universe consists of the *samāwātun* (heavens) and the *arḍun* (earth).⁴ God created them and still sustains them, according to Sheikh Amr's explanation of *rabbi l-ʿālamīna* (Arabic for "Lord of the universe") in Surah 2:2. He asserts that the phrase "Lord of the universe" implies that Allah is the Sustainer and Cherisher of the universe.⁵ Qur'an commentators, such as Yusuf Ali, endorse this as they agree that the Arabic word *rabbi* can also be translated as "cherisher and sustainer." Yusuf Ali further observes, "God cares for all the worlds He has created."⁶ Thus, the immanence of God is implied in this statement. Muslim teachers talked of this "nearness" of God, yet the pertinent question arises of whether they and the ordinary Borana Muslims they teach experience this "nearness" as they relate with the other created beings in the spirit world.

All living and non-living things fall under God's jurisdiction as created beings. Sheikh Amr explained that of all the created living beings that are found in the spirit and human worlds, God has *ametukuza* (Kiswahili for "exalted") three of them.⁷ These are the *waljinn* (jinn), the *malaika* (angels), and the *insi* (human beings).⁸ The concept of jinn will be discussed at length

---

3. I used Kiswahili in all my interviews with the Muslim teachers in Marsabit County. All the teachers were comfortable using Kiswahili and not *afan Borana*, their native language. They also quoted Arabic *ayah* and phrases, but they had to translate these into Kiswahili for my understanding. The Borana word for God is *Waaqa*, which also means the sky, the heavens, or the atmosphere. It is commonly translated as *God* in everyday conversations. Leus and Salvadori state that the word *Waaqa* does not have the anthropomorphic overtones that the English word, *God*, has. For a detailed explanation, see Leus and Salvadori, *Aadaa Boraanaa*, 639. However, I will use *Waaqa* for this study, especially in chapters 5–7, since the ordinary Borana Muslims use it frequently. It is the traditional name for God and was/is popular among other Cushitic tribal groups in Kenya, like the Somali (see Mohamed, "Sufi Poetry in Somali," 265), the Orma (see Faulkner, *Overtly Muslim, Covertly Boni*, 19), and the Gabra (see Tablino, *Gabra*).

4. *l-ʿālamīna*, the universe in Arabic, literally means "the worlds," or *ulimwengu* in Kiswahili. The Arabic word for heaven, singular, is *samāʾun*.

5. Sheikh Amr, May 17, 2017.

6. Ali, *Holy Qur'an*, 14.

7. Sheikh Amr, May 17, 2017.

8. My interviewees mentioned the Arabic words *waljinn* (for jinn), *malaika* (for angels), and *insi* (for human beings).

in the subsequent section as the main focus of this study. Suffice it here to mention that jinn are spiritual beings that are exalted together with human beings and angels. It is deemed expedient to briefly explain the relation between these three beings in order to form a basis of the official perception of the spirit world in Marsabit County.

To be exalted means that the three beings are esteemed above all other creatures. The reason for exalting them is their ability to *abudu* (Kiswahili for worship) God. Each of them worships in a unique way. Jinn and human beings are endowed with volition to worship, unlike angels.

Perception of Angels in the Context of *Al-Ghaib*

Angelology in Islam is a whole study in itself. Angels play a vital part in Islam, and they have been studied more than spirits. Delving much into the concept would derail the purpose of this research. A brief discussion is nevertheless necessary since they are included in the cosmological perspective of the Muslim teachers interviewed. It will be seen later in the analysis of *ayyaana* among Borana Muslims that the latter have a certain notion about angels in their cosmological perception. This notion will be gauged according to the perception of Muslim teachers about angels as briefly presented in this section.

I noticed that the Muslim teachers presented the topic of angels with much ease. The discussion on the three exalted beings according to the Islamic cosmology naturally began with angels as a more "pleasant" topic to discuss. One could see why angels were placed on a seemingly higher pedestal during the conversation. Angels are said to obey God in everything without questioning according to Sheikh Amr.

> *Kuna kipawa ambacho Mwenyezi Mungu amewapa. Hawamuasi Mwenyezi Mungu. Hawafanyi madhambi. Wanafanya kila kitu kulingana na maamrisho ya Mungu. Wanafuata kila amri na mapenzi yake. Hawamuasi Mwenyezi mungu, kila anawakataza wana kaa kando nayo. Kila jambo anawaamurisha wanatii kulingana na amri ya Mwenyezi Mungu. Hivo ndivyo Mwenyezi Mungu asema katika Qur'ani Takatifu, "laiya asuna (hawamuasi Mwenyezi Mungu) ilaya asun alahah ma amarahu (mambo Mwenyezi Mungu anawaamurisha wanafanya kulingana na amri*

> yake) wieif aruna (na wanatenda) mairub mairu (wanatenda kile Mwenyezi Mungu anawaamurisha. (Kiswahili)

Translation:

> There is an endowment that the Almighty God has given to them [angels] They never disobey or rebel against God. They do not commit sin. They do everything according to his commands. They follow his commands and his will. They do not rebel against God. Whatever he prohibits they stay away from it. Whatever God instructs them to do, they do accordingly. That is what God says in the holy Qur'an: "They do not disobey God. Whatever he commands them to do they do according to his will."[9]

The emphasis here is on the exemplary obedient nature of angels. They are *viumbe kando* (Kiswahili for exceptional) unlike the other two types of beings that are said to be glorified and endowed with the will to choose.

There are different angels according to the responsibilities and positions they have been allocated. The highest-ranking angel, who is believed to be in charge of all angels, is *Jibril* (Gabriel). He was entrusted with the task of taking the *waḥy* (Arabic for revelation) from God to the prophets like Muhammad, *Mūsā* (Moses), and *ʿīsā* (Jesus). Other angels are responsible for different cosmological realms of the heavens, such as rain or the sun. Every aspect of life is under the jurisdiction of respective angels, according to Sheikh Amr.

Man in the Context of *Al-Ghaib*

As one of the beings created by God, man is also esteemed in official Islam. Sheikh Amr and the other Muslim teachers, preferred to use the Arabic word *ins* for human beings.[10] Humans have been given the ability to choose between right or wrong. They have a greater propensity for disobeying the injunctions of God than for obeying them. There are nevertheless some who *wanamcha Mungu* (Kiswahili for fear God and obey), according to Sheikh

---

9. Sheikh Amr, May 17, 2017.

10. *Al-Ins* is the Arabic plural for *al-insān* [the human being]. An example is found in Surah 51:56 ."I did not create the jinn and mankind [*al-ins*] except to worship me." *Insān* is used when the focus is on the non-physical features of human beings, while *bashar* is used when the physical aspects are involved.

Gayo.¹¹ The other Muslim teachers also acknowledged that humans are prone to forgetfulness and thus disobedience to God. In spite of such limitations, humans are still placed on a higher pedestal than the other created beings. Surah 2:29 states that God created all other things because of human beings. This reinforces the official Islamic belief in the superiority of humans above every other created being including jinn. Jinn are subservient to humans, as will be shown in the discussion on jinn below. This is a relevant issue in understanding how humans ought to relate with the spirit world.

God created humans so that they could *abudu* (Kiswahili for worship) him. Humans revere God by submitting to his will and obeying his injunctions as postulated in the official texts. They thus become a *mu'minun* (Arabic for believer) and a true Muslim, according to Sheikh Abdi.¹² Such a believer must never place anything alongside God. All allegiance should be channeled to God alone. Otherwise, humans would be guilty of committing *shirk* (associating Allah with other beings), which is considered to be the most serious offense in Islam.

Unlike angels, humans have wills and can choose whether to submit to God or not. They have been endowed with the power to decide whether to obey God's instructions as revealed in the Qur'an and the Hadiths of Prophet Muhammad or not. These official Islamic texts have been given to offer *hidaya* (Arabic for guidance) toward the "right path" (Surah 72:2). True Muslims, according to Marsabit clerics, are those who also believe in the *nguzo tano za kiislamu* (Kiswahili for the five pillars of Islam) and perform the *shahāda*, *salāt*, *zakāt*, *ṣawm*, and *ḥajj* (Arabic, the five duties of Islam). A true Muslim is also expected to believe in *al-ghaib*.

Al-Ghaib as the Imaginal World in Official Islam

Amira El-Zein avows that "believing in *al-ghaib*, the unseen and the unknown, is central and fundamental in the Islamic faith."¹³ This centrality was also apparent from the interviews conducted with the Muslim teachers. They

---

11. Sheikh Gayo, May 16, 2017.
12. Sheikh Abdi, August 27, 2016.
13. El-Zein, *Islam, Arabs, and the Intelligent*, 1.

mentioned that *al-ghaib* is the unseen, "something that cannot be known by normal human beings."[14]

There are several dimensions of *al-ghaib* in the Islamic contexts. First, the unseen realm refers to the knowledge of imminent things that are yet to be manifest to human beings and to which only God is privy. Sheikh Amr further expounded this by referring to Surah 72:26: "He (alone) knows the Unseen [*al-ghaib*] nor does He make any one acquainted with His mysteries." Another dimension of *al-ghaib* is the unseen knowledge of the heart. Again, only God knows what human beings conceal within themselves. He also knows the *niya* (Kiswahilifor the intentions) of whatever actions humans take. Last, there is the nuance of the unseen that is implied by the spirit world. This realm is invisible to human eyes, and yet its existence is apparent to all Muslims. It is the imaginal world that is as real as the physical realm because it impinges on it.[15] The people's interaction with this invisible domain can go to unlimited magnitudes because of the broad conceptualization of the imaginal realm. This is evident when one examines the different articulations by various local Muslims as this study has done. It therefore makes it expedient for Muslim clerics to inform their congregants of the official boundaries when dealing with the imaginal world.

The Muslim teachers were emphatic in their caution against humans' desire to gain knowledge of the unseen. They confessed that it is a "temptation of man to try and know what his future holds. But it is only God who has the information according to this *ayah* [referring to Surah 72:26, previously mentioned about God not revealing his knowledge of *al-ghaib* to ordinary humans]." The next *ayah*, *ayah* 27, gives an exception: the person who had access to the knowledge of *al-ghaib* from God. This was "a messenger whom He has chosen" (Surah 72:27).[16] Sheikh Amr did not give an explanation for this *ayah*. The reason for this may be because of the scholarly deliberations regarding whether Muhammad had access to *al-ghaib* or not. Muhammad's

---

14. Sheikh Amr, May 17, 2017.

15. I borrow the word "imaginal" from Amira El-Zein, who also borrowed from the French philosopher Henry Corbin. She distinguishes it from "imaginary" because the latter denotes an "unreal, fantastic, or utopian" realm, which negates the Islamic belief in the unseen. See El-Zein, *Islam, Arabs, and the Intelligent*, 6. The fact that "imaginal" has a cognitive underpinning makes its usage appropriate for this study, which has a cognitive anthropological framework.

16. Yusuf Ali's 1946 edition of the Qur'an has "apostle" instead of "messenger."

relation with *al-ghaib* will be discussed more in the context of his encounters with the jinn as some of the beings that inhabit *al-ghaib* and yet are involved in the human world.

The Concept of Jinn in Official Islam as Represented by the Muslim Teachers

Muslim teachers in Marsabit County concur that jinn dwell in the *al-ghaib* that they perceived to be real. I noticed the teachers' firm belief in the concept of jinn from their vivid categorization and description of what these beings are and what they do. These are explored herein using three modes of analysis – textual, discourse, and domain analysis – which are used interchangeably to present a comprehensive and analytical frame of the clerics' perception of the concept of jinn. The textual analysis considers the official Islamic texts that the Muslim clerics in Marsabit know and teach concerning the concept of jinn. The texts include the Qur'an, Hadith, and materials written by other Muslim scholars on jinn that the clerics use to supplement their knowledge of the concept of jinn.

I interviewed the Muslim teachers, and I allowed them to give as much information as they could. I then analyzed the interviews as discourses as recommended by Bennardo and de Munck in discovering cultural model. The aim of the discourse analysis in this study was to realize the Islamic model that the Muslim teachers have concerning jinn.

Domain analysis is also a useful tool in discovering the kind of cultural model people have about a phenomenon. I used James Spradley's approach of domain analysis with some modification to illustrate the categorization of the Muslim teachers in Marsabit County. I found this approach to be relevant in identifying the way Muslim teachers categorize the inhabitants of *al-ghaib*. This reveals the way they conceptualize things, which is in line with the cognitive framework on which this study is based.

Categorization of Jinn by Muslim Teachers

Scholars have examined the concept of jinn in different Islamic contexts globally.[17] Most of them acknowledge that the official Islamic texts, the Qur'an

---

17. See chapter 3 of this dissertation.

and Hadith, influence the way Muslims worldwide conceptualize these beings of the spirit world. However, the interpretation of such official precepts is contextual as illustrated in this section. It is therefore indispensable to explore the way Muslim teachers in different contexts categorize the beings and powers in the spirit world. Such categorization further demonstrates the cognitive element that is a crucial aspect of understanding Muslims in their contextual settings. In this case, classification of jinn among Muslim clerics in Marsabit County will illumine the kind of cognition they have concerning the spirit world as representatives of official Islam in the county. This is necessary for an evaluative analysis of the phenomenon of *ayyaana* and possession as perceived by the ordinary Borana Muslims in Marsabit County.

The initial step in Spradley's domain analysis procedure is the discovery of "semantic relationships rather than cover terms."[18] Like Spradley, I also distinguish between "universal" and "folk" semantic relationships in classifying jinn. The former relates to the official Islam categorization according to the Islamic texts acknowledged universally, while the latter conveys the local, contextual categories as interpreted by the Muslim teachers.[19] In both these relationships, the categories are placed under the "strict inclusion" form (x is a kind of y).[20] Jinn, angels, and man are considered to be different kinds of created beings that are exalted by God.

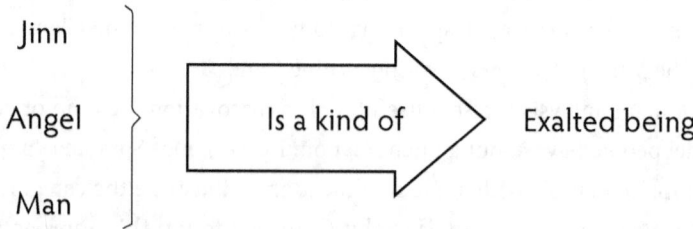

Figure 5: Semantic relationship of the exalted beings

God created each of the three beings from different substances. Angels were created from light, man from dust, and jinn from fire. This indicates

---

18. Spradley, *Ethnographic Interview*, 108.

19. Instead of "folk," I prefer to use "contextual" semantic relationship in referring to what the Muslim clerics in Marsabit County classify beings in the spirit world.

20. Spradley, *Ethnographic Interview*, 112.

that the Muslim teachers in the county adhere to the universal Islamic categorization as presented by Muslims scholars.[21] All the teachers interviewed consented that jinn can be either good or bad as illustrated in figure 6.

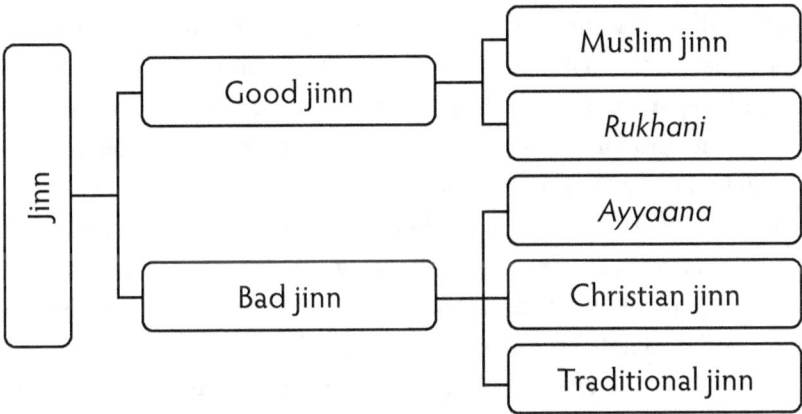

Figure 6: Categories of jinn according to Muslim teachers

In the perception of the Muslim teachers, the word *jinn* serves as the cover term for all kinds of *mapepo* (Kiswahili for spirits) that impinge on the human world. I noticed that the Muslim clerics preferred to use the Kiswahili term *jini* (plural: *majini*) instead of *pepo* (plural: *mapepo*) when referring to the spirits. Interestingly, the Muslim teachers used the term *mjini* to refer to *Iblīs*.[22] This confirms the general usage of the word *jinn* as a cover term among the teachers. Hence, all other kinds of spirits – including *ayyaana* – are a type of jinn, as indicated by figure 6 above. The perception of *ayyaana* according to the Muslim teachers will be offered later. Suffice it here to note that *ayyaana* are a kind of jinn. Such a perception, then, demands a common way of dealing with *ayyaana* that is accepted officially. It then becomes the procedure that all the other ordinary Borana Muslims are expected to follow. Any other practices are considered to be defiant and wrong. They are considered to be *bid'ah* (religious innovations) in Islam and should not be endorsed.

Before proceeding to discuss the other terms included under *jinn*, I will briefly examine how the Muslim teachers understand the word *jinn* in Arabic.

---

21. Philips, "Exorcism in Islam"; Al-Ashqar, *World of the Jinn*.
22. More details on *Iblīs* are discussed in a subsequent section.

Some of the teachers were fluent in the Arabic language, like Sheikh Amr.[23] Most of the teachers had rudimentary knowledge of the language especially when referring to the verses in the Qur'an. Sheikh Amr said that the word *jinn* is derived from the Arabic word *janna*, "which means to cover [Kiswahili: *kufunika*]." This is one of the encyclopedic meanings provided for Arabic words that use the root letters *jīm nūn nūn*. Other Muslim scholars agree that the verb *janna* has an indication of covering, concealing, to be dark, or to be mad.[24] The verb form *janna* appears only once in the Qur'an (Surah 6:76). The noun *jinn* appears twenty-two times and refers to spiritual beings. It is in the masculine gender, which is the same way that the Muslim teachers in Marsabit referred to the jinn spirits during the interviews. Kim notes that there are female jinn called *jinniyah* in Arabic. These are only mentioned in the Hadith and not in the Qur'an.[25]

Under the cover term *jinn* are the included terms that refer to the different types of jinn. From the interviews, the categorization of good and bad jinn was noteworthy. The benchmark used for this classification was whether a jinni was a Muslim or not. The teachers referred to the Qur'an, especially Surah 72 (*al-jinn*), which designated "good" jinn as those that heard the recitation by Pprophet Muhammad. These jinn believed what they heard and became Muslims. Sheikh Munur was emphatic in describing these jinn:

> There are some jinn that are good and that believe [*kuna majini wazuri ambao ni waumini*]. They even say it. These ones do not disturb unless they are disturbed, and they trouble a bit then they say "*poleni*" [sorry] [26]

This assertion represents the perception of the Muslim teachers in Marsabit County who submit to the Qur'anic avowal that there are good jinn. These teachers identified such *majini wazuri* (Kiswahili for good jinn) as the ones that adhere to Islamic tenets and thus are Muslims. Sheikh Alisa further explained that the "good jinn are the ones that obey and perform their

---

23. Sheikh Amr mentioned that he had studied at an Islamic university in Sudan and holds a bachelor's degree in Sharia. He did his research in Arabic, and his phone conversations were mostly in Arabic.

24. 'Omar, *Dictionary of the Holy Qur'an*; Philips, "Exorcism in Islam," 39.

25. Kim, *Islam among the Swahili*, 83.

26. Sheikh Munur, Personal interview by author, Saku Sub-County, May 18, 2017, Code: B07-2017, May 18th.

Islamic duties; they even go for pilgrimage."²⁷ These good jinn can also be annoyed with human beings and consequently can instill some discomfort in them. So, are they still "good"? This begs for clarity regarding whether there are jinn that are "inherently good." Kim realized that there is "no inherently good spirit in the Swahili spirit world."²⁸ For the Muslim teachers in Marsabit County, this did not seem to bother them at all. What was important was that some jinn are Muslims because they believe in the monotheistic God and in Muhammad his prophet.

The bad jinn are the antithesis of the good ones. They do not accept the message of the Prophet and thus do not believe in him as God's messenger. Neither do they believe in God or his oneness. Sheikh Amr describes them as:

> Jinn that are rude [Kiswahili: *wakorofi*], the ones that disobey the Almighty God [*wanamuasi Mwenyezi Mungu*]. They do bad things [*wanafanya mabaya*]. The ones that take alcohol, they commit adultery [*wanafanya zinaa*], they commit sin [*wanafanya madhambi*] of various kinds.²⁹

The impression from the above description of bad jinn is that they are evil because they defy God and do not follow his commands. They do all the wrong things prohibited in Islam like taking alcohol and committing adultery. They are inherently bad because they are not Muslims. These are the ones that trouble people and have to be dealt with according to the official texts. The Muslim teachers place *ayyaana* in this category of the bad jinn. They are not Muslim because they do not follow the precepts of the Islamic texts. They do not prostrate to God, they do not believe in the Prophet, nor do they have an Islamic predisposition. More details of the Muslim teachers' perception of *ayyaana* will be discussed later.

The other kinds of jinn, according to my interviewees, are called *rukhani*.³⁰ There was some ambiguity regarding whether *rukhani* are Muslim or non-Muslim spirits. Most of the teachers agreed that they are a type of jinn. Sheikh

---

27. Sheikh Alisa, May 16, 2017.
28. Kim, *Islam among the Swahili*, 107.
29. Sheikh Amr, May 17, 2017.
30. I did not research more on the etymology of *rukhani* among the Borana Muslims since I was more concerned with *ayyaana*. Their conceptualization is more toward jinn and *ayyaana* than *rukhani*, which is a prevalent notion among the coastal Muslims like the Swahili.

Abdi echoed the perception of the other clerics in explaining that the name *rukhani* (as well as *ayyaana*) is given to jinn because they "do not like to be called by their real names."[31] It seems the "real name" of the spirits is *jinn*. I noticed that they would sometimes mention it softly as though they were cautious not to annoy some unseen beings that may have been hovering around the conversation table. Sheikh Gayo was one of the teachers who stated that *rukhani* are jinn. He explained that the people who relate closely with jinn usually prefer to use the name *rukhani* to show that they do not indulge in a bad concept. *Rukhani* are considered to be in the category of good jinn that are Muslim, according to Sheikh Gayo's explanation.[32] Other scholars who have studied the spirit world of Swahili Muslims acknowledge that *rukhani* are Muslim spirits and that they are therefore good.[33] Faki, Kasiera, and Nandi define *rukhani* as "benevolent spirits" that are deemed to be beneficial to the Swahili Muslims in Mombasa, Kenya.[34] An interviewee, Maalim Haro, concedes to this and represents the consensus of other Muslim teachers in Marsabit in asserting that *rukhani* are Muslim spirits, which do not cause a lot of trouble.

The Muslim teachers also recognized the existence of non-Muslim jinn. There are two kinds: Christian jinn and traditional jinn. The former are not as bad as the latter because they "have a religion." The traditional jinn "do not have any religion" and they are the ones that "disturb people a lot," says Maalim Haro.[35] Sheikh Gayo also affirmed that the jinn that do not "have religion" are the ones "that disturb people very much [Kiswahili: *wanasumbua watu sana*]."[36] Religion in this sense includes both Islam and Christianity since both acknowledge the existence of God as a Supreme Being. As much as Christianity is recognized as a religion in this context, Christian jinn are not considered in the category of good jinn like the Muslim jinn are. The latter are regarded in a benevolent way, while the former are considered to be malevolent like the *Iblīs* discussed below.

---

31. Sheikh Abdi, August 27, 2016.
32. Sheikh Gayo, May 16, 2017.
33. Mackenrodt, *Swahili Spirit Possession*, 99; Kim, *Islam among the Swahili*, 107.
34. Faki, Kasiera, and Nandi, "Belief and Practice," 218.
35. Maalim Haro, Personal interview by author, Saku Sub-County, July 20, 2016, Code: A11-2016, 20th July.
36. Sheikh Gayo, May 16, 2017.

Iblīs *as a jinni*

The statement by interviewee Sheikh Amr that angels obey God in everything he commands offers a clear stance in the debate on whether *Iblīs* is a jinni or an angel. He narrated the story that *Iblīs* was a jinni that once lived with angels. Before God created humans, *Iblīs* used to see the piece of mud from which he was formed. When the latter was finally created, God told all the created beings to *kusujudu* (Kiswahili for prostrate) before Adam, the man.[37] Sheikh Amr explained that the kind of worship given to the man was different from that offered to God. The created beings were to pay homage by *kunyenyekea kwa salamu* (Kiswahii for "humbling themselves in the way of greetings"). All angels obeyed, as was their nature. Thus, *Iblīs* could not possibly be an angel because he declined to prostrate. He gave the excuse that man was created from mud while he was made from fire (referring to Surah 15:33; 38:71–81), which was a higher form of substance. Furthermore, *Iblīs* reckoned that he was created before man. The interpretation given for this defiance was that *Iblīs* had *fataqabara* (Arabic for pride) "that made him uplift himself that he was the one better than this man," according to Sheikh Amr.[38]

The Muslim teachers regarded *Iblīs* as a *shaiṭan*.[39] According to Sheikh Amr "*Iblīs* is the first *shaiṭan*" because his inclination is to defy God's commands. Subsequently, any jinni that follows him in rebelling against God is also a *shaiṭan*. People can also be referred to as *shaiṭan*, according to the Muslim clerics. Sheikh Amr explained, "Whoever disobeys the Almighty God becomes a *shaiṭan* [in Kiswahili: *Kila mwenye anayemuasi Mwenyezi Mungu ndio anakua sheitani*]." Sheikh Amr further expounded: these jinn and human beings that rebel against God and are called *shaiṭan* have a relationship that is essentially motivated by *Iblīs*, their leader. This association usually ends up in "what we call *sihr* [witchcraft]," according to Sheikh Amr, who further said that *Iblīs* and his followers among jinn and men therefore indulge in *ushirikina* (Kiswahili for idolatry) when they engage in witchcraft.[40]

---

37. The Arabic word used for "prostrate" is *sujūdu*, a verbal noun meaning "to prostrate oneself."

38. Sheikh Amr, May 17, 2017.

39. Kim helps to distinguish the Islamic usage of the word *shaiṭan* from the Christian usage. The latter refers to Satan as a fallen angel and the leader of evil. Since *Iblīs* is not a fallen angel, he cannot be equated to the biblical concept of Satan. See Kim, *Islam among the Swahili*, 85.

40. Sheikh Amr, May 17, 2017.

Attributes and Abilities of Jinn according to Muslim Teachers

The crucial task of discovering the Islamic model of jinn in Marsabit County entails examining the teachers' perception of the attributes and abilities of jinn. It has been mentioned before that this knowledge forms the official Islamic position that ordinary Borana Muslims in the county are expected to follow. Table 4 below is derived from the interviews with the nine teachers in both Saku and Moyale Subcounties. It shows how the Muslim teachers described the attributes and abilities of jinn as well as the references they cited from the Islamic texts. Most of the teachers did not give references from either of the texts to support their opinions as can be seen from the table.

Table 4: Attributes and Abilities of Jinn

Attributes and Abilities of Jinn	Number of Muslim Teachers who Mentioned the Attribute/Ability	Reference Cited from Islamic Texts
Intelligence	8	–
Resemblance to man	7	–
Ability to study and teach	1	–
Ability to choose (volition)	6	–
Ability to see (visual)	8	–
Ability to listen/hear	7	Surah 72:1–2
Ability to eat food	8	Hadith (specific book not given)
Ability to believe	5	Surah 72:2, 13
Invisibility	6	–
Created beings	9	–
Ability to worship (prostrate)	6	Surah 51:56
Ability to be happy or annoyed (emotional)	3	–
Ability to marry (relational)	4	–
Procreative	1	–
Residences in filthy places	3	Hadith (specific book not given)
Ability to reach the heavens	2	Surah 72:8
Ability to work for people	3	Qur'an, account of *Nabii* Suleiman

The aspect of jinn as created beings occurred most frequently among the Muslim clerics interviewed. Acknowledging that jinn were created implied that they are still lesser beings than God. They are, however, endowed with certain abilities that make them superior to human beings. This superiority has nevertheless been a subject of debate among Muslim scholars. Some assert that even though jinn were created with supernatural abilities, they are still subservient to human beings. It is suitable, herein, to examine what the teachers in Marsabit County perceive regarding humans in relation to jinn.

Of the three created beings, humans and jinn have been endowed with intelligence and volition. They have a semblance that positions them alongside each other. A number of *ayahs* in the Qur'an mention jinn together with human beings using the phrases "men and jinn" (Surah 6112); "jinns and men" (Surah 6:130; 7:179; 27:17); "men and jinns" (Surah 7:38); "mankind and jinns" (Surah 17:88), etc. This does not escape the attention of the Muslim teachers, who also mention how man and jinn resemble each other. Sheikh Amr said, "*Jini wako na akili kama sisi*" (jinn have intelligence like us). Human beings and jinn not only resemble each other in the ability to choose, but they also have some similar physical, emotional, and spiritual characteristics.

Jinn can see, hear, speak, eat, and work according to the table above. These are some of the somatic characteristics mentioned by the Muslim teachers that endorse the assertion of humans and jinn resembling each other. However, the ways that humans and jinn accomplish these actions differ from one another since they have different physical makeups. Jinn are said to consume bones from which people have removed all the meat. Sheikh Amr further cited the Hadith where the Prophet prohibited using these bones to clean oneself after excreting. Jinn also can speak, but they speak through people. The ambiguity of the physical makeup of jinn raises the question of whether they have a mouth to speak or eat through.

The religious characteristics of jinn enable them to "worship" and acknowledge the *tawhid* (the oneness of God) like men.[41] They are also able to recognize "the truth" and discern "a wonderful recitation" (Arabic: *qurānan 'ajaban*) from God as *hidaya* (Arabic for guidance) toward the "right path" (Surah 72:1–2) that was given through Prophet Muhammad. They can also perform

---

41. These characteristics that I have labeled religious apply only to the good, Muslim jinn; they are the ones that are monotheistic, according to figure 7.

the religious duties required of all practicing Muslims. Six out of the nine teachers interviewed said that jinn can "worship" by prostration. Sheikh Alisa, for instance, says that "Jinn are like humans and they also worship [Kiswahili: *abudu*]."[42] Sheikh Amr gave the *ayah* from the Qur'an (Surah 51:56) that says that jinn and humans were created by God to "worship" him. The Kiswahili translation reads, "*Sikuwaumba majini na watu ila wapate kuniabudu.*" The verb for "to worship" / "to serve" is *liyābudūni* in Arabic, from which *abudu*, the Kiswahili term for worship, stems. What was not very clear is how the jinn "worship" or "prostrate," whether they perform the prescribed ritual prayers or not. What was apparent was that the good jinn are the Muslim ones that have a religious inclination. The bad jinn are irreligious by choice. They decide to disobey God's commands even though they also have the propensity for being religious. They are aware that they have "rejected the faith" and refused to listen to the messengers that were sent to warn them of the Day of Judgment (Surah 6:130). The Qur'an is stern about their punishment. They will enter the fire of hell together with all unbelieving humans (Surah 7:38, 179).

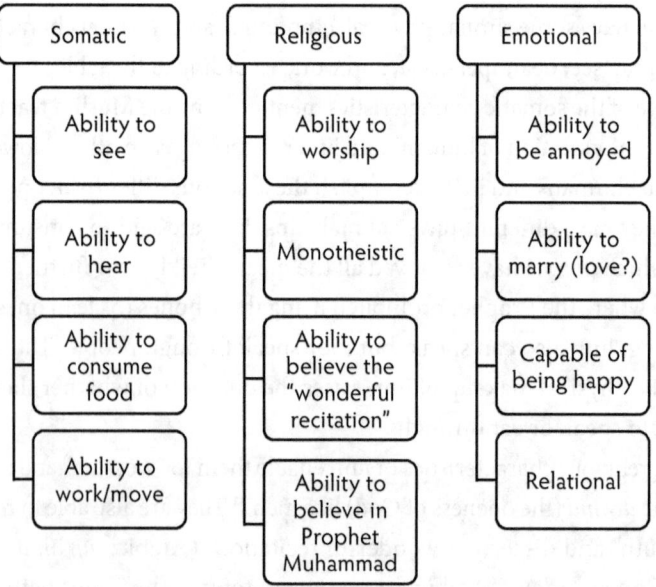

Figure 7: Characteristics of jinn

---

42. Sheikh Alisa, May 16, 2017.

Figure 7 above indicates that the Muslim teachers acknowledged the emotional element of jinn's nature. Three of them mentioned that jinn get annoyed especially when provoked by human beings. More about this will be discussed later in the section of jinn "possession." Yet another "emotional" dimension of the nature of jinn as perceived by my interviewees is their ability to marry and procreate.[43] Some of the clerics admitted that jinn get attracted to some people and seek to "marry" them. Robert Lebling asserts, "Most Muslim scholars agree that jinn can have sexual relations and marital relationships with humans."[44] Jimoh compares the Yoruba concept of the spirit husband with the Islamic belief in intermarriage between jinn and man. He mentions that there are love affairs and intermarriages between human beings and jinn in Islam, which finds support in Surah 17:64.[45] I did not pursue this concept of intermariage because it was not a focal point for this research. What sufficed is that human beings can relate with jinn in a social perspective because the latter can impinge on the human world.

Man's Relation with Jinn

This section examines the liaison that man is expected to have with jinn as stipulated by the gatekeepers of official Islam in Marsabit County. A pertinent question is whether man is subservient to jinn or vice versa. The Muslim clerics mentioned Prophets Muhammad and *Suleiman* (Solomon) as people who interacted with jinn and whose examples ought to be emulated. To answer the question of subservience, I begin by stating the perception of the teachers regarding superiority between man and jinn.

The clerics in Marsabit County agreed that there is a semblance between jinn and men. They also noted the significant differences between the two. My interviewees said that jinn can see human beings but that the latter cannot see jinn. El-Zein admitted that this theme of the invisibility of jinn to humans has been discussed among the different schools of thoughts in Islam. A scholar from the Hanafite School, for instance, compares jinn with the wind. Its visibility is possible when mixed with dust. It is therefore possible to see jinn

---

43. The term *emotional* is used cautiously here as it is assumed that the Muslim teachers' perception of "marriage" among the jinn would be similar to that of human beings, which involves an attraction of some sort.

44. Lebling, *Legends of the Fire*, 110.

45. Jimoh, "Yoruba Concept of Spirit Husband," 95.

when they take on a different form. The Sufi interpretation is interesting. Ibn 'Arabi, the Sufi scholar, wrote that jinn could be "seen" with the "eyes of the heart rather than with the physical senses," as quoted by El-Zein.[46] Whichever school one belongs to, the superiority of humans seems to be acclaimed by most Muslim scholars – and, in turn, by the Muslim teachers in Marsabit. Sheikh Amir was emphatic; "Of all his created beings, God has *amewatukuza* (exalted) *ins* (man) over all the other creatures in *alam* (the universe)." Amr emphasized this further by quoting Surah 2:29; "It is He who has created for you all things that are on earth . . ." Jinn were also created for the benefit of humans and not the other way around. This can be seen from the way they worked for Prophet *Suleiman*.

Prophet Solomon and the Jinn

The account of Solomon featured during the interviews with the Muslim teachers to illustrate the limitation of jinn in relation to man. Sheikh Amr recounted the story of Solomon from Surah 2 and Surah 27 respectively. Surah 2:102–103 is about *sihr* (Arabic for magic), which Sheikh Amr translates as "witchcraft" (*uchawi* in Kiswahili). He exonerated prophet Solomon from any practice of witchcraft when he dealt with jinn as described in Surah 27.

The story of Solomon and the jinn elicits different interpretations from Muslim scholars. Some, like Yusuf Ali, believe that those who worked for him were not jinn but "Sons of David."[47] El-Zein is among the scholars who admit that jinn worked for Solomon according to Surah 27:39 and Surah 34:12. However, her interpretation of "heretic jinn" that served Solomon does not match Sheikh Amr's explanation. The latter gives a lengthy account of Solomon and Queen Sheba, describing how one of the jinn carried a throne within a very concise time. The jinn that worked for Solomon were both the "learned" and "unlearned" – and not the "evil" ones as El-Zein writes.[48] When asked if people are allowed to use jinn like Solomon, Sheikh Amr said that it is *inakataliwa* (Kiswahili for prohibited). He explains that the weak nature of human beings may prompt them to go to the extent of "worshipping" the

---

46. El-Zein, *Islam, Arabs, and the Intelligent*, 23.

47. Kim, *Islam among the Swahili*, 86.

48. El-Zein also mentions that the jinn that are usually "enslaved by humans are the heretic jinn who refuse to submit to the new religion." See El-Zein, *Islam, Arabs, and the Intelligent*, 27

jinn if they are allowed to conscript them to work. Yet jinn also have their limitations as created beings.

Interviewee Sheikh Amr described the weakness of jinn using the historical account of Solomon's death. People believed so much in the unlimited power and knowledge of *al-ghaib* (the unseen) by the jinn. It was a popular belief that they could move extremely fast, get whatever information they needed, and relay it to people. One day, Solomon died while he was praying in the *miḥrāb* while supporting himself with his staff.[49] Sheikh Amr continued to narrate how Solomon stood like that for many years, yet no one noticed that he was dead – not even the jinni that was believed to know everything. Eventually, the staff was eaten by termites and could not support Solomon anymore. People realized that he was dead when he eventually fell. This story corresponds with the account in Surah 34:14, which highlights the weakness of jinn.[50]

Views of Muslim Teachers on Muhammad and Jinn

The *Sunnah* (traditions) of Prophet Muhammad are important for all Muslims. These are the ways he dealt with issues in life, which should be emulated by all Muslims. It is therefore necessary to know the perception of the Muslim leaders in Marsabit County about his encounter with the jinn. This forms the officially acceptable way to relate with jinn.

Surah 72 is a significant chapter in this discussion. The Muslim sheikhs kept alluding to it and mentioned how jinn heard the prophet's recitation and were attracted to it as a "wonderful recitation." I asked a question to my interviewees: "Could the prophet see the jinn that had surrounded him while he recited?" Interviewee Sheikh Amr answered affirmatively that the "Prophet (PBUH) could see them because he was sent not only to human beings alone, he was sent to the jinn, to the trees, even to the animals, all created beings, that is." The Shafiite School of jurisprudence may have influenced this admission that Muhammad could see jinn. Bilal Philips states that the founder,

---

49. *Miḥrāb* is the platform where the leader of prayer stands during the prayer sessions inside the mosque.

50. The accounts of Solomon and the jinn have stimulated hundreds of folk tales among Muslims worldwide. Various scholars examining the concept of jinn have noted this as well as the way different Islamic contexts have re-told the stories. See Kim, *Islam among the Swahili*, 89; and Lebling, *Legends of the Fire*, 46.

Ash-Shāfi'ī (767–820 CE), used Surah 7:27 which says, "for he (Satan) and his tribe watch you from a position where you cannot see them." Philips further says that this *ayah* is taken as "proof that only prophets could see the jinn."[51]

El-Zein's treatise on the encounter of Muhammad and the jinn concludes that those who believe that he saw the jinn physically are more inclined to a "popular" conviction. She claims, "The majority of Muslim scholars seem to believe that the Prophet did not see the jinn, contrary to what the popular accounts mention."[52] The Qur'an does not indicate that Muhammad ever saw the jinn physically, hence supporting her argument, notwithstanding the accounts in the Hadiths.

The Hadiths allude to the physical encounter of Muhammad with the jinn. One Hadith mentions that Muhammad was invited once by some jinn to recite the Qur'an to them.[53] Al-Ashqar says that the prophet met with the good jinn on several occasions.[54] Muhammad is also said to have confronted a bad jinni that was interrupting his prayers. He seized it by God's power, and he almost tied it to a pillar in the mosque, according to Hadith *Muslim* 1, no. 1104, p. 273. Hadith Bukhari records that the prophet would seek God's protection for his two grandsons, Hassan and Hussain, by saying, "I seek refuge for you two by Allah's perfect word, from every Satan and evil suggestion (Arabic: *haama*) and from every evil eye (*laama*)."[55] This is *Sunnah*, which every Muslim is expected to follow, especially where possession by jinn is involved as seen in the next section.

Jinn Possession as Perceived by Muslim Teachers in Marsabit County

Muslim teachers admitted that jinn could "possess" people.[56] Sheikh Amr consented, "There are some jinn that are bad and that enter people (Kiswahili: *kuna jinni wabaya wanaingia watu*)." The notion of "entering" in Kiswahili

---

51. Philips, "Exorcism in Islam," 54.
52. El-Zein, *Islam, Arabs, and the Intelligent*, 67.
53. *Muslim*, 244.
54. Al-Ashqar, *World of the Jinn*, 63.
55. "Book of the Stories," 361.
56. I put "possession" in quotes because it is an English term that does not mean the same thing to different cultural contexts that deal with spirit possession.

indicates that jinn are located outside a person and then find access into someone's body through a body part. It was not very clear which entrance the jinn use. Do they enter through the head or generally any part of the body? The teachers were not able to ascertain this. It had probably not occurred to them to examine such details. What was significant was that jinn "enter" a person's body and can cause them trouble.

Another phrase used for jinn "possession" in Marsabit is "caught" (Kiswahili: *kushika*). This was not as frequently used as "enter" to refer to jinn's action on someone. The teachers used the verb "caught" when they spoke of someone in whom a jinni has already "entered." They would say, "He has been caught by a jinni" (Kiswahili: *ameshikwa na jini*). "Caught" is the same word used for *ayyaana* possession in the Borana language, as will be seen in the section on cultural models of *Ayyaana* according to Borana Muslims.

It is not only bad jinn that can enter a person. The teachers explained that even good jinn enter people. These are considered to have a positive impact when they are in someone's body – unlike the bad jinn, which cause trouble. Bad jinn can also affect a person's relatives. Sheikh Umar mentioned that a jinni that is determined to "enter" a person and fails can easily "enter" his child or someone else close to him.[57]

Symptoms of Jinn Possession

My interviewees said that there are ways to discern whether a jinni has entered someone. One main symptom is *wazimu* (Kiswahili for madness). Loss of sanity is often attributed to the "entrance" of jinn into a person who was once normal but starts to behave abnormally. Sheikh Amr explained: "Some people who have jinn can become mad (Borana: *marata*). They start to behave in a way that is not normal (Kiswahili: *sio kawaida*)." He gave the example of a man who was once a renowned teacher. He worked well and was getting promotions because of his efficiency with school children. Unfortunately, someone became jealous and requested that a jinni be sent to him. The teacher became insane and now roams aimlessly in the marketplace.

---

57. Sheikh Umar, May 16, 2017.

The relation between jinn and insanity is not peculiar to the Borana Muslims. Scholars allude to the Arabic term *majnūn* to refer to a mad person.[58] This term is derived from the same root as the Arabic word *jinn*. This makes the scholars examining the phenomenon of jinn possession conclude that insanity is a "product of jinn-possession."[59] In the Qur'an, the word *majnūn* is mentioned eleven times as a passive participle.[60] Seven of these times refer directly to Muhammad. During the pre-Islamic, *jahiliyyah* times, his Arab opponents believed that a jinni possessed him like the other poets of the time.

Another common symptom of jinn possession, as recounted by the Muslim teachers, is an undiagnosed ailment. Someone becomes sick, and his health deteriorates. He is taken to the medical facilities, and no disease is diagnosed. If such a person continues to insist on taking the hospital remedies, chances of survival are minimal, according to the teachers.

The clerics are able to discern a jinni when a person brought to them for help starts behaving in funny ways. The person may start crying even before any remedy is administered. He cannot look straight into the eyes of the clerics. Sheikh Amr explained that the person feels shameful and prefers to look at the ground.

Reasons for Possession

The causes of jinn possessing or "entering" people are varied, according to the Muslim teachers. Jinn can enter people who invade their habitation. They are known to reside in certain places including holes, certain tall trees, toilets, and other dirty places. People who urinate into holes in the ground can easily fall prey to possession. Some holes are believed to be habitations of jinn. A jinni can be offended by such an action and decide to "enter" the person as a punishment. Quoting *Fiqh-Us-Sunna* 4:124, Sheikh Alisa referred to a Hadith where the prophet Muhammad told people not to urinate into holes

---

58. Philips, "Exorcism in Islam," 75; Kim, *Islam among the Swahili*, 82; El-Zein, *Islam, Arabs, and the Intelligent*, 74.

59. Philips, "Exorcism in Islam," 75.

60. Qur'an references to possession are: Surah 15:6; 26:27 (Moses accused of being possessed), Surah 37:36 (Muhammad accused of being a possessed poet), Surah 44:14 (Muhammad accused of being possessed), Surah 51:39 (Moses accused of being possessed), Surah 52:29 (Muhammad had been accused of being possessed), Surah 54:9 (Noah accused of being possessed), Surah 68:2; 68:51 (Noah accused of being possessed), Surah 81: 22 (Muhammad accused of possession).

because they are "dwelling places for jinn." Pouring hot water on the ground or throwing stones aimlessly can also offend a jinni that may be in the vicinity. Sheikh Amr added that a jinni can enter someone who steps on them. One such person who had sought for help had unknowingly "stepped on the child of a jinn." The jinn "mother" was infuriated and punished him by "entering" his body. When he was healed, he later said that he felt "something prick him (Kiswahili: *ilimdunga*) at some point."

Some bad jinn are malevolent and only seek to cause trouble. They intend to destroy people because they do not have any predisposition toward good in fear of God. Such jinn follow the footsteps of *Iblīs*, who is said to have been jealous of the created man, Adam, and to have refused to prostrate before him as commanded by God.

There are jinn that are attracted to people who have ceased to *kufuata imani* (Kiswahili for "follow the faith"). These are Muslims who no longer observe the duties required of all adherents. They do not pray, give the required offering, fast, etc. They are essentially nominal even though they continue to regard themselves as *Islana* (Muslims). The bad jinn enter such people in order to lead them further away from the right path of God.

Bad jinn also enter Muslims who indulge in forbidden activities such as *falfal* (Borana for witchcraft). Such activities are considered *uchafu* (Kiswahili for "filthy") and are abhorred by the Muslim teachers. When Sheikh Amr talked about them, he spoke with a visibly disgusted demeanor. This was specifically when he mentioned that such activities involved the offering of blood. He also reiterated that the rituals performed by *ayyaana* people were detested by God and that they attract the bad jinn to "enter" those who indulge in the cultic practices.

The good jinn mentioned above enter a person who is going in the wrong path away from God. Such jinn say that they have entered the person to try to make him live right. This is contrary to the way the bad jinn enter people to lead them further from the "truth." Sheikh Amr recounted a conversation of a good jinni that had "entered" a person. When asked why he entered him, the jinni said:

> He [the person] commits adultery [*anafanya zinaa*] yet he is a Muslim. He steals, he does this and that. Then tell him to stop

and I will come out. I do not have issues with him but the way I see him, this friend of mine does wrong [*mabaya*].[61]

All my interviewees said that jinn are more attracted to women than to men. Children are also affected, but not like women.[62] Sheikh Alisa recounted the case of children in a primary school who had frequent attacks from jinn until the Muslim clerics had to go and offer prayers. The reason given for jinn entering children was not clear from the interviewees' accounts. They narrated how children were prone to jinn "attacks" while in school. When children became unconscious, it was interpreted as having jinn. In one *madrasa*, children became hysterical and began shouting at the tops of their lungs. This occurred frequently and became the talk of the town. An issue that amazed people was the vulnerability of children to jinn. But local Borana Muslims said that it was the same Muslim teachers who engaged in jinn activities and *wanatupa* (Kiswahili for "threw") the jinn to the children.

The susceptibility of women to possession by jinn was based on their weak nature, according to the teachers in Marsabit County. Sheikh Alisa said that jinn enter women more because they have "easy or light hearts (Kiswahili: *mioyo myepesi*). They are easily swayed by something small."[63] Sheikh Gayo agreed saying that "Ninety percent of Muslim women are the ones possessed." He said the reason for this is that when they are in their menstrual cycle, they are not allowed to pray or go to the mosque since they are *wachafu* (Kiswahili for "unclean").[64] This makes them easy targets for jinn. Women are also prone to jinn possession because of their jealousy. Muslim men are allowed to marry up to four women. Women are aware of this because it is in the Qur'an. Yet the co-wives almost always have certain fears stemming from jealousy when they perceive their husbands' divided attention. This encourages them go to the *falfaltu* (*Afan Borana* for witchdoctors) for ways to gain their husbands' devotion. Such ventures eventually attract jinn to them.

---

61. Sheikh Amr, May 2017.

62. Lesley Sharp also narrated how *Njarininsty* spirits possessed adolescent girls in northwest Madagascar. See Sharp "Possessed and Dispossessed Youth"; and Sharp Possessed and the Dispossessed."

63. Sheikh Alisa, May 16, 2017.

64. Sheikh Gayo, May 16, 2017.

Dealing with Jinn in Marsabit County

In dealing with jinn, my interviewees classified them into two types according to how fast they are expelled from people: stubborn ones and cooperative ones. The former are said to be *wasumbufu* (Kiswahili for troublesome). They take a long time to come out of a person. Compliant jinn are easier to handle, according to Sheikh Abdi.

The officially recommended way of dealing with jinn is by "burning them with the Qur'an" (Kiswahili: *kuchoma na Kurani*). All the Muslim teachers consented that this was the permitted method even though it is not prescribed in the Qur'an. Sheikh Amur emphasized how the Qur'an is able to "burn the jinn badly, even the very stubborn ones" are not spared. There is a procedure to be followed in using the Qur'an.

First, the possessed person, who is usually sick or insane, realizes that the cause of their distress is a jinni. They go to one of the Muslim teachers in a mosque. Sheikh Munur stated that people are allowed to select any sheikh to attend to them. This can be either in the mosque or at home according to the patient's preference. It is permissible for a patient to be attended to by more than one sheikh. All of them must be in agreement concerning the source of suffering for the success of the process. The patient must be willing to be assisted and must have an optimistic attitude and belief in the power of God (Kiswahili: *nguvu za Mungu*). If the patient is unconscious or insane, those who brought him to the sheikh must have such a belief in God. It is also not recommended for such a patient to seek conventional medical assistance. These prescriptions are not "compatible" with the "ideal" way of dealing with jinn. Sheikh Abdi recounted an incident where the guardians of a patient insisted on taking him to the hospital. They were adamant, in spite of the diagnosis, that it was a jinni that was causing the patient's sickness. The man almost died as his condition continued to deteriorate while he took the medicine given. His life was spared when he was brought to Sheikh Abdi, and he was able to deal with the jinni.

The basic procedure for dealing with jinn begins with a conversation between the possessing jinn and the sheikh. Sheikh Amr made it sound so natural when he said, "We just talk to the jinn and they listen and speak (Kiswahili: *tunawaongelesha tu na wanasikia na wanaongea*)." The purpose of the dialogue is to make the jinn identify themselves so that they can be addressed correctly. The language used by the sheikhs depends on what the jinn speak. Sheikh Amr explained to me how some jinn say:

> I only know Arabic or Kiswahili. Some jinn say they are called Abdi, Hassan, and we know these are Muslim. Some have Habesh (Ethiopian) or Borana names. And others even have names like Njoroge and we identify them as Christian jinn. Some stubborn jinn refuse to speak and claim that they cannot hear the language used.[65]

Other jinn obstinately decline to speak and have to be coerced into speaking. This may take a long time, yet it is considered necessary in order to know the jinn being dealt with.

The sheikh addresses the jinni by name to establish the reason or reasons for punishing the patient. The jinni states the reason or reasons for exasperation, and the sheikh tries to apologize on behalf of the patient. If the jinni is a malevolent one that merely causes trouble, it is warned and threatened with eternal punishment according to the Qur'an. Sheikh Alisa said that he asks the jinn, "Will you come out or I burn you?" A jinni that cooperates would respond affirmatively and leave the patient without commotion.

For a stubborn jinni, the sheikh proceeds to "burn" the jinn by reciting the Qur'an. He does this by reading a particular verse. Surah 2:255 (*Āyah al-Kursī*, the "Verse of the Throne") is said to be "among the greatest weapons which may be used to exorcise the jinn."[66] Philips also quotes Ibn Taymiyyah's confirmation of the "incredible effectiveness" of this verse:

> It is greatly effective in repelling the evil jinn from human souls and exorcising them from the possessed as well as those prodded by devils like tyrants, those easily enraged, the lustful and lecherous, musicians, and those who ecstatically whistle and clap away the devils and neutralize their illusions. It will also disrupt satanic visions and devil-aided, supernatural feats performed by humans.[67]

---

65. Sheikh Amr, May 2017.
66. Philips, "Exorcism in Islam," 128.
67. Philips, 129.

My interviewees also consented that this verse is "powerful." They use it often and they say it "burns" the jinn and makes the patient scream as though in great pain. Sheikh Amr recounted how the patients shriek with anguish and even start shedding tears because of the pain. Sometimes the patients start shaking profusely (Kiswahili: *anatetemeka sana*) as though they were freezing. Other times they sweat, and their temperature rises. All these, explained Sheikh Amr, are the effects of the jinn being "burned." Other "burning" verses from the Qur'an that are used are Surah 113 and 114. Both are Surahs that exhort Muslims to seek refuge in God from:

> The mischief of created things; from the mischief of darkness as it overspreads; from the mischief of those who practice secret arts; and from the mischief of the envious one as he practices envy. (Surah 113:1–5)

> From the mischief of the Whisperer, who withdraws, who whispers into the hearts of mankind-among jinns and among men. (Surah 114:4–6)

Some of the Muslim teachers say they use "Qur'an water." They write the verses on a piece of board or paper and wash them with water. They give this to the patient to drink. Not all the teachers use this method. Most of them say they prefer to "burn" the jinn with direct words from the Qur'an. Others also use herbs to supplement the treatment after "burning" the jinn. Sheikh Alisa admitted that when he has tried all the ways he knew and not succeeded, he has advised the patient to "try" other sheikhs who had more advanced ways of dealing with jinn. Those who appeared to be more competent in dealing with jinn said they derived their knowledge from books written by Muslim scholars. Sheikh Amr said he refers to an Arabic book called *Saalimun Bataar*. Sheikh Alisa uses *Bulughu al-Maram*, a collection of Ḥadīths by al-Hafidh ibn Hajar al-Asqalani. The Ḥadīths are from Sahih Bukhari, Muslim, Abu Dawud, etc. However, he did not specify the particular ones he used.

Exorcism versus Adorcism in Marsabit County

Literature that has been reviewed in chapter 2 of this study points to the distinction between exorcism and adorcism in dealing with spirits.[68] It is relevant to understand this dissimilarity as I examine the perception of Muslim teachers and other ordinary Borana Muslims in Marsabit County concerning the world of spirits. This averts the mistake that some scholars have made of referring to "pacifying rituals" as exorcism. Kim critiques Swantz's usage of the term *exorcism* while referring to the rituals of possession observed among the Wazaramo people in Tanzania.[69]

The preceding section has described the official position of Islam in dealing with jinn according to the Muslim teachers interviewed. Evidently, jinn are not supposed to be appeased, hence no adorcism should be performed. Jinn are to be separated entirely from people's bodies. They should be summoned to leave, and if they do not comply they should be "burned" using the Qur'an as seen above. This applies to both good and bad jinn. The essence here is that jinn should not be befriended. They should be considered "enemies" as the prophet Muhammad perceived them. Muslim scholars cite the Ḥadiths (*Sunan Abū Dāwūd and Musnad Ahmad*), which mention various instances where the Prophet addressed jinn as "enemies of Allah" as he drove them out of the possessed patients. This raises a valid question: are the "good" jinn also "enemies"? I have shown how the Muslim teachers I interviewed stated the benefits of the "good" jinn in turning people back to the "right path" of Islam. Are they also to be exorcised like the bad jinn? Should they not be "accommodated" in a friendly relation to keep people from disregarding God's laws? The deduction I made from the interviews is that the "good" jinn are Muslims and thus are acceptable. Yet they should keep out of people's bodies and stay in the realm to which they have been assigned. Once they have done God's bidding of turning people to the "right path," they should leave their occupancy and seek their habitation. Therefore, there is no hint of accommodation therein.

The Muslim teachers in Marsabit refuted any form of adorcism when relating with jinn. I interpreted adorcism according to them as having a

---

68. See chapter 3 for more details on the term *adorcism*. It is a term used for the domestication of spirits instead of exorcising them.

69. Kim, *Islam among the Swahili*, 190.

relationship with jinn. Sheikh Amr quoted Surah 72:6, which stated that some people preferred to take "shelter with persons among the jinns, but they increased them in folly." Sheikh Amr explained that such people are "those who love being with jinn" (Kiswahili: *wanapenda kuwa na majini*). Such a relationship entails giving the jinn something to make them happy. It disgusted the teachers, who mentioned that one of the things such jinn relish is blood. People who give this to the jinn are practicing idolatry (Kiswahili: *ushirikina*; Arabic: *shirk*), according to Sheikh Amr. Sheikh Gayo also concurred that there are some Muslims who give blood to jinn. He said, "Once you give them blood you will always give them blood. They will ask for blood all the time." This indicates a vicious cycle that one is unable to break from and thus moves further away from the "right path" of Islam. This is the conduit that some Borana Muslims have chosen to take, according to Sheikh Amr. It was quite evident from the manner he, together with the other Muslim teachers, described how the *warra ayyaana* (people of *ayyaana*) relate with the jinn they call *ayyaana*.

Perception of *Ayyaana* by Muslim Teachers

I have described how the Muslim teachers in Marsabit County perceived the spirit world in the preceding section. I now conclude the chapter with an analytical description of the teachers' perception of *ayyaana* – and also what they think about the Borana Muslims who participate in the *Ayyaana* cult of possession.

Ayyaana as Jinn

I conducted interviews with the Muslim teachers in both Saku and Moyale Subcounties and did oral free-listing to determine what they think about *ayyaana*. This list was derived from the verbal statements made by the teachers. My intention was to understand their cognition on *ayyaana* and especially what would be foregrounded or would be "at the top of their heads" concerning *ayyaana*. The free-list is provided (See Appendix 8). The tables below display two main features of jinn that emanated from the statements free-listed.

Table 5: Perception of *Ayyaana*'s Existence by Muslim Teachers

Theme 1: Existence of *ayyaana*	
Created by Allah Are spirits (*mapepo*) Comprise an "army"	Came from Ethiopia Came from the Arsi people
⬇	
Sub-theme 1: *Ayyaana* are real spiritual beings	

All the Muslim teachers interviewed consented that *ayyaana* are real and that they are spiritual beings that originated from the Arsi people in Ethiopia. It is important to note that the teachers do not refute the existence of *ayyaana* as supernatural beings that are involved in the lives of the ordinary Borana Muslims in Marsabit County.

Table 6: Perception of *Ayyaana* as Evil Jinn by Muslim Teachers

Theme 2: *Ayyaana* are jinn	
Bad jinn Bad jinn that mislead people Evil jinn (*mashetani majini*) No good *ayyaana* Bad spirits (*pepo*) Are deceptive (*upotovu*)	*Ayyaana* mean jinn entering a person *Ayyaana* are the jinn that speak in a person Speak through people "Explain things" (used in divination) Enter people Involved in witchcraft (*falfatu*) Want to be sung for
Sub-theme 2: *Ayyaana* are evil jinn and therefore involve *shirk*	

The second theme I highlight from the free-listing exercise is that *ayyaana* are jinn and that they are evil. They do not fall under the category of good, Christian, or traditional jinn. They are bad or evil because of several reasons: they mislead people, they are involved in divination and witchcraft, and they like to be "sung for." The following section continues the discussion on how the teachers perceive *ayyaana*. This is discussed from both an epistemological and ontological perspective. In a subsequent chapter, these sentiments will be used to evaluate the lived experiences and beliefs of the ordinary Borana Muslims as they participate in the *Ayyaana* cult.

Epistemological View of the Muslim Teachers regarding *Ayyaana*

The term *ayyaana* is pluralized according to my interviewees' usage.[70] It will be seen later in the discussion about the lived experiences of Borana Muslims that the term is indeed a compound word that includes different types of *ayyaana* spirits. The Muslim teachers did not want to delve much into the discussion about *ayyaana*; thus it was not a surprise that they would omit any reference to the different kinds of *ayyaana*. However, they acknowledged the cultural connotation of the word. Most of them said that it is a borrowed word from the Arabic and Borana languages. The original usage in Borana means "good fortune" (Kiswahili: *bahati*). It also has another cultural meaning that the teachers admitted. The Borana calendar has days that are referred to as *ayyaana*. The Oromo Borana people in Ethiopia appropriated it for their cultural use but borrowed it from the Arabic language, according to Sheikh Munur. This indicates that the word *ayyaana* is a homonym. The different meanings will be discussed in the next analytical chapter.

In the context of the spirit world, all the Muslim teachers consented that *ayyaana* is another name for jinn. Sheikh Abdi reiterated that the people who introduced the *Ayyaana* cult to Borana Muslims looked for a camouflage word that was popular, attractive, and not scary. The word *jinn* had a negative connotation, and they knew people would not accept it. They chose the word *ayyaana*, which had a very auspicious sense in traditional Borana culture. The word appealed to the "ignorant" people who did not have much knowledge of religion (*dini*). They were not aware that they were getting themselves into forbidden practices under the guise of "good fortune" (the original Borana term for *ayyaana*). They did not realize that they were dealing with jinn and that these were bad ones.

The Muslim teachers conceded that *ayyaana* belong to the class of bad jinn (see figure 6). Sheikh Amr was emphatic that there are no good *ayyaana*.

---

70. Østebo refers to the plural of *ayyaana* as *ayyaanota* according to the Oromo Muslims in Ethiopia. See Østebo, *Localising Salafism*.

Apart from this reference to *ayyaana* as jinn, they are also referred to as bad spirits (*pepo mbaya*). *Pepo* is a Kiswahili word for "spirit." This is contrary to what Kim reports. The Swahili Muslims in Zanzibar perceive the word *pepo* as mostly used by Christians who are "ignorant of what spirits are." They also relate the inconspicuousness of jinn to *upepo* (Kiswahili for "wind") from which the word *pepo* is derived.[71] Similarly, "*Ayyaana* is *upepo* [wind]" according to the Muslim teachers in Marsabit. This understanding of *ayyaana* as "wind" may have been influenced by the Borana word for wind (*qileensa*), as will be seen in the next chapter.

Ontological View of the Muslim Teachers regarding *Ayyaana*

All the Muslim teachers concurred that *ayyaana* were created by God like the rest of the jinn even though they are placed in the category of bad jinn. They have the same abilities and attributes listed by the Muslim teachers for any jinn. What causes *ayyaana* to be classified as "bad" is that they fail to perform the religious activities required

Good Jinn	*Ayyaana*
1. Worship God	1. Do not worship God
2. Acknowledge oneness of God	2. Do not acknowledge oneness of God
3. Believe the Qur'an as a "wonderful recitation"	3. Do not believe in the Qur'an as a "wonderful recitation"
4. Believe in Prophet Muhammad	4. Do not believe in Prophet Muhammad
5. Go for pilgrimage	5. Do not go to Mecca for pilgrimage

Figure 8: Comparison of good jinn and *ayyaana* by the Muslim teachers

Jinn can worship God and acknowledge his oneness. They are also able to hear and believe in the message of the Qur'an as given through the prophet Muhammad. The jinn that perform these religious duties are classified as Muslim and are the good ones. Those that do not execute them are termed as non-Muslim and are considered to be bad. The latter include *ayyaana*, as illustrated in figure 7 above. They do not prostrate themselves, they do not

---

71. Kim, *Islam among the Swahili*, 106.

acknowledge the oneness of God, and they do not believe in the Qur'an or the prophet Muhammad. In essence, they do not perform any Islamic duties. Their aim is always to lead people away from the straight path.

In spite of the badness of *ayyaana*, they sometimes do good, like "explaining something" (Kiswahili: *ayyaana wanaeleza kitu*) to people. Sheikh Amr clarified that *ayyaana* are able to reveal hidden secrets. They are able to access the secrets of heaven and then go to relay them to the practitioners involved in the *Ayyaana* cult. This makes "people believe they have extraordinary powers," says Sheikh Amr. They are also prone to lie and make people believe they are helpful. But they are always inclined to do bad things and lead people away from God. They are very deceptive and make people indulge in the worst sin of all, *shirk*, which is unforgiveable by God.

Ayyaana also enter people's bodies and cause trouble. They often cause sickness that defies medical diagnosis. They speak through the mouths of the patients they enter and make their demands known. One of the things they ask for is blood, according to my interviewees. Good jinn never ask for blood because it is tantamount to offering sacrifices. Thus, when *ayyaana* demand blood, it shows they are not good jinn.

Something else that makes *ayyaana* bad is the way they like *kuimbiwa* (Kiswahili for "to be sung for"). The adepts prepare séances for a whole night and sing for the *ayyaana* to make them happy. It is believed that this will make them stop disturbing their victims. This, according to the Muslim teachers is equivalent to "worship." It diverts people's attention and allegiance away from God.

I deciphered a negative attitude toward *ayyaana* among the Muslim teachers. One of them said that it is archaic (Kiswahili: *imepitwa na wakati*), implying that people should not continue to uphold it. Two of the teachers further estimated that 99 percent of Muslims in Marsabit County reject it.[72] The fact that it is not referred to in the Islamic texts makes it obsolete and not to be followed, according to Sheikh Abdi. And so, with such a negative stance

---

72. This estimate may not be very accurate because there is no empirical investigation that has been carried out so far about the attitude of Muslims in Marsabit County toward *ayyaana*. It will be seen in the next chapter that in spite of the negative perception that stems from the fundamentalist tendencies of some Muslims, the *Ayyaana* cult is still popular among the ordinary Borana Muslims especially with the endorsed registration from the government.

against *ayyaana*, the teachers would not be expected to perceive the *warra ayyaana* who participate in the cultic activities in any better way.

Perception of the Muslim Teachers regarding *Warra Ayyaana*

The Islamic model of the spirit world as described above includes a solid belief in jinn, as created by God, and an assumption that there are good and bad jinn. The immediately preceding section has presented the understanding of *ayyaana* by Muslim teachers in Marsabit County as representatives of the official Islam. This section will describe their perception of the Borana Muslims who interact with *ayyaana* and participate in the resultant *Ayyaana* cult. The Borana term *warra ayyaana* means "people of *ayyaana*." It denotes anybody who upholds the beliefs and practices regarding *ayyaana* and who joins together with like-minded people to form a cult.[73] Some Muslim teachers also referred to them as *garib*, which according to them is an Arabic word that means "visitor." The Muslim teachers therefore acknowledge the existence of such a group that meets and performs rituals. What do these teachers then think about the group? Do they perceive them as Muslims or not?

There was a consensus among the teachers on who is a true Muslim. They say that someone who believes in God and his prophet, Muhammad, who obeys the injunctions of the message in the Qur'an, and who performs the duties stipulated is a true Muslim *mu'minun* (Arabic for "believer"). Such a person is also obligated to believe in the world of spirits and hence to believe that jinn exist and impinge upon the human world. So, can the *warra ayyaana* qualify as true Muslims? Outwardly, they appear to be true because they try to comply with the requirements. The Muslim teachers also attest to this. They testify that the *warra ayyaana* believe in God, Muhammad, and the Qur'an like other Muslims. They also believe in the existence of the spirit world whose beings can encroach on the human world. They further affirm that the *ayyaana* people also pray like the other Muslims. This is evidenced

---

73. I use the word "cult" to represent the group of people who share basic beliefs and practices revolving around *ayyaana*.

by the following statements made by some of the teachers concerning the "Muslim-ness" of the *warra ayyaana*.[74]

Sheikh Amr:

> They worship God [*wanaabudu Mungu*].[75]

Sheikh Abdi:

> They pray the way other Muslims pray ... When they come to pray, they are like Muslims.[76]

Sheikh Munur:

> They do the prayers [*wanafanya maombi*].[77]

Sheikh Abdi:

> They believe in prophet Muhammad [*wanaamini mtume Muhammad*].[78]

Sheikh Khadi:

> *Ayyaana* people say they are Muslims and even say they love Muhammad.[79]

Sheikh Ibra:

> They do not have funds to start their own mosques so they join us [*wanainigiliana na sisi*].[80]

Sheikh Munur:

> They sacrifice [*wanachinja*] ... It is true that this sacrificing is also in the mosque.[81]

Sheikh Munur:

---

74. I use this term, *Muslim-ness*, to describe the extent to which Muslims adhere to the Islamic tenets.
75. Sheikh Amr, May 17, 2017.
76. Shiekh Abdi, August 27, 2016.
77. Sheikh Munur, May 18, 2017.
78. Shiekh Abdi, August 27, 2016.
79. Sheikh Khadi, August 30, 2016.
80. Sheikh Ibra, August 27, 2016.
81. Sheikh Munur May 18, 2017

You will see someone on Friday in the mosque...You will see that person is very religious [*mtu wa dini sana*].[82]

Primarily, the Muslim-ness of the *warra ayyaana* may seem apparent from the above sentences. Watching the *warra ayyaana* perform the religious duties leaves one in no doubt concerning their Muslim-ness. The Muslim teachers cannot be incorrect in their assessment because they watch them stream into the mosques to join the other Muslims in prayer. When the *warra ayyaana* die, they are buried in the Islamic way. Funerals, in Marsabit County, are a major indicator of the religion that the deceased followed. Yet in spite of all these testimonies, Muslim teachers admit that it is superficial, according to the following statements made during the interviews:

Sheikh Amr:

> [Reading from the Qur'an] Surah 72:6 says, "And verily there were men among mankind who took shelter with the masculine among the jinn, but they increased the jinn; the jinn increased them in sin and disbelief." That among mankind, these are those who love being with jinn [*wanapenda kuwa na majini*]. These are the *ayyaana* and others, who choose that they want to be together and get help from side of the jinn.[83]

Sheikh Amr:

> About the *ayyaana* people, I can say they worship God and they worship jinn [*wanaabudu Mwenyezi Mungu na wanaabudu majini*]. Because the jinn are created beings like they themselves. So they worship God as well as jinn. So they are between God and jinn. So this is associating God with something else. It is *shirk*.[84]

Sheikh Abdi:

> These things of *ayyaana* are not different from *shirk*. They just call themselves Muslims, they say they are Muslims, they pray the way other Muslims pray but their actions are those of Shia. Islam prohibits the relationship between man and jinn. They do

---

82. Sheikh Munur May 18, 2017.
83. Sheikh Amr, May 17, 2017.
84. Sheikh Amr, May 17, 2017.

their work and we do ours. But those people of *ayyaana*, they relate with jinn, *ayyaana* is jinn. Now that jinn wants songs [Borana: *faaru*]. They stay there and praise jinn and the sheikhs who brought that religion [Kiswahili: *dini*]. Now they start to praise Sheikh Hussein and prophet Muhammad and the level in which they place the Prophet behind Hussein who is before the Prophet according to them . . . Now they take that Hussein and Ali, they pretend that they are Muslims. When they come to pray in the mosque, they are like Muslims, yet they still go back to their station [*darga*] of jinn.[85]

Sheikh Abdi:

They say they are Muslims but they are not according to Islam. Because they prefer *ayyaana* to God, they believe in Sheikh Hussein more than Muhammad because they keep singing songs that praise Sheikh Hussein. This is not allowed in Islam. It is what we call *shirk* [Kiswahili: *kushiriki*] when they do other things apart from what we as Muslims should do.[86]

Sheikh Gayo:

Ayyaana people claim to be Muslims but they just hide under the umbrella of Islam. *Garib* people always ask for a sheep or a goat as a sacrifice. They even drink blood or pour [it] on the possessed person. There are other things that the *ayyaana* people do that are not Islamic. Like beating the drum, mixing of men and women. *Ayyaana* people sit in the same room and they say they are praying. This is not Islamic at all. Many people prefer to follow a *garib* sheikh than an ordinary Muslim sheikh. You see in the Qur'an many prophets who followed the truth were rejected.[87]

---

85. Shiekh Abdi, August 27, 2016.
86. Shiekh Abdi, August 27, 2016.
87. Sheikh Gayo, May 16, 2017.

Sheikh Ibra:

> The *ayyaana* people call themselves Muslims but according to our faith of the real Islam (Kiswahili: *imani yetu kabisa ya Islamu*) they are not Muslims. [88]

Sheikh Khadi:

> These *ayyaana* people just know how to sacrifice in the wrong way because they accept the way of the jinn that want sacrifices. Their sheikhs do not have Qur'anic knowledge.[89]

Sheikh Munur:

> So now this is like a sect/group of Islam [*kundi la waislamu*] who are not really on the right path [*hawako katika njia kamili*]. They believe much in jinn. They believe too much [*sana wanaamini*]. They do not want to follow God's word. They believe much. Because they are stuck on these things of jinn, that is what we say about *ayyaana* people.[90]

The statements made by the Muslim teachers in the county show that they do not regard the *warra ayyaana* as Muslims – although only one sheikh considered them a "sect/group" (*kundi*) of Islam). Weighed on the scale of Muslim-ness they are found wanting as illustrated below. Tilting the scale downward indicates less Muslim-ness.

Participation of the *warra ayyaana* in the cultic beliefs and practices made the Muslim teachers assert firmly that they are not Muslims. They seem to place excessive faith in the *ayyaana* although these are merely created beings. Sheikh Munur explained, "If you believe in them [*ayyaana*] or any other created being, then you enter into the sin of *shirk* [Kiswahili: *ushirikina*]. If you reject the faith of God [Kiswahili: *kama umetoka kwa ile imani ya Mungu*] and you believe in *mahlub* [Arabic for created beings of God], then you have left the right path of God." Thus the *warra ayyaana* are on the wrong path and are committing the most unforgiveable sin in Islam: *shirk*. Their deviation from the right path is primarily because of lack of *elimu* (Kiswahili for

---

88. Sheikh Ibra, August 27, 2016.
89. Sheikh Khadi, August 30, 2016.
90. Sheikh Munur May 18, 2017.

"knowledge"), according to Sheikh Munur. Such deficiency is because the sheikhs who led them in the cultic activities do not have the knowledge of the Qur'an.

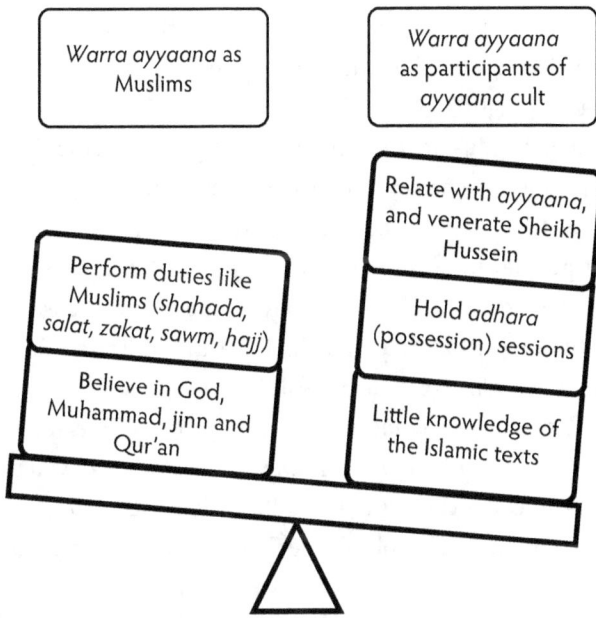

Figure 9: Weighing the Muslim-ness of the *warra ayyaana*

The Muslim teachers admitted that the founder of the cult, Sheikh Hussein of Bale, was a "strong man," supposedly, in religious matters. But his followers continue to be fascinated by what he did. They recount the stories they heard about his supernatural power to see jinn with his naked eyes. Consequently, they revere him during their séances, in which they beat the *dibbe* (drums in *afan Borana*) and sing for him. They praise him more than they honor Muhammad, even though they say they "love" the latter according to Sheikh Khadi.[91] All these make their *imani dhaifu* (Kiswahili for "faith weak"). They are easily enticed into the cultic activities that include dealing with sicknesses by appeasing *ayyaana*. This pacification requires offering sacrifices and beating drums. It is believed to make the *ayyaana* happy and thus cease to cause trouble. This is similar to the people referred to in Surah 72:6, quoted above

---

91. Sheikh Khadi, August 27, 2016.

by Sheikh Amr – people who love being with jinn (Kiswahili: *wanapenda kuwa na majini*). They believe and worship the Supreme God like the other Muslims. Unfortunately, they indulge in additional worship of *ayyaana* when they placate them, and hence they commit *shirk*. Such tendencies then tilt the weighing scale of measuring the Muslim-ness of the *warra ayyaana*, hence the declaration by the teachers that they are not Muslims. They need to be taken back to the right path.

I inquired of the Muslim teachers whether they assisted the *warra ayyaana* in coming back to the correct Islamic beliefs and practices, especially those regarding how to relate with the spirit world. All of them admitted that they taught their people either through the madrasa or during the Friday *hutba* (Kiswahili for "sermons"). However, there seemed to be a sense of hopelessness as I listened to what they said. Sheikh Amr confessed that the *warra ayyaana* were "really firm on that [Kiswahili: *wameijenga kabisa*]. They cannot be shaken [Kiswahili: *hawatingiziki*]. It is only God who can remove them from there [Kiswahili: *ni Mwenyezi Mungu tu awatoe kule*]; you cannot help them." This firmness can be attributed to the benefits accrued by participating in the cult. Sheikh Munur spoke of the financial benefits that the practitioners got when people went to them for assistance. The former charge a lot of money. They can even ask for "lions' teeth" which is translated into money because it is almost impossible for the ordinary Borana Muslim to acquire that. Many of these people have been impoverished while the practitioners have continued to amass wealth. The latter ensure continuity by "deceiving" the ordinary Muslims and not offering them the right knowledge about the spirit world as required in the Islamic texts.

Summary

This study seeks to understand Borana Muslims in Marsabit County as they participate in the *Ayyaana* cult of possession. Before delving into this, I have endeavored to present the official teaching of the spirit world as represented by the Muslim teachers in the county. I began with a general overview of their perception of the world of spirits before delving into the specific perception on *ayyaana* and the *warra ayyaana*.

The spirit world is an officially accepted notion in Islam. The authorized texts bear witness to a reality of this world with its beings. The fact that all

Muslims are required to believe in this gives them a springboard to launch from with regards to any perception or involvement in the spirit world. This chapter has shown how the concept of jinn as part of the spirit world is endorsed in the official Islamic texts. The Muslim teachers I interviewed affirmed their knowledge of jinn and possession according to what they have been taught or read. Based on this knowledge, they assessed the concept of *ayyaana* and how the followers appropriate it in their daily lives as Muslims. I have shown how these teachers believe that *ayyaana* are bad and that the followers are not Muslims. They ought to be taught so that they can go to the right path. But do the *warra ayyaana* consider themselves wrong as perceived by their Muslim teachers? This is the essence of the following chapter that describes the phenomenon of the *Ayyaana* possession cult and consequently, how the participants view themselves.

CHAPTER 5

Religiocultural Model of *Ayyaana* According to Ordinary Borana Muslims in Marsabit County

Introduction

Practitioner Diid commented, "The story [of *ayyaana*] is long, and we cannot finish it."[1] Nurea concurred, "*Ayyaana* does not have many things that can be explained to someone else. Whatever God brings, who can be able to explain fully such things?"[2] Indeed, the concept of *ayyaana* is broad and multifaceted, as I realized during the interviews. Yet it is a core aspect of the life of ordinary the Borana Muslims who participate in the *Ayyaana* cult in Marsabit County. This chapter seeks to show how they organize their conceptual framework within their religiocultural context.

A cognitive anthropological perspective is used herein to examine their beliefs and experiences in order to understand the critical issues underlying their participation. Thus, this study goes beyond merely observing behavioral practices. I sought to understand the proclivity of the Borana Muslims to the *Ayyaana* cultic activities despite the negative perception from their Muslim teachers as described in the preceding chapter. The perceptions of the Muslims who participate in the *Ayyaana* cult are described in this chapter.

---

1. Diid, March 9, 2017.
2. Nurea, July 16, 2016.

The intention is to discover the religiocultural model of *Ayyaana* that is consequently examined in light of the Islamic model of jinn as construed by the Muslim teachers. Giovanni Bennardo and Victor de Munck propose a methodology to discover cultural models, which I modified to fit my study. I have discussed this in chapter 3, on the particular methods and methodology that I employed. The goal of a cultural model research is generally to provide a description of the organization of cultural knowledge in a specific context. In this study, I sought to find out how the Borana Muslims organize their religiocultural knowledge about *ayyaana* and the consequent behavior that results from such a model. Since it is not possible to enter their minds to access such cognitive contents, I listened to their discourses as they narrated their experiences with *ayyaana*. I had the opportunity to watch some of them keenly when they welcomed me into their homes. I also attended *Ayyaana* ritual sessions in both Saku and Moyale Subcounties of Marsabit County.

This chapter goes beyond a mere discussion of what I heard and saw. It gives an analytical description of the religiocultural model of *Ayyaana*. I used linguistic tools to analyze the discourses narrated in order to understand the perception of *ayyaana* and hence the mental model shared by my interviewees. I begin this chapter with a key word analysis of the term *ayyaana* and show that it is polysemous in the view of the ordinary Borana Muslims who participate in the cultic activities. This is followed by a sentence-level analysis that primarily considers some key conceptual metaphors used to denote *ayyaana*.

Conceptualizing *Ayyaana* among Ordinary Borana Muslims

This section discusses the way Borana Muslims conceptualize the word *ayyaana* in their daily lives. This conceptualization was derived from the interviews conducted in the Borana language. The majority of the interviewees were more conversant with Borana than with Kiswahili. The prevalent usage of Borana was an added advantage in discovering the conceptual content evoked by the term *ayyaana*. Language is considered the "privileged entry into the mind, or mental organization of knowledge," as Bennardo and de

Munck summarize in their third chapter on structure and culture in mind.³ They also assert that linguistic data is a fundamental element in discovering cultural models. I have specifically used discourse analysis as a primary analytical tool to discover the religiocultural model of *Ayyaana*.⁴

Ayyaana as a Polysemous Word

Ayyaana is a polysemous word with several related meanings, according to the ordinary Borana Muslims.⁵ Chapter 3 of this study reviewed some scholarly works on the concept of *ayyaana* especially among the Oromo people of Ethiopia. Zitelman states that the word has Arabic-Islamic roots and was used within the Sufi legacy of Islam in a "highly mystical and gnostic" way. The Oromo people adopted the word and used it within their religiocultural setting.⁶ The Borana, who are part of the Oromo fraternity, however, have changed these meanings probably because of their distance from Ethiopia. One point of departure is that the Borana concept of *ayyaana* does not emphasize the aspect of *ayyaana* as a derivative of *Waaqa*, the Sky-God. This is the conceptual belief propagated in the traditional Oromo religion found in Ethiopia. *Ayyaana*, according to the Oromo, "refers to that by which and through which God (*Waaqa*) creates anything and everything."⁷ I did not find such conceptualization among the Borana Muslims in Marsabit. For them, the concept of *ayyaana* has three related meanings: calendric days, fortune, and spiritual beings that inhabit the *al-ghaib* yet impinge on the world of human beings. These meanings were derived from the statements made by the interviewees when I asked them what they understood by the word *ayyaana*. Below is a sample of the statements they made:

Boru, a Borana tradition specialist in Saku:

---

3. Bennardo and de Munck, *Cultural Model*, 49.

4. It should be noted that other Borana speakers like the Orma people of Tana River County might use the word in a different way.

5. The Muslim teachers in Marsabit County do not perceive the term *ayyaana* as polysemous. This contrasts with what the ordinary Borana Muslims said. The latter viewed *ayyaana* in a polysemous way that revolved around the theme of *nagaa* (Borana for "wellness"). Since the focus of this chapter is analyzing the discourses from the ordinary Borana Muslims, I chose to classify the term *ayyaana* as polysemous rather than homonymous in this chapter.

6. Zitelmann, "Oromo Religion, Ayyaana," 83.

7. Megerssa, "Oromo World-View," 71–72.

Ayyaana is a common word used in daily communications even today. It stands for good fortune from God; favored. When someone is in need of money and then gets it, he/she will comment, *ayyaana dansa*, meaning good fortune. In times of misfortune, one can be heard saying, *ayyaana kiyya hama*, meaning 'my luck is bad'. There are also bad and good seasons in the Borana calendar that have to do with *ayyaana*.[8]

Fatuma, a participant in the *Ayyaana* cult in Moyale:

You cannot know anything until that *ayyaana* is counted. Whenever you have a ceremony you must count the calendar of Borana first.

The one I know is that Borana calendar; the second, we slaughter coffee, and then we plan to pray.[9]

Halkano, Borana traditionalist:

No event can happen among Borana without this *ayyaana*.[10]

Interviewer: "If the word *ayyaana* can mean 'good fortune,' does it have another meaning in Borana? Do they mean similar things?"

Mzee Godana: "No, it is not one, it is not the same. This one, you know, the elders count the days without following any book. They count the days; if you want to know which day it is today, he can tell you. But it is not *sheitani*."

Interviewer: "So, what is this other meaning of *sheitani*?"

Mzee Godana: "That one of *sheitani* is what they say *ayyaana*. Yes, we say *ayyaana* means days but these people of *sheitani* are the ones . . . [pause] the words resemble but they are not the same thing. The *ayyaana* as calendar are things of *aadaa* [custom/tradition].[11]

---

8. Boru, January 8, 2016.

9. Fatuma, July 21, 2016. "Slaughtering coffee" is the literal translation of the Borana phrase *bunna qala*, which is the name of a traditional ceremony where *bunna* (coffee) is roasted in ghee. Aguilar has described this ceremony in his article, "Recreating a Religious Past in a Muslim Setting: 'Sacrificing' Coffee-beans among the Waso Boora of Garba Tulla, Kenya." "Recreating a Religious Past in a Muslim Setting: 'Sacrificing' Coffee-Beans among the Waso Boorana of Garba Tulla, Kenya." See *Ethnos* 60, no. 1–2 (1995): 41–58.

10. Halkano, August 24, 2016.

11. Godana, July 27, 2016.

The three nuances of the word *ayyaana* are evident from the statements above. I did not delve into the philological examination of how the meanings evolved. Instead, I inquired about the contemporary usage of the word *ayyaana* among the Borana people in Marsabit County. It is apparent that it evoked strong stances from the interviewees. Halkano's statement represents the perception of many Borana people (both Muslims and non-Muslims) concerning the word: "In a real sense *ayyaana* is a very respected word among Borana." The Muslim teachers consented to this as noted in chapter 4. They admitted the auspicious notion as prevalent among the Borana people generally. However, in spite of the traditional significance that the word *ayyaana* carries, these teachers did not discuss it as much as the ordinary Borana Muslims did. Like Mzee Godana in the above interview exerpt, the Muslim teachers construed a negative aspect of the term when applied to the concept of spirits. Chapter 7 of this study discusses this disparity in a comparative analysis of the different conceptualizations of *ayyaana* by the Muslim teachers and the ordinary Borana Muslims. For now, the preceding section examines the three nuances of the term *ayyaana* as described by the ordinary Muslims who engaged in the cultic activities.

Ayyaana as Calendric Days

The concept of *ayyaana* as calendric days was used among Borana people and is still observed in contemporary times.[12] It is a complex system of counting days that differs from the Gregorian calendar. As Schlee observes, "it does not share anything with the oriental seven-day week except the general functioning of structuring time."[13] One of the interviewees showed me a calendar that was produced by the Bible Translation and Literacy (BTL) program in 2005. It bears the title *Borana Calendar: Ayyaana Wogga Ka Ganna Shaneeso Gada Libani Jaldeesa* (literally: "*Ayyaana* season of the fifth year of the rule of Abba Gada Libani Jaldeesa"). Unlike the Gregorian calendar, the Borana calendar has twenty-seven days in a month. Each of these days has a Borana name. (See appendix 3 for the specific names.) Each day is said to have *ayyaana*.

---

12. Oromo people in Ethiopia also have this calendar system that is "based on the astronomical observation of the moon in connection with six or seven stars moving together." See Gerba, "Typology of Oromo," 19.

13. Schlee, *Identities on the Move*, 90.

Gerba explains this *ayyaana* aspect of each day as "fate."[14] This concurred with what interviewee Yaatani explained – that this means that each of these "rotating/recurring days" was associated with a specific fortune.[15]

There are specific people among the Borana who know the *ayyaana* (the auspiciousness) of each day and thus give appropriate advice on when to perform essential events like *fudda* (weddings), *gubbisa* (naming ceremonies), and others. Some days are considered good for certain occasions, while others are bad. When a Borana person intends to carry out an event, the leader of the family consults with the Borana calendar specialists *ayyaantu* ("calendar specialists" in *afan Borana*) who will advise regarding the best day. The father, as the head of the family, goes to the *ayyaantu* with *tamboo* (tobacco) and *bunna* (coffee), and he requests, "*Ayyaana naa heddi*" (calculate the *ayyaana* for me). This seems to be mandatory for all Borana people keen on observing the tradition even in contemporary times. Fatuma was emphatic that no Borana should hold a ceremony before "counting the calendar of Borana first."[16] Halkano agreed:

> What is called *ayyaana*, Borana do nothing without it. You know when a girl is about to marry the calendar must be counted to know the suitable time accepted in Borana culture. For a child that is born, *ayyaana* is counted. If you mention the name *ayyaana* in Borana, it is a thing that is highly esteemed.[17]

The Borana calendar cannot be said to follow the lunar system. However, there are some aspects of the auspiciousness of the days that are related to the phases of the *baati* (the moon). Important traditional Borana ceremonies like *fuuda* (weddings) are performed during the new moon especially for young people. This component of the moon is also crucial for the *warra ayyaana*. They choose the days to perform their ceremonies based on the sighting of the moon. *Goobana*, for instance, is a common ritual ceremony they perform. Fatuma reported that *goobana* is done on the fifteenth day after the

---

14. Gerba, "Typology of Oromo," 19.
15. Yaatani, December 26, 2015.
16. Fatuma, July 21, 2016.
17. Halkano, August 24, 2016.

appearance of the new moon. She explained that the *warra ayyaana* gather for *maombi* (Kiswahili for "prayers") during every *goobana* (new moon).[18]

Ayyaana as Fortune

Ayyaana also means fortune. Leus and Salvadori affirm this when they state that *ayyaana* is "good luck, good fortune, blessing. *Ayyaana* can be either good or bad. When it is good- *ayyaana dansaa*."[19] The ambiguity in these translations of *ayyaana* shows that there is no simple English equivalent for the meaning of the term *ayyaana* as "fortune."

Waqo, a Borana elder who understands a number of the cultural features said, "There is no equivalent translation to English that can bring out the real intended meaning" of the word *ayyaana*.[20] Such imprecision of translation is patent in the Borana Bible translation of the Beatitudes as found in Matthew 5:3–11:

> Vs. 3 *Ayyaana* [blessed] *worra aka garaa keesa hiyyeeyi ufi beekhu* . . .
>
> Vs. 4 *Ayyaana worra lalefatu* . . .
>
> Vs. 5 *Ayyaana worra ufi diqeesu* . . .
>
> Vs. 6 *Ayyaana worra d'ugga jed'e*. . .
>
> Vs. 7 *Ayyaana worra naasu qabu*. . .
>
> Vs. 8 *Ayyaana worra garaa qulqullo qabu*. . .
>
> Vs. 9 *Ayyaana worra nagaya tolchu*. . .
>
> Vs. 10 *Ayyaana worra d'ugaafi gaargalchani* . . .
>
> Vs. 11 *Ayyaana keesani hojja beeni isani arabse gaargalche* . . .[21]

---

18. The word *goobana* can mean either the "full moon" or the "day of the full moon." Leus and Salvadori explain that in the past, the Borana people planned attacks on their enemies on the thirteenth or fourteenth day immediately preceding the new moon, when the nights would be very bright allowing for both day and night travel. See Leus and Salvadori, *Aadaa Boraanaa*, 270. Based on my interviews, *warra ayyaana* still use the word *goobana* to refer to both the new moon and the ceremony performed on the fifteenth day after the new moon.

19. Stroomer also defines *ayyaana* as luck or fortune. See Stroomer, *Comparative Study of Three*; and Stroomer, *Grammar of Boraana Oromo*.

20. Waqo, May 19, 2017.

21. Kitaaba Waaqa, Bible Society of Kenya, Nairobi, 1994.

The word "blessed" or "happy" was translated as *ayyaana* in the Borana Bible. In a bid to understand this meaning more, I interviewed Yaatani, who was one of the key people involved in producing the Borana translation of the Bible. He asserted that the use of *ayyaana* as the translation for "blessed" was preferred because it was a stronger word than synonyms like *gammada* ("happy," "happiness," or "glad"). According to Boru, the word *ayyaana* in the Borana Bible means either the "favored one [by God]," or "spiritual empowerment from God."[22] Primarily, the word *ayyaana* evokes largely positive schemas in the minds of Borana people.

Ayyaana is used in daily communications of both Muslim and non-Muslim Borana people in Marsabit County.[23] Leus and Salvadori agree with this by giving similar sentiments made by Borana people. When someone acquires wealth, people will comment, "*Ayyaana nama kanaa*" (it is his blessing/good fortune). In the event that someone did not have food then he gets it later, he may say, "*Silaa arra sagalee hin qabu galgala name dhufee boshe naa kenee ayyaana qaba*" (I would not have had any food today, but in the evening someone came and gave me some maize flour, [it was] *ayyaana*).[24]

The perception of *ayyaana* as fortune alludes to an external, causal agency. Happiness or being favored does not result from any inherent characteristic of a Borana person where the schema of *ayyaana dansa* (good fortune) is evoked. It is perceived that an external agent beyond the person causes either good or bad *ayyaana*. This causative agent can be either *Waaqa* or other supernatural beings that have creatively been given the same name: *ayyaana*.

Ayyaana as Spiritual Beings and Cult

The word *ayyaana* also refers to possession spirits and denotes the resultant cult where the *warra ayyaana* (people of *ayyaana*) engage with the *ayyaana* spirits. These two meanings of *ayyaana* (as spirits and as a cult) are linked metonymically in a referential way, where one entity is used to refer to another. This referencing also serves the purpose of distinguishing the *Ayyaana* cult from any other cultic activities that may ensue with other possession

---

22. Boru, January 8, 2016.

23. This contemporary usage of *ayyaana* in daily communications seemed to be confined to the older generation of Borana people.

24. Leus and Salvadori, *Aadaa Boraanaa*, 35.

spirits like the jinn described in chapter 4 of this study. Hence, the metonymic concept of *ayyaana* is used primarily for identification among the Borana Muslims in Marsabit County.

The metonymic concept of *ayyaana* is basically grounded in the experiences of the participants of the cultic activities revolving around *ayyaana* as spirits. These experiences identify the participants as *warra ayyaana* (people of *ayyaana*) and thus distinguish them from non-participants. The creativity of the *warra ayyaana* is evident in the way they use various metaphors in the context of *ayyaana* as spirits and as a cult.

Metaphorical and Domain Analysis of *Ayyaana* as Spirits

Metaphors are basic cognitive processes of the mind that are derived from individual and collective cultural experiences. As mental constructions, metaphors are overtly expressed in language. From the interviews I conducted with Borana Muslims, I derived three metaphorical references to *ayyaana* that express the themes of invisibility, warfare, and relationship. The theme of relationship is connected with the anthropomorphic construal of *ayyaana* discussed later.

Ayyaana as *Qileensa Rabbi / Waaqa*

A frequent *afan Borana* metaphor used by the interviewees was: *ayyaani qileensa Rabi*, which means "*ayyaana* is wind/breath of/from the Lord." The word *qileensa* means "wind," "air," or "breath" in *afan Borana* and is commonly used both metaphorically and literally as illustrated in table 7.

In the literal sense, strong winds are said to be an indicator of an impending drought and a consequential lack of pasture for their livestock. This enables Borana people to start preparing to move their animals to greener pastures. The metaphorical usage of *qileensa* has two references. First, it denotes an outbreak of an epidemic disease that occurs without any predication. Second, it refers to *ayyaana* as an invisible entity.

Table 7: Usage of the Word *Qileensa* (Wind)

Borana Term	Interlinear Translation	Meaning
Qileensa Waaqa	Wind God/Heaven	Wind from heaven (*ayyaana*)
Qileensa bonaat	Wind of drought	Bad wind of drought in dry spells (literal sense)
Qileensa hamma baujirt	Wind bad passing by	Outbreak of disease
Qileensa Rabbi	Wind Lord	Wind from God (*ayyaana*)
Qileensa Rabbit	(The -*it* ending indicates that this is the possessive form.) Wind Lord	Wind of the Lord (*ayyaana*)
Qileensa	Wind/air	Wind (literal sense)

Metaphor analysis involves identifying the source and target domains.[25] These domains are related and are connected conceptually through a mapping of common themes. The source domain in the above metaphor is wind, a feature that is well known. The Borana Muslims understand the conceptual domain of spirit by relating it to the invisible wind. The invisibility of *ayyaana* makes it associated with the wind, which is felt but not seen although it is perceived to originate from somewhere.

The source of *qileensa* is believed to be *Waaqa*. Similarly, the Borana Muslims accept that the source of *ayyaana* is *Rabbi* (Arabic for "Lord") or *Waaqa* (God). Practitioner Diid, for instance, stated emphatically, "First of all, *ayyaana* is the breath of the Lord." Adho also affirmed this by asserting, "This is the breath of the Lord that he has brought to me." Adho further clarified that *ayyaana*, as *qileensa Rabbi*, was not a spirit of God (*afur Rabbi* in *afan Borana*[26]). Rather *ayyaana* is considered to be a "spirit sent by God" or a "wind from God." This differentiation is crucial as it indicates the perception by the ordinary Borana Muslims who would not want to equate

---

25. Source and target domains are analytical elements of a metaphor. The source domain is understood in terms of the target domain.

26. *Afur Rabi* (Spirit of God) is synonymous with *Afur Qulqulo* (Holy Spirit), which is the Borana word used in the Bible to refer to the third Person of the Godhead.

anything with *Waaqa*. They do this to avoid any tendency toward the sin of *shirk* (association).

Furthermore, in the last phrase of table 7, *Qileensa Rabbit*, the suffix *-it* on the noun *Rabbi* in *afan Borana* indicates possessiveness. Interviewees used this phrase to indicate their firm belief that *ayyaana* are from *Waaqa* and not from *Sheitani* (Satan). *Ayyaana* were thus perceived as *waan dansa* (*afan Borana* for "good things"). The theme of *nagaa* (peace) is also implicated with this notion of goodness from *Waaqa*.[27]

Ayyaana as a *Jeshi* (an Army)

The thematic expression of war was apparent from the interviewees' statements. There was frequent mention of *ayyaana* as an army: "*Ayyaana* is the army of *oblia* (*ayyaani jeshi oblia*)."[28] Before discussing this metaphor, it is necessary to explain what *oblia* is.

Oblia is a group of angels who are ranked higher than *ayyaana*, according to my interviewees in both Saku and Moyale Subcounties. They believe that *oblia* were sent by God to help Borana people to be more devoted to him as Muslims. *Oblia* were sent together with *ayyaana*. The latter came to serve *oblia* in making people more religious. Practitioner Diid affirmed this by stating, "*Ayyaana* is [are] an army [*jeshi*] that the Lord released from heaven so that they help *oblia*."[29] The theme of warfare is further alluded to in the following statements:

Diid:

Ayyaana can be commanded.[30]

---

27. *Waaqa* is the Borana name for the Supreme God. This word is more popular among Borana traditionalists and Christians. However, I also realized that it is used interchangeably with *Rabbi* (Lord) by the ordinary Borana Muslims. *Waaqa* is also the word for "sky." In his 1983 work, Bartels' description of the Oromo God is similar to that of the Marabit Borana people, who believe that *Waaqa* and the sky are synonymous. See Aguilar, "God of the Oromo," 57–61, in which Aguilar discusses Bartels' religious paradigm on the "God of the Oromo" and mentions its similarity to that of other Oromo groups like the Waso Borana of Kenya.

28. *Jeshi* is a Kiswahili word that has been adapted in *afan Borana* and is widely used to refer to an army.

29. I did not delve much into the concept of *oblia* as a group of angels. I realized it was a complicated concept that needs to be understood on its own. It seemed to be more associated with the Sufi tendencies since the *warra ayyaana* would call themselves *oblia* people whose work is to "pray and bless people," according to practitioner Jillo.

30. Diid, March 9, 2017.

Fatuma:

All the *ayyaana* that an *abba sera* [father of law] commands, they are all his followers or battalion.[31]

Boru:

Ayyaana is an army with divine spiritual powers.[32]

Nurea:

Ayyaana can attack.[33]

Fatuma:

When *ayyaana* is in somebody it is called *hankanya baari* [...] *Hankanya* means army, army men of the sea.[34]

Fatuma:

Ayyaana struggles with jinn.[35]

Fatuma:

Ayyaana have ranks.[36]

Fatuma:

You appease all these [*ayyaana*] so that you are at peace. This sacrifice is for that.[37]

Fatuma:

All these are weapons of *ayyaana* [referring to the stick and chain], weapons that are used when fighting with jinn.[38]

---

31. Fatuma, July 21, 2016.
32. Boru, January 8, 2016.
33. Nurea, July 16, 2016.
34. Fatuma, July 21, 2016. *Hankanya* is word a commonly used within the *ayyaana* circles. See Fatuma, July 16, 2016; and Ako-Garqasa, March 11, 2017).
35. Fatuma, July 21, 2016.
36. Fatuma.
37. Fatuma.
38. Fatuma.

Dabasso:

The chain of *ayyaana* is the spear.[39]

Dabasso:

Yes, *ule* [stick], this is G3, AK47[...] It stands for AK47, that thing has been given power by God, Kalashkov[...] This one if you go with it to a house, the sick person inside will be healed.[40]

The conceptualization of warfare is based on the experiences the Borana have had over the years. They have constantly engaged in conflict with neighboring tribes using spears as weapons of warfare. It is, therefore, easy to conceptualize the domain of spirits in terms of a contestation involving an obedient army with weapons to attack an adversary when commanded.

The shared conceptual metaphor of warfare illustrates another aspect of the religiocultural model of *Ayyaana* construed by Borana Muslims. *Ayyaana* is an army that is under the command of *abba sera* (*afan Borana* for "father of laws"). The latter is given authority because of possessing the *ule ayyaana* (the stick of *ayyaana*) and a *shibo* (a chain). These artifacts of *ayyaana* are construed as weapons (see Dabasso's statement above) and have been discussed in more detail in a subsequent section of this dissertation.

Conceptual Domain of *Ayyaana* as Spirits

The domain of spirits in the conceptualization of Borana Muslims includes *ayyaana*, jinn, and *ekhera* (ancestral spirits). This domain forms a significant part of the conceptual framework of Borana Muslims who are inclined to non-orthodox practices and beliefs. The concept of ancestral spirits did not feature much during the interviews as has already been mentioned. *Ayyaana* and jinn featured more prominently during the discourses. This indicates the inclination of my interviewees' thoughts concerning the spirit world. Unlike the view by the Muslim teachers interviewed in Marsabit County, ordinary Borana Muslims do not classify *ayyaana* as jinn. These are two distinct kinds of beings as shown in figure 10.

---

39. Dabasso, August 1, 2016.
40. Dabasso.

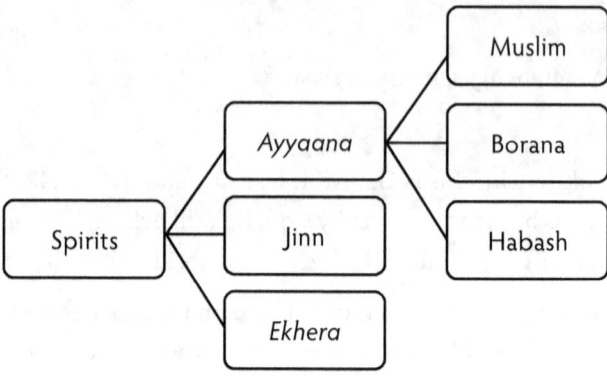

Figure 10: Domain of spirits

Before delving into the different types of *ayyaana*, I describe below how the ordinary Borana Muslims perceive the relation between *ayyaana* and jinn. They consented that *ayyaana* are superior to jinn, as shown from the following interview with Fatuma.[41]

> Interviewer: "And what is the difference between *ayyaana* and what we hear called jinn?"
>
> Fatuma: "The difference is this: You know all are spirits [Kiswahili: *mapepo*]. All are spirits. But *ayyaana* and jinn do not cooperate [Kiswahili: *hawasikilizani*]. Now, if someone has a jinni... when [an] *ayyaana* comes,[42] first it "catches" [Kiswahili: *anashika*] that person."
>
> Interviewer: "The person with a jinni?"
>
> Fatuma: "Yes, that person who has a jinni. First, it is a must that the *ayyaana* first removes the jinni... *ayyaana* and jinn cannot relate or coexist together."

---

41. Fatuma, July 21, 2016. Fatuma is a schoolteacher at a local school, and she spoke in Kiswahili. Other interviewees also used some Kiswahili words that I have noted throughout this dissertation. The word *Kiswahili* refers to the national language used in Kenya, while the term *Swahili* or *Waswahili* refers to a people group majorly found along the East African Coast. See Kim, *Islam among the Swahili*, 41–46 on defining Waswahili identity from a sociocultural perspective.

42. The word *ayyaana* here is used in singular to refer to what happens when a particular *ayyaana* enters a person with a jinni. Otherwise, throughout this dissertation, the word *ayyaana* is used as a collective.

> Interviewer: "Do you want to say that someone who has a jinni, *ayyaana* is more attracted to them?"
>
> Fatuma: "No, it is not more attracted. *Ayyaana* attacks to remove that jinni from the person. *Ayyaana* attacks the jinni so that he removes it."
>
> Interviewer: "*Ayyaana* is more powerful than the jinni?"
>
> Fatuma: "Yes, he is more than jinn [laughter]."
>
> Interviewer: "Very interesting. Now, how does he remove it? Do they fight?"
>
> Fatuma: "Yes, you can see them struggling... *ayyaana* is a spirit [Kiswahili: *pepo*] and jinni is a spirit [Kiswahili: *pepo*]. You will not see these two struggling, but this person with *ayyaana*, you will see them struggling with the person. Then after a short while you hear, 'He has taken [Kiswahili: *amechukua*].' The person will start saying, 'The problem I had has been removed from me. Whatever has been sitting [Kiswahili: *inanikalia*] in me has been removed; I do not know what has taken it.'"

Fatuma's perception is representative of the *ayyaana* people's view. *Ayyaana* are seen to be stronger than jinn. The latter are even said to be more problematic when they "catch" someone. *Ayyaana* thus comes to remove the jinn that are perceived to be troublesome. Insanity is one major problem believed to be caused by jinn, as Fatuma stated:

> When a jinni enters a person, that person must be mad... *ayyaana* does not make someone lose his mind. *Ayyaana* only comes to enter the body and speaks. That it is time someone loses consciousness. When the jinni leaves, someone becomes fine and not insane. Even all the other times someone is fine.[43]

Losing one's mind is therefore attributed to jinn and not to *ayyaana*. This shows how the ordinary Muslims who believe in *ayyaana* rank jinn on a lower niche. Jinn are said to be "servants" or "messengers" of *ayyaana*. However, despite this lower rank of jinn, interviewees admitted that *ayyaana* are not

---

43. Fatuma, July 21, 2016.

mentioned in the Qur'an like jinn. This did not bother them as Muslims who still esteem the Qur'an. It was more pertinent to rank *ayyaana* higher than jinn even if the former were not mentioned in the Islamic texts. This was further indicated by the way they classified *ayyaana* and gave them different names. There was no mention that jinn had other sub-names like *ayyaana*.

Categorizing *Ayyaana*

According to George Lakoff, categories are pertinent in understanding how people think and act.[44] Therefore, examining the way Borana Muslims categorize *ayyaana* is germane to the discovery of their cultural model of *Ayyaana*. Figure 10 above shows how they classify *ayyaana* into three main groups: Muslim, Borana, and Habasha (Ethiopian).[45] The *ayyaana* in each of these groups have variant names for identification and communication. Table 8 below lists some of the names:

Table 8: Nomenclature of *Ayyaana* Spirits

Muslim/Arabiya	Habasha/Amharic	Borana
Hajji Nuri	Abdallah Nura	Odha
Hajji Hussein	Abdalla Geta	Jillo
Hajji Sharif	Fano	Boru
Hajji Risa	Mali	Fanole
Rukhani	Haile	Etc.
Jani	Maarite	
Etc.[46]	Ayiti/Hayiti (female)	
	Etc.	

Ayyaana are mostly identified by their names, language, and demands. The names also indicate their origin. The Muslim/Arabiya *ayyaana* are said to originate from Arabia. A number of the Muslim *ayyaana* have the title

---

44. Lakoff, *Women, Fire and Dangerous Things*, 6.

45. I use the term *Habasha* here the way my interviewees pronounced it. I noticed that they used this word to refer to all Ethiopians in general. Conventionally, Habesha are the people who inhabit the northern part of Ethiopia, especially the Tigre, Agew, and Amhara. They were also known as Abyssinian people.

46. The list of names of *ayyaana* in each of the three groups is not exhaustive. I have only listed a few to indicate that *ayyaana* have been given names according to where they are deemed to have originated.

Religiocultural Model of *Ayyaana* According to Ordinary Borana Muslims 149

Hajji attached to their names. Usually *Hajji* precedes the name of a Muslim man who has made the annual pilgrimage to Mecca.[47] Pilgrimage is similarly a crucial aspect of the *Ayyaana* cult, as will be discussed later. Fatuma also explained that these Muslim *ayyaana* manifest when songs praising the prophet Muhammad are sung.

There was a consensus among the interviewees that *rukhani* is a Muslim *ayyaana* that is identified by its preference for sweet smelling things like perfume.[48] The perception of *rukhani* as *ayyaana* differs from the view of the Muslim teachers, who consider *rukhani* to be a jinni and not *ayyanna*. According to the ordinary Borana Muslims, *rukhani* as a kind of *ayyaana*, requires the person they enter to pray more and be a diligent Muslim.[49] Tarimo recounted the story of her niece who lived with her. *Rukhani* entered the latter and demanded that she observe the *salat* prayers regularly.[50]

In spite of the *rukhani's* inclinations to Islam, they still demand to be appeased with sacrifices. Fatuma mentioned that her *rukhani* demanded the "sacrifice of sheep," and he also "comes at that time when all [*ayyaana*] are called to eat or drink." Ashaka likewise referred to the *ayyaana* that "caught" her as "*rukhani tiya* [my *rukhani*]" that "drinks lemon" and even liked the *hadhara* songs.[51] This implies that even though *rukhani* spirits are considered Islamic, they are not dealt with in the required Islamic way of exorcism as taught by the Muslim teachers.

The Amharic/Habasha *ayyaana* prefer to speak in Amharic.[52] They are believed to originate from Ethiopia and have names from there, such as *Haile*, *Ayiti*, and others. Ayiti is a female *ayyaana* that prefers a special type of

---

47. Muslim women who have made the Islamic pilgrimage to Mecca bear the title *Hajja*.

48. Some of my interviewees also mentioned that this type of *ayyaana* also makes people literally drink perfume. See Turunesh, July 29, 2016.

49. It will be noted later in this chapter that *warra ayyaana* believe that *ayyaana* were generally manifested in order to Islamize Borana people. Yet, where *rukhani* was mentioned, it was evident that they associated it more with Islam than the other *ayyaana*.

50. Tarimo, March 10, 2017.

51. Ashaka, March 4, 2017. The name *hadhara* has been borrowed from the Arabic *haḍra*, which stands for the Sufi ritual performaces. *Hadhara* is the name given for the singing, clapping, and drumming sessions for *ayyaana*. It is also used as a verb meaning, "to sing songs." Leus and Salvadori call it *adara*. See Leus and Salvadori, *Aadaa Boraanaa*, 10. I prefer to use *hadhara* because that is the pronounciation I heard from my interviewees.

52. See footnote 592@@ for an explanation of the term *Habasha*.

perfume. The Borana *ayyaana* speak *afan Borana* and have Borana names, like Odha, Jillo, and Boru.

There are ranks within all these types of *ayyaana*. Fatuma, a keen participant of *Ayyaana* sessions, explained that the ranking was based on speech. The *ayyaana* that are considered to be of lower status are the ones that have not yet "spoken." These are said to be dormant and usually disturb people when they cannot be identified. Such *ayyaana* are called *ch'ullo* in *afan Borana*, which means "a child who does not yet know how to talk."

There is another kind of *ayyaana*, called Odha, that was mentioned frequently during the interviews. Odha is classified under the Borana type,[53] and it is said to be the highest in rank of all *ayyaana*. Odha identifies himself as *abbaa maati* (father of many in *afan Borana*), indicating his superior position, according to Galgallo.[54] Odha usually demands blood when he "speaks." Another type of *ayyaana* that asks for blood is Hajji Risa. Risa is the Borana name for eagle, an animal that plays a significant role in the *Ayyaana* cult.[55] It is commonly believed that *ayyaana* are able to enter the bodies of eagles and hence the name Hajji Risa. Konso, a practitioner from Moyale, claimed that Hajji Risa usually preceded Odha in drinking blood.[56] Again, Hajji Risa's supremacy is evident from the way he is always given meat. When a sheep or a goat is slaughtered during the sessions, the heart and the meat that surround it are placed on a tree. Hajji Risa appears in the form of an eagle and takes all the pieces.

The above categorization of *ayyaana* by the ordinary Borana Muslims has become normative in their conceptualization based on their experiences with *ayyaana*. This is in accord with Lakoff's submission:

> Human categorization is essentially a matter of both human experience and imagination – of perception, motor activity,

---

53. The specific names of *ayyaana*, like Odha, are not italicized because they are used as proper nouns. Some of these names are also names of people (for instance Jillo). This differs from the term *ayyaana*, which is used as the collective term of the spirits in *afan Borana*.

54. Galgallo, April 14, 2017.

55. Eagles are significant in the *Ayyaana* cult. There was a big portrait of an eagle in one of the *dargas* (sacred places for *ayyaana* ceremonies) I visited.

56. Konso, August 26, 2016.

and culture on the one hand, and of metaphor, metonymy, and mental imagery on the other.[57]

Both the cultural experience and the creative imagination are evident from the categorization of *ayyaana*. The participants interviewed used their cultural knowledge to classify *ayyaana* into orderly categories. They not only creatively give names and categories; they also describe pertinent features of *ayyaana* that further enhanced the mental construction of the kind of cultural model they have about *ayyaana*.

Descriptive Features of *Ayyaana*

The number of specific *ayyaana* is not very formidable. Ashaka, for instance, mentioned that they could be approximately seventy. This makes it an arduous task to try and describe all their features, which even my interviewees were unable to do. This section presents a description of some of the features that I deem significant. I have selected these features to provide a platform where I can examine the perception of the *warra ayyaana* in light of the official precepts of Islam as propagated by the Muslim teachers in Marsabit.

Religious Features of Ayyaana

The word *religion* is used here to denote Islam, Christianity, or *aada Borana* (traditional Borana beliefs and customs). *Ayyaana* is associated with the Islamic religion.[58] This is clear from the following statements I derived from the interviews with the ordinary Borana Muslims.

Table 9: Religious Features of *Ayyaana*

Theme 1: *Ayyaana* are religious.	
Borana	**English**
Ayyaani waan duri gabusani aka naami islanisis	*Ayyaana* came to make people Muslims.
Wonti inni tolchu d'ufe d'ibini hinjirtu nama Isilansu male	There was nothing else they came to do but to Islamize people.
Ayyaani Isilana fed'a maan jennani ini Isilanin ufi hima	*Ayyaana* like Muslims because they claim to be Muslims.

---

57. Lakoff, *Women, Fire and Dangerous Things*, 8.
58. The loanword in *afan Borana* used to refer to the religion of Islam is *Islana*.

Theme 1: *Ayyaana* are religious.	
Borana	**English**
Ayyaani Isilana jalata. Worrin mishenilleni (Kristani) yo ayyaani qabatu, inisilana	*Ayyaana* love Muslims. Even when Christians get it, they become Muslims.
Ayyaani akka nabi Muhamadi gafa jihadi qarqarufi gadi ergani, eegi duisa nabigi, Sheikh Hussein qarqare	*Ayyaana* were sent to help the prophet Muhammad during jihad, and after the death of the prophet assisted Sheikh Husssein.
Kara ayyanatini, Borani hedduni ya Isilane	Through *ayyaana*, many Borana people have become Muslims.
Jalalti rabi jalalti nabi dufte. Jalalati taanan one umata seene jijiir diniit	In the love of God, the love of the prophet, then *ayyaana* came. For this love, *ayyaana* entered the hearts of people and changed them toward the religion.
Yo name ayyaana qabu, inni/isini dulachu feed'a, ayaani suni fed'a. Isilamadini atini ammantana gartu tunini marro ayaanatiifi akkana guddatte.	When someone has *ayyaana*, he/she wants to pray; *ayyaana* like that. This Islamization you see now is because of *ayyaana*.
⬇	
Sub-theme 1: *Ayyaana* are inclined to Islam.	
Sub-theme 2: *Ayyaana* make people more religious.	

Ayyaana, according to table 9, are religiously inclined to Islam. It was noted previously that *ayyaana* were manifested to Islamize the Borana people. Galma described her people as those who "did not have a *dini* (Kiswahili for "religion") before."[59] Hence, *ayyaana* brought them *dini*. This concept therefore differentiated *dini* from *aadaa Boorana* (Borana customs).

---

59. *Dini* is different from the traditional usage of the term *religion* (*afan Borana*: *aadaa*). *Aadaa* (customs) of Borana were inclusive of religious beliefs and practices. A "lack of religion" is the interpretation that most Muslim teachers have when they refer to the time Borana people

Traditionally, Borana people regard religion as a way of staying at peace (*afan Borana*: *nagaa*) with *Waaqa* by following his *aadaa* (rules). *Ayyaana* are perceived to play a vital role in making people live in *nagaa* by submitting to God through Islam. Such a role is mediatory. The *warra ayyaana* believe that *ayyaana* assisted Prophet Muhammad and Sheikh Hussein to Islamize people (see Diid's statement above). After the demise of these two religious leaders, *ayyaana* are believed to continue their Islamization through physical and behavioral attributes.

Anthropomorphic Attributes of Ayyaana

The *warra ayyaana* ascribe human traits to *ayyaana* despite their invisibility as *qileensa Waaqa* (wind of God). This ascription made my interviewees personify *ayyaana*. They used the masculine pronoun "he" when referring to a single *ayyaana*. I did not hear much reference to *ayyaana* in the feminine sense. Only one interviewee said there were female *ayyaana*. This may be because of the patriarchal system inherent in the Borana culture. Table 10 lists some of the statements made in *afan Borana* concerning the behavioral features of *ayyaana*.

Table 10: Behavioral Features of *Ayyaana*

Theme 2: *Ayyaana* behave like human beings.	
Borana	**English**
Yo horin dib ede laf d'ae, yom sun yamani d'ig d'uga	When an animal has been slaughtered, *ayyaana* are immediately called to come and drink the blood.
Waan inyane inqabu foon inyata d'iga ind'uga	There is nothing that *ayyaana* do not eat; they eat meat, drink blood.
Bun d'abaniif (ayyaana buuna kennannifi)	Coffee is cooked for them (*ayyaana* are given coffee).
Ayyaani dandae ennumma ufi hima	*Ayyaana* are able to identify themselves.
Ayyaani hindubata	*Ayyaana* speak.
Ayyaani hind'agaa ammalle yo woi tai jed'anini hintolcha	*Ayyaana* can hear, and when they say they will do something, they do it.

---

had not yet embraced Islam. Notwithstanding, the traditional religion was prevalent from time immemorial. This religion encompassed every part of the Borana sociocultural sphere.

Theme 2: *Ayyaana* behave like human beings.	
Borana	**English**
Ayyaani sigara kad'ata	*Ayyaana* ask for cigarettes.
Ayyaani worra waan inni fed'u keenufi diidu himballessa	*Ayyaana* punish people who neglect to give their demands.
Ayyaani waan jed'e, "Abbani nama kana kokkottesse ananiti, ka qalbi isa jijjire duudda isa d'ukkubeselleni ananiti."	An *ayyaana* has said, "Am I not the one who paralyzed him, changed his mind, and made his back sick?"
Ayaani d'ufe nama keessa qubata	*Ayyaana* come to reside on people.
Fulani guddo dansa ka boqota ayyaana koba riimmee.	The best resting place for *ayyaana* is the anthill [*koba*].
Ayyaani ch'ireeyyi qajeelcha fula worri hundafi dame nama wollaanufi argatuutti.	*Ayyaana* direct the medicine people where to get roots and stems in treating patients.
⬇	
Sub-theme 1: Anthropomorphic descriptions of *ayyaana*.	
Sub-theme 2: Socialization of *ayyaana*.	

Ayyaana are anthropomorphized since they are believed to have some characteristics that resemble human beings. They can eat, drink, smoke, speak, listen, obey, and punish people. Since *ayyaana* are said to be invisible, they use the sensory organs of people to perform the behavioral acts mentioned above. These acts also illustrate that they are relational and that they socialize with people.

Relational Features of Ayyaana

Ayyaana can be emotive and are said to express their volition as well. They choose to be angry or happy. When their demands are not met, they feel neglected and thus cause trouble. They are not happy until their requests are met, at which point they cease troubling their victims. A binding relationship is then established between *ayyaana* and the afflicted person. This relationship is to be ongoing to ensure that the *ayyaana* are not neglected.

The result is the formation of a cult that comprises all the people who relate with *ayyaana* in such a way.

Articulating a Cultural Model of *Ayyaana*

Formation of the *Ayyaana* cult is a result of the conceptual knowledge possessed by the ordinary Borana Muslims concerning the spirit world. This is specifically how they conceptualize *ayyaana* as spirits within their Borana religiocultural spheres. Such knowledge is organized into mental representations that constitute the cultural model of *Ayyaana*. Figure 11 summarizes the essential features included in the cultural model of *Ayyaana*, which is based on the preceding analysis of the discourse provided through the ethnographic interviews I carried out.

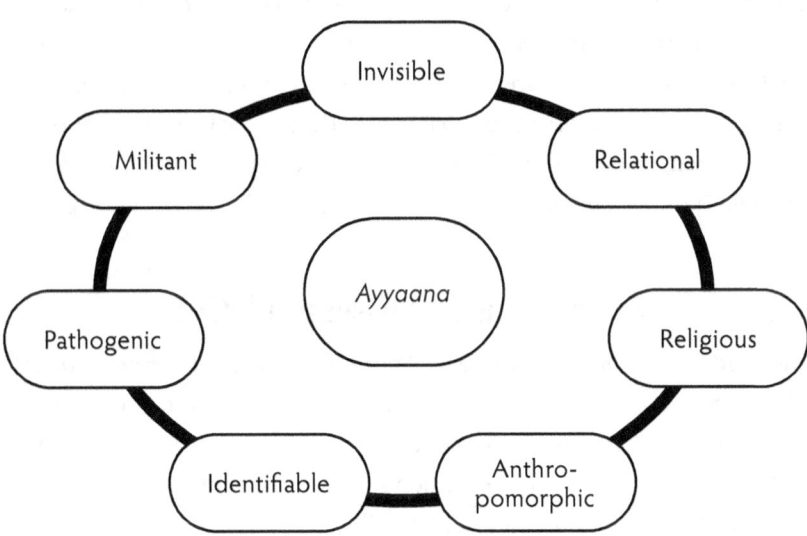

Figure 11: Diagrammatic representation of the religiocultural model of *Ayyaana*

The metaphorical expression of *ayyaana* as *qileensa Waaqa* (*afan Borana* for wind from God) illustrates their invisible character as well as their origin. It is important for the ordinary Borana Muslims to acknowledge that *ayyaana* originate from *Waaqa*, who sends them with a purpose. Another metaphor is used to illustrate how *ayyaana* are sent down. They come as an army, hence the militant motif that entails the usage of weapons. *Ayyaana* can also be pathogenic because they cause illness when they "catch" people. The relational traits are evident from their anthropomorphic character. They are identified by the specific names they have been given by the Borana Muslims who relate with them.

This religiocultural model of *Ayyaana* is intersubjectively shared by the ordinary Borana Muslims. The model is instantiated by individual members according to their frequent experiences with *ayyaana* or what others recount about their experiences. The individual experiences and knowledge are then embedded as mental representations in people's minds, which consequently form the individual schemas of *Ayyaana*. These individual schemas may not be exactly the same since the people cannot have identical experiences with *ayyaana*. However, there are salient idiosyncratic elements of the schemas that are shared among the Borana Muslims and that enable the formation of a cultural model of *Ayyaana*. This model is significant because it is used to "make sense of and interpret sensory input and also to produce and shape purposive and communicative behaviors."[60] The kind of behavior that results from the religiocultural model of *Ayyaana* then is exhibited through the *Ayyaana* "possession" cult.

Ayyaana as a "Possession" Cult

The word *possession* in English cannot be imposed on *afan Borana* to refer to what *ayyaana* do to people. I intentionally adopt the word my interviewees used instead of "possession." This is because my study is phenomenological and seeks to describe their perception in order to come up with a cultural model of *Ayyaana* that is as emic as possible.

The Borana expression used instead of "possession" by *ayyaana* was to be "caught" (*qaba*) by *ayyaana*.[61] When somebody has been "possessed" by *ayyaana*, Borana will say, "*Ayyaana qabat*" (literally: "He was caught/taken hold of by *ayyaana*").[62] The passive verb *qabat* means "to be taken hold of."

---

60. Bennardo and de Munck, *Cultural Models*, 3.

61. In *afan Borana*, the verb *horra* means, "to possess, be rich, increase, bear fruit, prosper." The word is used in a common expression to appreciate hospitality especially after a meal: *horra bula!* This means, "prosper and rest well!"

62. Demon possession in the Borana Bible, for example in Matthew 8:28, is translated *jiini qabu* (literally: "they have jinn").

This indicates that the person is not in control of the entrance of *ayyaana*. Yet, this does not imply that the *ayyaana* "possess" the person in the sense of ownership. I did not perceive such an assumption from my interviews. Instead, they said that *ayyaana* "caught" people and then entered them to cause an internal bodily discomfort, which resulted in sickness that eluded diagnosis at the health facilities available.

Thus, one of the symptoms that *ayyaana* had "caught" somebody was their having an ailment that defied medical attention. It was noted above that one of the reasons *ayyaana* "catch" people is that they are *dallana* (*afan Borana* for "angry") because of being neglected. If this anger is not averted, someone ends up suffering immensely, and many eventually die. Some of my interviewees recounted their frustrations when they would try to seek medical assistance in the health clinics and would not find any redress. When these patients eventually acknowledge that their ailments need non-medical attention, they take the necessary steps to pacify *ayyaana* in order to ensure peace.

Pacification of *Ayyaana*

Chapter 4 of this study showed that the accepted procedure for dealing with jinn in official Islam is exorcism. The Muslim teachers classifed *ayyaana* as jinn. They recommended "burning" jinn with the Qur'an as one of the main methods of exorcism. The ordinary Borana Muslims, especially those who participated in the cult, did not share this view. They did not classify *ayyaana* as jinn and thus did not believe they should be exorcised. The cultural model of *Ayyaana* according to the ordinary Borana Muslims directs them to accommodate *ayyaana* within their religiocultural context. The anthropomorphic and relational elements in that model enable the people to perceive *ayyaana* as beings that should be domesticated or tamed instead of being exorcised.

Domestication of *ayyaana* is done by the *warra ayyaana*, who are a section of the ordinary Borana Muslims in Saku and Moyale Subcounties.[63] These Muslims have been initiated into the cult and regularly perform the necessary activities to pacify *ayyaana*. There is also another group of ordinary Muslims

---

63. I use the term *domestication* here as a concept that explains how the ordinary Borana Muslims deal with *ayyaana*. Domestication is about taming *ayyaana* by pacifiying them with *darara* (*afan Borana*: gifts), which the *ayyaana* demand.

who prefer to call themselves *warra oblia* (*afan Borana*: people of *oblia*).⁶⁴ The latter meet together under the leadership of a *garib* (a prayer leader).⁶⁵ They refer to themselves as "Sufi followers" or "Sheikh Hussein followers."⁶⁶ These two groups illustrate the two types of sessions that encompass the domestication of *ayyaana*. Some *warra oblia* (people of *oblia*) I interviewed tried to distinguish themselves from the *warra ayyaana*. One of them insisted, "We do not serve things of *ayyaana*. Don't take us to the *abba* (the leader) of *ayyaana*. It is only that we love them, do not take us to the things of *ayyaana*."⁶⁷ Diid gave the following explanation about the *warra oblia*:

> People of *oblia* are people who follow the way of the Lord [*warra oblia warra khara rabi yau*]. They follow the way of the Lord and do not digress from that way. They speak only the truth and they do not have any lie in them. They are the ones who call on the Lord and he fulfills their prayers.⁶⁸

The *warra oblia* perceive themselves as "good" people who did not deviate from the Islamic way. The statements above show that they considered themselves to be religious in following the "way of the Lord," which is Islam. However, as I observed in Saku and Moyale Subcounties that there is a point of intersection between the *warra oblia* and the *warra ayyaana*. The former asserted that *ayyaana* is the "army of *oblia*." This confirmed the connection between the *warra oblia* and the *warra ayyaana* as presented in figure 12.

---

64. It was mentioned before that *oblia* was used to refer to a type of "angel" associated with Sufism in Marsabit County.

65. The word *garib* (an Arabic or Persian name) has been adopted by Borana Muslim as a title for the leaders of *warra ayyaana*.

66. I include, here, a brief note on *warra oblia* because I found it interesting when they tried to distance themselves from *ayyaana*, and yet my observation showed otherwise. From the minutes of a meeting they held in March 2016, there was nowhere they referred to themselves as *warra ayyaana*. Yet, when I inquired from other members of the communities in Saku and Moyale Subcounties, they all agreed that *warra oblia* and *warra ayyaana* were the same.

67. Qumbo, March 10, 2017.

68. Diid, March 19, 2017.

Religiocultural Model of *Ayyaana* According to Ordinary Borana Muslims

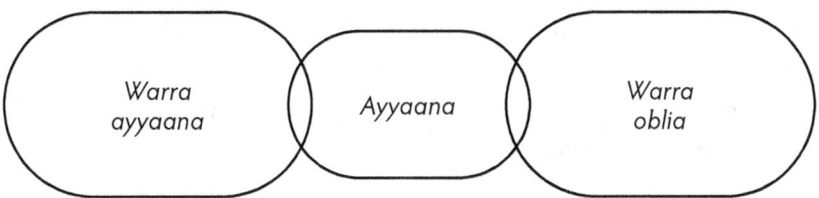

Figure 12: Intersection point between *warra ayyaana* and *warra oblia*

Ayyaana play a vital role in the lives of both the *warra oblia* and the *warra ayyaana*. During one of the interview sessions with *warra oblia*, two of them became uncomfortable and asked for perfume. When I asked the reason for this, I was told, "Their *ayyaana* are trying to manifest because of being mentioned." Furthermore, I identified some people who said they were *warra oblia* and yet participated in the *ayyaana* healing sessions that I attended. Eyewitnesses who were neither *warra ayyaana* nor *warra oblia* but knew about the cult and its participants affirmed this. This made me realize there are two different subdomains within the *ayyaana* domain in Marsabit: the subdomain of intercessory *ṣalawāt* prayer and the healing subdomain for patients of *ayyaana*-related ailments.

Subdomain of Intercessory *Ṣalawāt* Prayer

The *warra oblia* are "people of prayer," according to Jillo, one of their leaders who summarized their activities in the following sentences.

> The world of *oblia* people is to bless, pray, and fast. We pray for the government, the president, national flag, the educated people, peace, and others. We do not feed *ayyaana*, but we pray for anyone possessed to be healed. Those contesting in the election come and tell us to pray for them. They bring an animal and rice for celebration and we bless [*afan Borana: ebisa*] them.[69]

Ṣalawāt is an Arabic word for "prayer." It can have various meanings depending on who is using the word.[70] For the *warra ayyaana* in Marsabit, *salawat* stands for the regular prayers performed to invoke *ebba* (*afan Borana*

---

69. Jillo, March 11, 2017.
70. *Ṣalawāt* is the plural form of *ṣalāt*. It also means "salutation" or "greetings" (see Surah 33:56; 2:157, etc.).

for "blessings") from God.[71] These prayers differ from the obligatory Islamic prayers. *Salawat* prayers are equivalent to the Islamic supplication prayers called *du ʿā ʾ* in Arabic. I attended several sessions in both Saku and Moyale Subcounties, as shown in table 11.

Table 11: Participant Observation Schedules of *Salawat* Sessions

Site of observation	Subcounty	Leader (Male or female)	Event	Time
Site A: *Darga*	Outskirts of Marsabit Town, Saku	Male	*Salawat* session	9 p.m.–4 a.m.
Site B: *Darga*	Outskirts of Marsabit Town	–	*Salawat* session	4 p.m.
Site B: Participant's house (indoors)	Outskirts of Moyale Town	Male	*Salawat* session	Nighttime
Site C: Participant's home (indoors/outdoors)	Outskirts of Moyale Town	Male	*Salawat/ Muuda*	Daytime
Site D: Outdoors	Outskirts of Moyale Town	Female	*Salawat* session	Daytime

The *salawat* sessions are not restricted to a particular space. They are either held in a *darga* or in a participant's house. A *darga* is a place designated for ritual activities by the *warra oblia* and *warra ayyaana*.[72] It is primarily a "treatment place," but prayers were also held, as Chuqule acknowledged concerning her *darga*.[73] Fatuma also consented that the kind of prayers held at the *darga* included the *dhikr*-type that began by praising the Prophet, for instance: "*Muhamadi, Muhamadi . . . asalam aleikum, salam ala, rasul lalahi asalam*" ("Muhammad, Muhammad . . . peace to you, peace Prophet of the

---

71. Henceforth, I use the Boranized word *salawat* instead of the Arabic *Ṣalawāt*.

72. *Dargah* is a Persian (and Urdu) name that refers to a shrine built over a grave of a revered Sufi leader. Devotees often visit such *dargahs* for pilgrimages. *Warra oblia* and *warra ayyaana* have adopted the word *darga* to designate their special places for ritual activities. To my knowledge, these were not graves of Sufi leaders. Each *darga* was called the name of the current leader. For example, *darga* Garib Jillo was led by Garib Jillo.

73. Chuqule, August 24, 2016.

Lord, peace").⁷⁴ I attended a *salawat* prayer session in one of the *dargas* and heard the *dhikr* songs mentioning Sheikh Hussein. The other *dua* prayers were directed to God, who was invoked as Rabb or Allah. The traditional Borana name for God, *Waaqa*, was not frequently used like the Islamic titles during the *salawat* prayers.

There was always a break during the prayer sessions, during which popcorn and coffee were served to all the participants. I observed that the leader of the prayers first threw the popcorn to the ground before distributing to people present. The snacks seemed to rejuvenate the participants and prepare them for a rigorous time of clapping and singing with rhythmic drumming.⁷⁵

Salawat prayers are performed in people's houses as well as outdoors in open places. I observed a session that was held next to a water well. There were about eight women, three men, and several children between the ages of four and fourteen. The purpose of this *salawat* session was to pacify an angry *ayyaana* that had been neglected and had made four goats fall inside the well. The interpretation was that that particular *ayyaana* was thirsty for blood and hence the death of the goats.⁷⁶ Further negligence would result in more deaths. To curb this, there was need to offer prayers and acknowledge the *ayyaana* by singing and offering the usual *darara* (gifts) like coffee, popcorn, and khat (*miraa*). A middle-aged woman who led the prayers also served the popcorn and coffee. I was informed that the presence of *ayyaana* was acknowledged by throwing popcorn to the ground before distributing it to participants. Everyone was seated on mats laid on the ground. Women and children sat together with the men. The singing and praying were done while seated. Only the elderly women who had back or leg problems were allowed to sit on chairs. This kind of sitting arrangement wass common across all the sessions I observed.

Something else that drew my attention during the sessions was the show of brotherhood displayed. I noticed that the participants shook each other's hands in a different way from what I knew as the conventional way of greeting. They took the right hand of the person next to them and kissed the palm.

---

74. Fatuma, July 21, 2016.

75. These singing and clapping sessions are called *hadhara* and will be explained later. They are also a significant part of the *salawat* prayers.

76. *Ayyaana* do not have to catch a person to display their anger. This case shows that the goats were the victims of their anger.

Every participant then went around the room greeting somebody else. This was neither a traditional nor an Islamic way of greeting.[77] When I inquired what that meant, I was told it was a sign of unity and love within the group.

Analyzing the *Salawat* Prayer Sessions

The *salawat* sessions has both Islamic and traditional Borana features. The Islamic features included Islamic greetings, the use of Islamic phrases, references to Prophet Muhammad, mentions of Allah, and recounts of Prophet Moses's plea for a reduced number of prayers.

Table 12: Islamic Features in *Salawat* Sessions

Islamic features in *salawat* sessions	Specific references of the Islamic features
Islamic greetings (in Arabic)	*Asalam aleykum*
Islamic phrases (in Arabic)	*Bismi llāhi* (In the name of God) *Al-ḥamdu li-llāhi* (Praise belongs to God) *Allāhu akbar* (God is greater)
Reference to Prophet Muhammad	Frequent mention by the *salawat* session leader of the prophet as *Rasuallah*
Islamic name for God	Addressing God as Allāh or Rabb
Prophet Musa's plea	Practitioner Jillo recounted Moses's plea to God to reduce the fifty times of prayers to five
Islamic dressing for women	All the women were veiled during the session[78]

Table 12 lists the elements that gave the *salawat* sessions an Islamic outlook. There was no mention of worship to other gods. There was a conspicuous reference to God as Allah and that he alone is to be worshipped. Prophet Muhammad was also highly respected as the prophet of Allah. This made the *warra ayyaana* / *warra oblia* authenticate themselves as Muslims who adhered to the *shahada*, the first pillar of Islam.

---

77. The Bajuni Muslims along the Coast of Kenya have a similar form of greeting. The younger children and youth greet older people by kissing the palm of their right hand as a sign of respect.

78. Traditionally, Borana women are not required to veil their heads. Since the inception of Islam, Muslim women in Marsabit have accepted the veil as normative.

A few un-Islamic elements were manifested in the *salawat* sessions. A prominent one was the intermingling of men and women in the same place of prayer. This did not seem to be a problem to the participants as I observed. The kissing of the hands in greetings was not restricted to the same gender either. Apart from Prophet Muhammad, there were many references to Sheikh Hussein during the prayers and *dhikr* chanting/singing. An example of this veneration is evident in the following statement in *afan Borana* made by practitioner Jillo who was leading a *salawat* session I attended in Moyale: "*Waan jalanu ka Shekana Husseini ira ebiti nu ha duftu, robale kha rabi nuu nagaan dikrian*" (What we love is blessings from Sheikh Hussein, rain from the Lord and that we pray in peace).[79]

Apart from the elements borrowed from Islam, some other traditional ones have become part of the *salawat* prayer sessions. These include the use of traditional Borana items and rituals. It has been mentioned that participants of the prayer sessions drink coffee and eat popcorn. This coffee is prepared in a traditional coffee frying ceremony called *buna qala* (*afan Borana* for "Sacrifice of coffee"). It is an important ritual that has been transmitted from one generation to the other. Aguilar Mario explains that the *buna qala* is a ritualized way, which the Waso Borana use to remember their traditional and historical roots.[80] Similarly, the Marsabit Borana people try to maintain the traditional heritage through the *buna qala* ceremony. The *warra oblia* and the *warra ayyaana* equally respect their cultural heritage by performing the ceremony. They fry *bunna* (dry coffee berries) with cooking oil in a special pan (*afan Borana*: *qorii*).[81] Once it is ready, it is cooled and passed from one participant to the other during the *salawat* sessions.

The Subdomain of Healing: Therapeutic Sessions

Apart from performing the *salawat* sessions, the *warra oblia* I interviewed also admitted that they "have a cure for diseases and those possessed by evil spirits through animal sacrifices and the sacrifice of fried coffee berries. However, this is hidden knowledge from others," according to the minutes of a meeting

---

79. Jillo, March 11, 2017.
80. Aguilar, "Current Religious Practices," 241.
81. *Qorii* is the Borana name for the wooden bowl used to serve fried coffee. Every Borana household is expected to have one.

held in March 2016 by "Sufi followers" in Moyale. The ambiguity evident in the above statements is summarized in the phrase "hidden knowledge from others." The evil spirits referred to in the quote above are not identified. The reader is thus bound to question whether this referred to jinn or *ayyaana*. Another difficulty arises when one considers the inclusion of "animal sacrifice" in the process of "cure." This procedure does not allude to the exorcism advocated by the Muslim teachers (see chapter 4). It points to the pacification of *ayyaana* as explained by *warra ayyaana* during the interviews. Adho, a practitioner in Saku, described the general sequence of the healing process:

> When a person falls sick from *ayyaana*, you will not recognize it until the sick person is brought to the session and the *ayyaana* in another person will say he caused him sickness and then demands something. Once the *ayyaana* gets the demand, the person gets well. You will take the person to every doctor but finally they bring him and they beat the drums. So when a person is sick with *ayyaana* if he hasn't said his demands, somebody cannot be healed.[82]

The above excerpt presents a sub-model of healing within the cultural model of *Ayyaana*. Germs, parasites, or ther microorganisms do not cause disease as explained in the bio-medical context. It is therefore futile to seek treatment from facilities that use such an outlook. The religiocultural model of *Ayyaana* includes the pathogenic component of *ayyaana*. The *Ayyaana* practitioners affirm diagnosis and the necessary steps are taken to pacify the causative *ayyaana*. Once this process is initiated, the patient is obligated to sustain a pacification relationship that may last for a lifetime. Hence, there is a recursive process that has been summarized in Figure 13.

---

82. Adho, April 13, 2016.

Religiocultural Model of *Ayyaana* According to Ordinary Borana Muslims 165

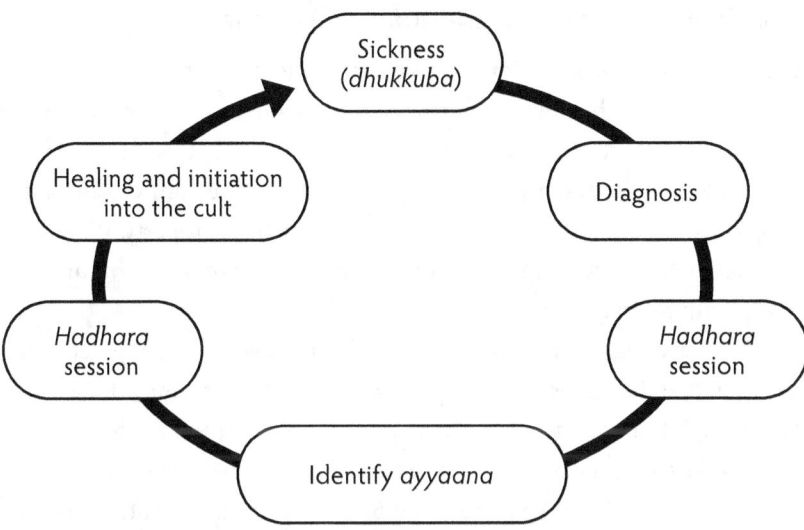

Figure 13: **Episodic sub-model of healing in the *Ayyaana* cult**

Diagnosis of Dhukkuba *(Sickness)*

The healing process involves various stages and is initiated by the diagnosis of a disease. The patient is first taken to an *Ayyaana* practitioner who determines that the causative agent is an irate *ayyaana*. I was not able to ascertain the percentage of Borana Muslims who sought this advice from practitioners of *Ayyaana* against those who went to the medical facilities available in the county when they fell sick. A number of Borana people do not attend these facilities. They prefer to seek the advice of local practitioners. This is because of the schema evoked by the concept of *dhukkuba* (*afan Borana* for "sickness"), which also explains causality.[83] The shared cultural model of *Ayyaana* by the *warra ayyaana* enables them to construe that the cause of most *dhukubba* is *ayyaana* that need to be appeased. Thus, the initial step is to visit an *Ayyaana* practitioner who affirms the diagnosis.

---

83. Various spellings are used for the Borana word for sickness. For instance, Stroomer uses *d'ukuba*. See Stroomer, *Grammar of Boraana Oromo*, 171. I follow Leus and Salvadori's spelling, *dhukkuba*. See Leus and Salvadori, *Aadaa Boraanaa*.

First Hadhara *Session: Identification of* Ayyaana

After diagnosis, the practitioners advise the patients to prepare for the first *hadhara* session. The purpose of this initial session is to create a favorable atmosphere that would make the troubled *ayyaana* talk. It is imperative for *ayyaana* to identify themselves during the sessions. The family of the ailing person is required to organize *hadhara* sessions on their property. When they are ready with the items required, they invite the rest of the *warra ayyaana* to help with the clapping.

On the evening of the day of the first *hadhara* session, the practitioner arrives first and ensures that everything is ready. If there are animals to be slaughtered, the practitioner selects the parts of meat to be offered to the *ayyaana*. The sessions begin late in the evening and involve beating the *dibe* (*afan Borana* for "drum"), vigorous clapping, singing, and chanting in praise of Sheikh Hussein, Prophet Muhammad, and Bale, the place of pilgrimage.[84] Galma affirmed that the *dibe* made the *sirba* (*afan Borana* for "songs") more lively and attractive (*afan Borana: diben sirbum owiftiini*) to *ayyaana* in order to make them speak (*afan Borana: hoja sirbi sun owe ayyaanai dubachu jal qabarta*).[85] The *hadhara* lasts the whole night with various activities in addition to the singing. Prolonged *hadhara* sessions are interspersed with the drinking of black coffee, which is served while participants sit on the mats strewn on the floor. *Miraa* (khat) is also provided for everyone, presumably to keep people awake throughout the night. Men and women sit together as they sip coffee and chew *miraa*. Another session of drumming and clapping proceeds until the practitioner senses that the *ayyaana* in the patient is pacified and is ready to talk.

The most anticipated moment is usually when the practitioner converses with the *ayyaana*. People wait with bated breath to see if *ayyaana* are pleased with the *hadhara* and are willing to speak. *Ayyaana* speak through the mouth of the patient and converse with the practitioner. They start with the Islamic greetings, and the practitioner then pleads with them to identify themselves as well as their demands, which are met in a second *hadhara* session. (See

---

84. I attended daytime *hadhara* sessions in both Saku and Moyale. Basically, the procedures would be similar to those of evening *hadhara* sessions.

85. Galma, August 18, 2016.

appendix 4 for an excerpt of a conversation I listened to between a practitioner and *ayyaana*.)

Second *Hadhara* Session

A second *hadhara* session is organized on a different day after the *qaal* (the demands) of the *ayyaana* are available. The purpose of this session is to present the *qaal* to the *ayyaana*. Every *ayyaana* demands different types of *qaal*, and that is why the first *hadhara* session is important in order to know the specific requirement for a specific *ayyaana*. I attended a session where the *ayyaana* had asked for blood and meat. The head of the home slaughtered a *korma* (*afan Borana* for "he-goat"), and the practitioner selected the specific parts of meat as required by the *ayyaana*. Blood was poured into a shallow hole on the ground, and the *ayyaana* were invited to drink. They did this through the patient, who knelt and licked the blood until satisfied. Other *ayyaana* that craved blood also got their share through their respective "hosts."

Other food items included in *qaal* are *qursi* (*afan Borana* for popcorn) and *bunna* (*afan Borana* for coffee), which should always be available during the *hadhara* sessions. These are also given to *ayyaana* through the patient. The popcorn is usually thrown around the room procedurally from right to left and not vice versa, as practitioner Diid explained. He further cautioned that anyone who ate the popcorn before it was given to the *ayyaana* would be punished by death since he or she "had eaten the top layer of *abaye* (father, referring to *ayyaana*)."

Apart from eating food, *ayyaana* also delight in sweet scents. All the *hadhara* sessions must have *lubadini* (frankincense) fumigating the place to attract the *ayyaana*. Some *ayyaana* also requested to literally drink a particular kind of perfume. Gudrun Dahl examined the *Ayyaana* "possession" cult among the Waso Borana in Isiolo District (now Isiolo County), and he attests that there is generous use of frankincense at these sessions, which promotes hyperventilation and trance.[86]

Healing and Initiation into the Cult

The *Ayyaana* release the patients after accepting the *qaal* (demands), and the ailing person is supposed to start recovering. The healing period can be

---

86. Dahl, "Possession as Cure," 157.

either immediate or prolonged. Some patients continue to take traditional medicine that the *ayyaana* directed the practitioners to give.

Healing, according to the practitioners I interviewed, was guaranteed. Sickness that defied the medical management had been treated during the *hadhara* sessions. Practitioner Diid affirmed, "Things that cannot be treated at the hospital are all treated here, including a mad man [*maraataa*] who was tied with ropes. All human problems, including major ones." With such a glowing testimony of successful treatment, word goes around the village, its vicinity, and beyond. This increases the salience of the model of healing and hence the popularity of the *Ayyaana* cult. Diid revealed that he had treated people from as far as, "Uganda, Sudan, Mombasa, Somalia, and many other places and they have recovered . . ." He continued,

> I have not put any signpost to tell people that I am a medicine-man [*chi'ressa*]. I do not call people or write anywhere on my house. The place from where the sick people who get healed come from, they go and tell others and they come. People come for the sake of their soul [*lubbu*].[87]

This statement from Diid shows the confidence the practitioners had in their ability to deal with *ayyaana*-inflicted problems. It gave them have a following that is begrudged by the Muslim teachers. In the practitioners' homes and the *darga* (healing places) that I visited, I always found people resting within the compound. Some were on treatment for a number of days, while others went there to have a time of tranquility. That was probably the reason Diid mentioned that people went there "for the sake of their soul [*lubbu*]. That is why they come from all over."

Summary

The overall intention of this chapter was to describe the religiocultural model of *Ayyaana* as derived from the cognition of the ordinary Borana Muslims in Marsabit County. I used linguistic tools to analyze the discourses. I began with a key word analysis of the term *ayyaana* and showed that it is polysemous in the view of the ordinary Borana Muslims who participate in the

---

87. Diid, March 9, 2017.

cultic activities. The sentence-level analysis included identification of some key conceptual metaphors used to denote *ayyaana* and which displayed the creativity of the *warra ayyaana*.

Further domain analysis of *ayyaana* revealed the anthropomorphic attribution of *ayyaana* that consequently led to their personification by the *warra ayyaana*. This anthropomorphism is a major component of the religiocultural model of *Ayyaana* and the ensuing possession cult. I have described the two sub-domains of the *Ayyaana* cult – *salawat* prayers and the healing sessions – both intended to pacify *ayyaana* and hence ensure a peaceful life. The following chapter continues the analytical description of how the *warra ayyaana* articulate this theme of *nagaa* (*afan Borana* for "peace") as they instantiate the religiocultural model of *Ayyaana*.

CHAPTER 6

Lived Experiences as Instantiation of Religiocultural Model

Introduction

The previous chapter gave an analytical description of the religiocultural model of *Ayyaana* as construed by the ordinary Borana Muslims in Marsabit County. A major component of the model is the way *ayyaana* are anthropomorphized. This is one of the factors that make the *warra ayyaana* foreground the model of *Ayyaana* and background the Islamic model of jinn. Socialization of *ayyaana* then becomes inevitable as people experience *ayyaana* within the cultic context.

In this chapter, I examine these experiences as instantiations of the religiocultural model. I illustrate how a dynamic relationship ensues between the experiences of *warra ayyaana* and the construction of the religiocultural model of *Ayyaana*. The model is informed by the kind of experiences *warra ayyaana* have with *ayyaana*. The foundational model then informs the kind of experiential behaviors exhibited by *warra ayyaana*. Hence, a recursive dynamism results that is enhanced by other symbolic expressions, like tangible items and cultic songs.

Dynamism of the *Ayyaana* Model and Lived Experiences

The model of *Ayyaana* has a higher degree of salience than the Islamic model of jinn. This makes *warraa ayyaana* instantiate the former more within their contextual framework. Instantiation initially occurs at the individual level as people experience *ayyaana* in personal ways. Hence, it was expedient to interview individual participants instead of using focus group interviews. It is the intersubjective sharing of these experiences that contributes to constitution of the religiocultural model described in the preceeding chapter. Such a model is further enhanced and developed as *warra ayyaana* continue to experience *ayyaana* in their daily lives. The people also assign relevance to the model of *Ayyaana* as they continue to find explanations to their quotidian issues. Thus, there is a recurring cycle between the lived experiences and the religiocultural model of *Ayyaana* as displayed in the figure below.

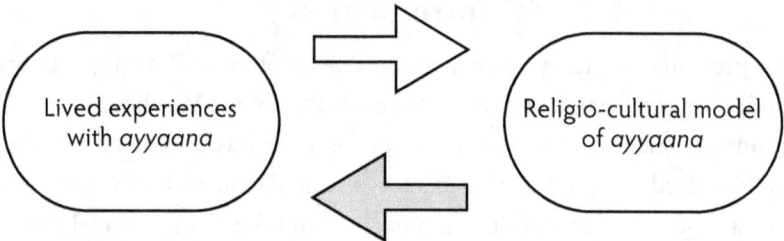

Figure 14: Dynamic relationship between lived experiences and the *Ayyaana* model

In discussing how the ordinary Borana Muslims instantiate the religiocultural model of *Ayyaana*, I examine the ritual experiences of both the practitioners and ordinary participants of the cult. It is expedient to analyze these experiences because they are significant in the formulation of the mental models. These individual models that are shared among the ordinary Borana Muslims consequently become the religiocultural model described in chapter 5. The dynamic interplay between the ritual experiences and the religiocultural model is further enhanced by the music and artifacts used during the cultic sessions. Hence, I will discuss the use of songs and items in the later part of this chapter.

Ritual Experiences of *Ayyaana* Practitioners

Bradd Shore states that rituals tend to conventionalize memory and hence lead to mental models or schemas that become shared as cultural models. Even if cognitive homogeneity cannot be fully achieved, rituals have a tendency to make experiences overlap and hence induce the formation of cultural models.[1] Shore's assertion is quite valid in the context of the religiocultural model of *Ayyaana*. Frequent participation in the cultic sessions conventionalizes the conceptual knowledge of the participants who eventually construct mental models that are shared within the group.

I have chosen three main thematic areas that I consider notable in describing the religiocultural model of *Ayyaana*, namely, the participation of female practitioners, the initiation experiences of practitioners, and the benefits they accrue from participation.

I interviewed fourteen practitioners from both Saku and Moyale Subcounties.[2] Six of them were female and held different leadership positions within their respective groups. Eight of the practitioners were from Saku, while six were from Moyale Subcounty. All the practitioners said they were Muslims who tried to adhere to the requirements of Islam.

Experiences of Female Practitioners in the *Ayyaana* Cult

The individual experiences of female practitioners contribute immensely to the construction of the religiocultural model of *Ayyaana* by *warra ayyaana* in both Moyale and Saku Subcounties. *Ayyaana* do not discriminate against gender. In both places, the female practitioners are esteemed as highly as their male counterparts. The former are allowed to lead *salawat* prayers as well as *Ayyaana* healing sessions. This is a significant point of departure from the Islamic structural organization that does not allow women to lead prayers in the presence of men. The story of Nureah epitomizes the experience of female practitioners as accepted leaders in the ritual circles.

---

1. Shore, *Culture in Mind*, 48.

2. One of the male practitioners in Saku Subcounty succumbed to illness several months after I interviewed him.

Nureah's Vignette

Nureah grew up watching her parents participate in the ritual leadership of *Ayyaana* healing sessions. They had the ritual titles *abba sera* (father of laws) and *hadha sera* (mother of laws).[3] Nureah was therefore aware of *ayyaana* since her childhood as she says, "Since I was a child I knew this thing and I inherited it [from my parents]." She participated in the annual sessions her father held as demanded by his *ayyaana*. Nureah was inducted into the cult as a novice practitioner as she recounted in the following conversation.

Nureah: Mine is not the *ayyaana* that comes to speak. There are *ayyaana* that speak. When the *ayyana* come, I am the one who feeds them. My *ayyaana* comes that time also. I have known these things since I was a child. I am now 45 years old. My father is *abba sera*. My mother is *hadha sera*.

Interviewer: Are there no people who call you here for any help?

Nureah: I do not have permission, and I have not matured enough to do the rituals. My mother is the one who can do it.

Interviewer: How do you start the sessions when your father comes in April, and how does it end?

Nureah (explaining how they slaughter a sheep and goat): I am the one who prepares all these things or supervises with instructions. When they are ready, the *ayyaana* is then called. The *ayyaana* in my father comes, and I then give him a small portion of the food. When the *ayyaana* people have washed their hands, I place the meat and *qita* [bread] as small pieces in their hands.

Interviewer: Do you like this?

Nureah: Since I was born I have known it and I like it. I do not see any wrong.

Interviewer: Are you a Christian or a Muslim?

Nureah: A Muslim.

Interviewer: What makes you a Muslim?

Nureah: I pray. I try to pray, as often as I can though I sometimes do not. I fast during month of Ramadan. I give [alms] to poor people.

Interviewer: How do you pass it on to your children?

---

3. The titles *abba sera* (father of laws) and *hadha sera* (mother of laws) are common traditional titles given to esteemed leaders (especially to men) who ensure the customary laws are kept. *Warra ayyaana* adapted the titles and included women leaders.

Nureah: They do not know. I do it with my father, maybe one day I will be given the permission to pass it to my children. For now I see myself as a *raaga* [prophet]. When something comes to me or somebody I usually know.[4]

The above excerpt from the interview with Nureah presents three considerations that were common among the female practitioners I interviewed:

1. Female practitioners as Muslims: Nureah did not hesitate to state her religious affiliation. Neither did the other female practitioners I interviewed. All of them acknowledged they were Muslims. One of them had a small room behind her shop that served as her regular prayer place.
2. Acceptance by men practitioners and community: Nureah's father, a lead practitioner, recognized her position as a novice *murraa* and was training her. The other female practitioners were similarly accepted as leaders and allowed to lead both *salawat* and healing sessions in the presence of men.
3. Elevated self-esteem: Nureah is employed by a local orgarnization as a social/community worker. This did not give her as much esteem as her position as a *murraa*. Nureah and the other female practitioners perceived themselves as *raaga* (prophets).[5] Leus and Salvadori assert that this was an "extremely important" position, mostly inherited and held by men.[6] Nureah and the other female practitioners were aware of this, yet they did not hesitate to regard themselves as prophets.

The raised self-esteem of women practitioners gives salience to the religiocultural model of *Ayyaana*. In a religiocultural context that allocates a lower status to women, the elevated position accorded to them in the *Ayyaana* cult is significant. This, however, does not submit to Lewis's deprivation theory.[7]

---

4. Nureah, July 18, 2016.

5. Nureah, July 18, 2016; Adho, April 13, 2016; and Chuqule, August 24, 2016. *Raaga* is the Borana name for a prophet, a seer, or a person of God. See Leus and Salvadori, *Aadaa Boraannaa*, 550.

6. Leus and Salvadori, 550.

7. Lewis, Ecstatic Religion; Lewis,"Exorcism and Male Control of Religious Experience"; and Lewis, *Religion in Context*. Lewis proposed the famous deprivation theory to explain why women are predominant in spirit possession cults. His assertion is that women participate in peripheral cults as a reaction against oppression or societal deprivation.

Women are still predominant in the *Ayyaana* cult. Yet their involvement is not because they find redress in a deprived context. The increased participation of women in the *Ayyaana* cult is because they find significance in participating in religious matters. This makes them construct (unconsciously) a religio-cultural model that helps them make sense of their sensory input according to their supernaturalistc context. Their initiation as practitioners into the *Ayyaana* cult is congruent with the experiences of their male counterparts.

Initiation Experiences of Practitioners

Induction of practitioners into the *Ayyaana* cult has been conventionalized and is part of the conceptual knowledge that is eventually organized into the religiocultural model. It is accepted by participants that induction into the *Ayyaana* cult as a practitioner is either by inheritance or after an illness that defies hospital remedies. A few of the practitioners I interviewed inherited the practice from their parents or relatives. Nureah, whose story was highlighted above, was apprenticed to her position by her parents. Dabasso also mentioned that he was "blessed" by his father to continue his lineage as a practitioner.[8]

Other practitioners experienced a distressing situation prior to their engagement as leaders in the *Ayyaana* cult. Nureah narrated how her father, before he became a practitioner, experienced "odd things like trying to throw himself into fire."[9] Diid was a popular practitioner who described how he was initiated into the cult. He went through a difficult childhood with the demise of his parents. An *Ayyaana* practitioner adopted him as his child and inducted him into the cult.[10]

A number of the practitioners experienced inexplicable ailments that defied hospital remedies, as the example of Adho illustrates. She recounted how she once fell critically ill and was taken to a hospital. She was diagnosed with tuberculosis. The sixty injections she was given did not improve her condition. She was discharged from the hospital, and a *hadhara* session was held. She was healed and became a practitioner. Adho's father was similarly inducted into the cult after an illness. Adho narrated his story as follows:

---

8. Dabasso, Personal interview by author.
9. Nureah, August 1, 2016.
10. Diid, March 9, 2017.

Before my father got the *ayyaana* ... he fell sick and was unable to urinate. He was taken to various hospitals including Meru and Sololo. Instead of getting better he was getting worse. They took him back home and held a *hadhara* session where the *ayyaana* said, "*Abbaa maati* [father of many], I am Odha who caused this sickness." The old man was healed after that. He joined the other people and even became their leader.[11]

The above accounts raise a question: Do the practitioners join the cult involuntarily or out of their own volition? Like the shamans discussed by Kim, the *Ayyaana* practitioners' calling into the profession differs from that of the ordinary priestly calling of the *qallu* (Borana priests).[12] The latter do not go through initial sickness even though the office was heritable. The aspect of involuntariness was more evident with *Ayyaana* practitioners than with the *qallu*. Yet this did not diminish the significance of the model of *Ayyaana* in the cognition of participants of the cult. This can be attributed to the benefits they get through the ability to control *ayyaana*.

Positive Perception: Benefits of Being a Practitioner

All the practitioners I interviewed admitted they had benefited by participating in the *Ayyaana* cult in various ways. They mentioned economic, societal, spiritual, and psychological benefits. Adho affirmed:

Ayyaana has no problem. I have no harm with him. He has brought wealth and no harm. He has made me a *chi'ressa* [traditional doctor]. I treat people, and when they get well, they bring me a lot of money or gifts. I have nine children, and a lot of cattle while having it. This is *qilenssa rabbi* [the breath/wind from God] that he has brought to me . . . He [the *ayyaana*] speaks to me even telling me when a person will die. Even my son died while *ayyaana* was telling me that he was dying. Odha said, "*Nati ejeese* [I killed him]." The greatest profit is that the *ayyaana* has made me to be a prophet [*raaga*]. Even when misfortune comes, for instance the death of someone, I am told in advance

---

11. Adho, April 13, 2016.
12. Kim, *Islam Among the Swahili in East Africa*, 123–48.

that so and so would die, and this is what would happen... He [the *ayyaana*] also protects me against sickness. He directs me to drink or directs me to get traditional medicine.[13]

Adho stated that her greatest gain from what she did as a practitioner was the recognition she received as a *raaga* (*afan Borana* for "prophet"). Economic profits were secondary to Adho. She was not the only female practitioner to acknowledge this societal respect. A prophet was – and still is – an esteemed person in traditional Borana society. This raises the self-image of these women in a patriarchal society. Furthermore, whereas Islam does not allow women to teach or minister to men in public, *Ayyaana* provides a space where Muslim men recognize and respect the female practitioners.

Another significant benefit of the *Ayyaana* cult according to the practitioners was that it provided an avenue for improving the *nagaa* (well-being) of the people. Many of the *Ayyaana* practitioners serve as *ch'iressa* (*afan Borana* for traditional medicine healers). They treat myriads of people, who have found a remedy for the maladies that afflicted them. The practitioners also revealed that *ayyaana* direct them to the medicine they administer to their patients. Chuqule narrated how she has served as a medicine woman in Moyale Subcounty. She said that in a day she receives at least ten patients. I asked her about her experience in treating so many people daily. This was her confession:

> I get very tired; people come to me as if I am God. And because these are Borana, I have to treat them. This thing has given me headache. All those people who are staying [at the *darga* outside my house] even now are all mad people waiting to be treated. Others have problems with the bones, others with their stomach. I get tired. But I am also happy when people feel well after treatment.[14]

Chuqule's mixed feelings about her practice show that the *warra ayyaana* prioritize the religiocultural model of *Ayyaana*. The work of the practitioners is overwhelming, yet empathy for the welfare of their fellow Borana people motivates Chuqule and her fellow practitioners. Others, like Dabasso,

---

13. Adho, April 13, 2016.
14. Chuqule, August 24, 2016.

resigned from formal employment and ventured fully as *Ayyaana* practitioners because of the significance they place on the concept of *ayyaana*.

Diid narrated how he had benefited immensely from *ayyaana*. He remembered his humble background as a "poor orphan." *Ayyaana* raised his status in the community. He described his participation as a *karama* (Kiswahili for "gift") that accorded him *gara gandidu* (*afan Borana* for "great favor") among his people. The phrase *gara gandidu* in *afan Borana* is a "strong word" that refers to an exceptional favor that supersedes the normal blessings. It is used to signify someone whose socioeconomic status has been raised significantly. Diid perceived himself as an example of a *gara gandidu*. He described how he had been uplifted as follows:

> [I was] a poor person without a clan or relatives. I was not known anywhere. Until I knew the secret of [*ayyaana*] and people from all over cut the trees and come to me. Even this it is God who has given me, so I can give to people.[15]

Practitioner Jillo is visually impaired. I listened and observed how he led the *salawat* and *hadhara* sessions. He seemed to be well respected according to the title people gave him. He is fondly addressed as Abba Jillo (Father Jillo).[16] This was also evident from what I observed when I went to interview Abba Galma (Father Galma), as people fondly addressed him. Galma was a popular practitioner who had "climbed the ladder" from a novice practitioner to a leader of all the practitioners in Saku Subcounty.[17] I was informed that he owned a lot of livestock. Most of these were gifts that people gave him after recovering from *ayyaana*-afflicted ailments and other ailments. He said his greatest joy, as a practitioner of *Ayyaana*, was that more Borana people had embraced Islam. His continual approval of *ayyaana* was also evident when he mentioned how people got healed of various diseases including some that had defied the hospital medicine.

The *salawat* prayers by the *warra oblia* were intercessory and not merely recitation. These prayers were directed to God, whom they called *Rabbi*

---

15. Diid, March 9, 2017.

16. I was present when Abba Jillo quelled the anger of a woman who threatened to start a physical fight. He spoke very calmly, and the woman listened and quieted down.

17. Galma died a few months after my interview with him. He was sick during the interview and did not recover.

(Arabic for "Lord"), although the *warra ayyaana* attribute some interventions to *ayyaana*. Nurea, for instance, said that her father was once dismissed from his work place but that "*ayyaana* helped and he was reinstated to work after one month. *Ayyaana* helped to return him back and he had to perform a *jilla* (ceremony) to appreciate the help from *ayyaana*." I, however, observed that during the *salawat* prayers the power of God was invoked more than that of *ayyaana*. The contents of the prayers varied. They sought divine intervention for adverse weather, the political goodwill of the nation and Africa at large, peace among the Borana people, etc.[18] Politicians also recognized the prayers by *warra oblia* / *ayyaana* people. In both Saku and Moyale Subcounties, prominent politicians requested prayers in order to succeed in the general elections held in 2017. Some were successful, and others were not.[19]

These benefits accrued by *Ayyaana* practitioners outweighed any negativity that may have been faced. Apart from Chuqule, who mentioned that she "prayed to *Waaqa* to remove this thing" from her, none of the other practitioners displayed any deleterious effects of the practice. When asked if there was anything wrong with *Ayyaana*, most of them did not see any negative aspects. Such positivity was further endorsed when the practitioners conceded that Allah brought *ayyaana* "as a punishment for those who are arrogant. *Ayyaana* turns some people back to prayers," according to Nureah. It was useful to find out if there were similar positive attitudes among the ordinary participants of *Ayyaana*. The following section discusses their experiences as non-practitioners.

Ritual Experiences of Ordinary Participants

The experiences recounted by the ordinary participants of the *Ayyaana* cult showed some variations from what the practitioners went through as discussed in the preceding section. After the initial induction period, the practitioners were able to control the *ayyaana*, unlike the ordinary participants.

---

18. During my observation of the *salawat* prayer session in Butiye, Moyale Subcounty, Jillo, the leader of the prayers, prayed for us that we would succed in our education and that we would have a safe journey back to where we had come from.

19. One local poilitician gave a bull and a sack of rice to the *warra oblia* group in Butiye, Moyale Subcounty, so that prayers would be conducted for his political success. I was told that he was not successful. Yet this did not deter the *warra oblia* from their intercession.

The latter sought the assistance of the practitioners because they were unable to control the adverse effects of the *ayyaana* single-handedly. This desperation from the ordinary people was evident in the experience of Ashaka. (See more details of her story in appendix 5.)

Ayyaana are not constrained by spatial boundaries. This is clear from Ashaka's account. An *ayyaana* called Jaani "caught" her while she was in Nairobi. Jaani troubled her for a long time, leaving her in a deplorable state. It took several sessions of *hadhara* for Jaani to speak and make his demands. Ashaka believed that she was healed after Jaani was pacified and was henceforth obligated to participate in the *Ayyaana* cult. She is also required to make regular domestic sessions as she had been inducted into an ongoing relationship with Jaani.

Induction into the Cult

Most of my interviewees were inducted into the cult after an initial distressing experience like an untreatable illness. Some people, like Ashaka, became mad. Qumbo, another participant, recounted her initiation experience. She had once become insane and imagined that a lion was attacking her. She was married with two children. She could not take care of her family in that condition. Her relatives were desperate and sought help from different practitioners, including the Muslim teachers who dealt with jinn. There seemed to be no relief for her situation. In that hopelessness, they were advised to seek the help of *Ayyaana* practitioners. She recovered and had to hold regular *hadhara* sessions to placate her *ayyaana*.[20]

Induction into the *Ayyaana* cult is not restricted to women, even though women are the majority. One participant described how he tried to seek assistance from a hospital and from the Muslim teachers. In great despair, he eventually visited an *Ayyaana* practitioner who diagnosed his condition as inflicted by *ayyaana*. The latter admonished him for going to the Muslim teachers because *ayyaana* do not like the Qur'an.[21] He then became a regular participant of the cultic activities.[22]

---

20. Qumbo, March 10, 2017.

21. No *ayyaana*, not even the Muslim ones, accept the "burning with the Qur'an," which is the official way employed by the Muslim teachers to exorcise jinn.

22. Susare, July 18, 2016.

An initial illness is not every participant's entry point. Akule explained how she was strongly drawn into the cult. When the practitioners went to her village, she had just given birth to a baby girl. She felt such an intense urge to join in the *hadhara* sessions, but she feared her husband, who despised *warra ayyaana*. Eventually she could not resist the urge. She ran to where a *hadhara* session was being performed. She joined in the singing and clapping, and after an intensive time of *hadhara* she eventually became unconscious. She could not "feel" herself. What she knew was that *ayyaana* had "caught" her. When she went home, her husband threatened her, "If you have *ayyaana*, you cannot live with me in this house I will chase you away." Despite the threats, Aluke continued to attend the sessions.[23]

Other participants were drawn into the cult after watching some of the unusual feats performed by the practitioners. Seeing how the participants behaved was an entertainment venue. Some roared like lions, others tried to flap their arms as though flying, and others crawled on the ground like snakes.[24] An incredible act was when someone licked a red-hot machete with his tongue, and there was no trace of burning after the stupor was over.[25] Such feats attracted onlookers, including children. Some of these later became adepts after being "caught" by *ayyaana*.

Socializing Experience with *Ayyaana*

Once someone has been initiated into the cult, an ongoing relationship ensues between him or her and the *ayyaana*. This association requires the former to constantly "remember" their *ayyaana* by holding regular *hadhara* sessions. Neglecting this would be costly, as Halima realized. She had disregarded her *ayyaana* by failing to give "his things." One day she fell inside a pit latrine. She was convinced that it was her *ayyaana* that was retaliating. She recovered after she gave the demands required. She became an active participant of the *Ayyaana* cult. She walks with a limp and with difficulty due to her old age. In spite of her condition, she still attends the *hadhara* sessions organized by

---

23. Aluke, March 13, 2017.

24. I was able to witness all these during my participant observation sessions.

25. I did not witness this licking of a red-hot machete. Yet, all my interviewees conceded that there were people who have such powers of licking red-hot machetes without getting burned. Most of my interviewees said they had witnessed "possessed" people, especially practitioners, licking hot blades or holding coals of fire with their hands without being burned.

her colleagues. She also invites them to the sessions she holds regularly in her compound. She makes the *jabanna* ritual coffee every Friday, together with popcorn, which she throws to the ground for the *ayyaana* before distributing to all who are present. The picture below shows some of the items used for one of the weekly sessions I attended at Halima's homestead.

Picture 1: Items of a weekly domestic session
(Original photo: Marsabit County, 2017)

Religious Experiences with *Ayyaana*

In chapter 4, which dealt with the representation of official Islam, the Muslim teachers in Marsabit County showed their negative view of *warra ayyaana*. They do not consider the latter to be true Muslims. This is because of their participation in the *Ayyaana* cult that is considered to be *shirk*. In the following section, I discuss the experiences of *warra ayyaana* within the context of Islam.[26] I look at how they experience *ayyaana* as ordinary Muslims. This discussion is pertinent because the essence of this study is to understand the conceptual framework of the ordinary Borana Muslims from their experiences with *ayyaana*.

---

26. I continue to use the term *warra ayyaana* henceforth inclusive of *warra oblia* (*oblia* people) who are involved in the *salawat* or *dhikr* sessions.

Experiencing *Ayyaana* as Local Muslims

Warra ayyaana believe that *ayyaana* were manifested as punishment from God for those who have deviated from Islam.[27] It is a widespread perception that *ayyaana* were sent for the sake of Muslims; hence, they prefer to "catch" Borana Muslims. This makes the *warra ayyaana* consider themselves to be true Muslims, notwithstanding the view of the Muslim teachers about their Muslim-ness. Fatuma justified her participation as a Muslim who makes *jabanna* and still prays. She said, "I cook *jabanna* every Friday and burn incense, but I do not pray to that coffee or that incense. I pray to God who has power and helps me."[28] I attest to this, as I watched the family that hosted me perform the Islamic prayers every morning and evening. The elderly ones carried the prayer beads (Arabic: *tasbīḥ*), popularly used by Muslims to repeat the names of Allah. The walls of most of the houses, including the *darga*, were adorned with Arabic calligraphy. They also used common Islamic terms like *bismillāhi*, especially when slaughtering animals during the ritual ceremonies. Practitioner Diid emphasized this point:

> Those who have not thrown the staff and have not rejected the Sunna of the prophet; these ones when they pray, they have not ceased to say the phrase, *bismillāhi* even when they slaughter. They say this because the food without this is not *halal*. Those who have stopped saying *bismillāhi*, we are not together and we do not agree. The ones we are together are the ones who have not left the word *bismillāhi*.

It seems from this discourse that the word *bismillāhi* is significant in determining the Muslim-ness of *warra ayyaana* in their own perspective.

All my interviewees said they try to observe the five duties of Islam although they confessed that they falter sometimes. They acknowledge the *shahada* (the *aš-šahādah* confession in Arabic), they give *zakat* (*zakāh* alms in Arabic) to the poor, theyperform the *salat* (prescribed prayers), and they fast during the month of Ramadhan. Most of them are not financially able to make the pilgrimage to Mecca. They said they had the option of making the pilgrimage to Bale instead, which to them was acceptable in Islam since it is

---

27. There is a popular adage that asserts that Borana people were Muslims before they were traditionalists. Hence *ayyaana* came to make them return to Islam as their "original" religion.

28. Fatuma, July 21, 2016.

equivalent to the Islamic hajj. Diid said that Muslims go to Mecca to "anoint the prophet (Muhammad)." Similarly, Bale is "the home of Sheikh Hussein, where he is anointed" when people make the pilgrimage. Hence, all these practices make *warra ayyaana* consider themselves to be authentic Muslims who adhere strongly to the *shahada* submission of oneness of Allah and the prophethood of Muhammad. Furthermore, they adhere to the "kernel of Sufi discipline" of *dhikr* (remembrance of God) as shown in the next section.[29]

As Muslims with Sufi Tendencies

Most of the Borana Muslims who participate in the *salawat* or *hadhara* sessions know that they are part of a group registered as Eastern Africa Sufi Council in Kenya. Practitioner Diid admitted that they are a "branch of Sufi . . . who have continued to follow the Sunna of the prophet."[30] Diid further described the group as God-fearing, prayerful, morally upright (since they "do not steal from anybody"), and their aim is only *eeb* (*afan Borana* for "prayer and blessings"). They often make the *ziyara* (pilgrimage) to Bale and join other followers of Sheikh Hussein to pray. They are guided by Sufi orders, according to an excerpt from the recorded minutes of a meeting they held in Moyale:

> The Sufi followers practice Sufi orders. Their common place of worship is Gamo- the grave of Aulia Allah, and *darga* [italics mine] where they carry out their worship activities such as offering animal sacrifices, burnt sacrifices and frying coffee berries as part of their worship besides the five daily prayers commanded by Allah.[31]

This excerpt shows how *warra ayyaana* consider themselves to be Sufi Muslims who adhere to a *tariqa* (Sufi order). They also value *auliya* (Arabic for "saints"), and they frequent their graves like other Sufi Muslims along

---

29. Chittick, *Sufism*, 20.

30. There was a meeting in which all Sufi groups nationwide convened in March 2016 in Isiolo. The then-permanent secretary in the Ministry of Culture and Sports, Hon. Hassan Wario, chaired it. Prior to this meeting the council officials had met the president, who insisted that they should be registered in order to be recognized by the national and county administrators. This information came from a manual I was given by one of the leaders.

31. Minutes of the meeting held in November, 2016.

the Kenyan Coast.³² Like other Sufi orders in East Africa, the *warra ayyaana* believe that the founding of their cult was to Islamize the Borana people.³³

Another characteristic of the *Ayyaana* cult with Sufi tendencies, both in Saku and Moyale Subcounties, is the emphasis on the brother- and sisterhood of its members. They refer to themselves collectively as *jamaat* (Arabic for "brotherhood"). A strong bond of fellowship is visible to an outsider watching the way they prepare and cook food together during their joint sessions. They invite each other regularly when individual members hold *hadhara* sessions in their respective homes. I also observed how they frequently visited one another casually. They occasionally mentioned their love for each other. Dabasso stated, "People love each other and call each other for coffee any time one wants."³⁴

Generally, Sufism denotes a mystical practice that invites people into an ecstatic session to connect with the divine.³⁵ *Warra ayyaana* also have such euphoric episodes as I witnessed when they performed joint *salawat* and *hadhara* sessions. Vigorous clapping, rhythmic drumming, and collective singing induced trances for both women and men during the sessions I observed.³⁶ Jillo summarized their attitude to all these activities by asserting that these are "things we love and follow of Sheikh Hussein that grant us blessings, and a rain of peace."³⁷

Offering Sacrifices as Local Muslims

One of the reasons given by Muslim teachers in Marsabit to discredit the Muslim-ness of *warra ayyaana* was that they "sacrificed in the wrong way,"

---

32. Olali, "Alawiyya Sufism," 3.

33. Imtiyaz asserts that the Hehe and Ngindo of Tanzania were converted to Islam through the Qadiriyyah Sufi order, which was brought to East Africa around 1884 by Sheikh Uways ibn Muhammad (d. 1909), who hailed from Somalia. See Imtiyaz, "Islam and African Socialism," 63. Wario similarly states that the Sufi brotherhoods played a major role in converting indigenous groups in Africa to Islam. See Wario, "Networking the Nomads," 57.

34. Dabasso, August 1, 2016.

35. Gearhart suggests that the Alawiyaa order may have been the first established Sufi *tariqa* in East Africa. It was founded by Mohammed bin Ali bin Mohammed in Yemen in the year 1255. See Gearhart, "Ngoma Memories," 71.

36. I saw elderly women in a state of trance as they clapped very vigorously without getting tired. These were otherwise frail when they were their normal selves. I was also told that the clapping was not lightly but was very vigorous. One of my interviewees recounted how her hands ached for three days when she was a novice in the *ayyaana* sessions.

37. Jillo, March 11, 2017.

according to Sheikh Khalid.[38] Sacrificing in Islam is allowed especially during the *idh-ul-adha* Islamic ceremony to commemorate the time Abraham was told to sacrifice his son.[39] *Warra ayyaana* as Muslims are aware of this. They know that Abraham, the prophet of Allah, offered animal sacrifices as part of his religious practice.[40]

Fatuma explained that sacrificing is part and parcel of the lives of *warra ayyaana* because "sacrifice is like worshipping."[41] There is a strong assertion of the significance of offering sacrifices as worship. Fatuma's explanation did not specify who/what the object of the "worship" was. Was it *ayyaana* or God? This ambiguity was evident in what she explained next. She avowed that offering sacrifices was *ingamashifti* in *afan Borana* (Kiswahili: *kufurahisha*). *Ingamashifti* means to appease: "You appease/gladden all these so that you are at peace. This sacrifice is for that."

Performing *Salawat* as *Dua*

Warra ayyaana acknowledge the two kinds of prayers in Islam: the regular *salat* and the informal *dua* prayers. They try to perform the prescribed *salat* as often as possible. Yet, it is evident that they find much delight in making the *dua*. They perform these prayers during the joint *salawat* sessions.

These prayers have inspired confidence in *warra ayyaana* and have made them perceive themselves as people who offer successful supplications to God. They boldly assert that it is through their prayers "that most nations of the world have survived hard times," according to the minutes of a meeting held in March, 2016. It has already been noted that they pray for the political situations that they know. I heard them pray for peace in Kenya and in Africa as a whole. *Nagaa* (*afan Borana* for "peace") was a major theme in these prayers. They beseeched God to give peace as they acknowledged his sovereignty over all situations. A prayer made by one participant who assisted in leading the sessions showed how they believe in the effectiveness of their prayers:

---

38. Sheikh Khalid, August 30, 2016.
39. The account of Abraham sacrificing a son is mentioned in the Qur'an (Surah 37: 99–109). The name of the son is however not included. Muslims infer that it was Ishmael and not Isaac.
40. Muslims generally believe that Abraham (*'Ibrāhīm*) was a prophet of Allah and hence was a Muslim who preceded Prophet Muhammad. References to Abraham in the Qur'an can be found in Surah 16:120; 2:128.
41. Fatuma, July 21, 2016.

> *Rab wor baha nu tolchina wor woni biyaat jabaatu laftuf nam Shekahana Hussein it d'eetan male ira indeetani baran gambot ollan buute jamaa Shekhana Hussein yamani guyum suni rabin naam jede roobi d'ufe.* (May God make us safe, people to whom what is heavy for others is easy to us. People run to the followers of Sheikh Hussein but cannot run from them. [Once during] drought on the side of Ethiopia, people of Sheikh Hussein were called, [and] on the same day the Lord answered their prayers and the rain fell).[42]

It is common to hear *warra ayyaana* assert how they have prayed for many things and God heard them, as exemplified in the words of Guyoh, above. Such confidence seems to give them resilience amid opposition from the Muslim teachers. It further enhances their construction of the model of *Ayyaana* as they also visit the sacred places or hear about them.

Making the Pilgrimage as Local Muslims

The pilgrimage to Bale is compared to the Islamic one to Mecca in magnitude and significance. Bale is one of the main pilgrimage places in southern Ethiopia frequented by *warra ayyaana*.[43] It is believed to be where the shrine of Sheikh Hussein is situated.[44] This is evident from the way *warra ayyaana* describe what they refer to as *ziyara*[45] (pilgrimage) to Bale in Ethiopia, as Diid describes below:

> *Baalen nam achi daqeti mama biya millionat dufa. Sheikhit qara achit tolche lafa Ethiopia ininu achit dalate nam isilanse kafira laf tenaaleen rab baase.*

---

42. Guyoh, March 11, 2017.

43. Bale is also referred to as *Bale Sheikh Hussein* or *Dirre Sheikh Hussein*. See Merga, "Archaelogical Survey of Islamic." It has become a tourist attraction site and has the support of the Oromia Culture and Tourism Bureau of Ethiopia. See Tola, *Conservation of Dirre Sheikh*.

44. Some scholars refer to this Sufi *tariqa*, founded by Sheikh Hussein, as *Husseiniya*. Sheikh Hussein is a Muslim saint venerated by *warra oblia* together with Prophet Muhammad. He is believed to be the founder of the Sufi group to which *warra oblia* belong. He should not be confused with Hussein who is venerated by the Shiites and who was the grandson of prophet Muhammad.

45. *Ziyara* is a word borrowed from the Arabic *ziyārat*, which means pilgrimage, from the word *ziyārah* (to visit).

(Anyone who has gone to Bale is amazed because millions of people come. Sheikh Hussein first made that place in Ethiopia where he was born. He made people become Muslims and the Lord removed the pagans from our land).

Going for *ziyara* to Bale is considered a significant spiritual undertaking. It is perceived as a sacrificial venture when one chooses to leave his family and property for the sake of Allah and not merely to see the historic town of Bale. *Warra ayyaana* say they go for *ziyara* throughout the year. If an individual or a group of them receives a divine message, they "leave immediately without seeking formal documents like a passport or a pass." (Minutes of a meeting held on November 1, 2016. Such flexibility is perceived to be of greater value than the Islamic pilgrimage that confines Muslims to only two times (*Hajj* and *Umrah*, greater and lesser pilgrimages respectively).

Revering Prophet Muhammad and Sheikh Hussein

Bale and Sheikh Hussein are frequently mentioned during the *salawat* prayers because of the high value the *warra ayyaana* accord them. Bale, as a locality, is revered because of Sheikh Hussein. The latter is respected because of the *karama* (gift) around him. Some of the statements from my interviewees show how they esteem him as an exemplary man who was also associated with *ayyaana*. He is referred to as the leader of *ayyaana*:

Konso:

> He [Sheikh Hussein] is the leader of *ayyaana* given power by God. The staff passed through Moses and then to Sheikh Hussein. He is the one who was left by the Prophet [Muhammad].[46]

Diid:

> Sheikh Hussein, according to the prophet, was the Sheikh over jinn and humans. If jinn possess somebody, you can command it to go in the name of Sheikh Hussein. The one who has refused [to get out], you can proclaim, "In the blessings of my Sheikh

---

46. Konso, August 26, 2016.

[Hussein] I strike you." And then it gets out, and this is the honor that the Lord [*Rab*] has given to him [Sheikh Hussein].⁴⁷

These statements show that Sheikh Hussein is revered because God endowed him with *irre jabdu* (*afan Borana* for "special power"). *Warra ayyaana* believe strongly that he was sent to "rule over jinn" and ensure they do not trouble people. The name of Sheikh Hussein is used to "strike" jinn, unlike what the Muslim teachers recommended. The latter endorsed striking the jinn by burning them with the Qur'an. Neither the practitioners nor the participants of the *Ayyaana* cult mentioned this usage of the Qur'an.

Some *warra ayyaana* believe that Sheikh Hussein has a spiritual connection with Prophet Muhammad.⁴⁸ Diid traced to the Prophet the origin of the *ule* (the staff) that Sheikh Hussein had carried. He asserted that it had passed from Moses, then to Prophet Muhammad, and eventually to Sheikh Hussein. It is viewed as a sign of authority and leadership handed to Sheikh Hussein in a similar way that Moses and Muhammad were endowed with authority to lead God's people.

A pertinent question is whether *warra ayyaana* revere Sheikh Hussein more than the prophet Muhammad. The former is perceived to have wrought more outstanding miracles than the latter. My interviewees referred to exceptional performances in the name of Sheikh Hussein but not in the name of the Prophet. The only miracle they mentioned that was performed by the prophet Muhammad was the *mi'rāj* (the night journey).⁴⁹ There was no mention by the *warra ayyaana* that the Prophet had ever dealt with jinn. They were probably not aware of his encounter with the jinn as recounted in the Islamic texts. This made them associate more with Sheikh Hussein than with the Prophet because of their supernaturalistic worldview.⁵⁰

---

47. Diid, March 9, 2017.

48. It seems to be popular assumption that Sufis trace the spiritual descents of their saints to the prophet Muhammad, according to Umashankar, who examined the redefining of Indian Islam by the shrine-based Sufis. See Umashankar, "Defending Sufism, Defining Islam," 206.

49. *Mi'rāj*, in Arabic, means "dream." Muslims believe strongly about Prophet Muhammad's night voyage on a winged horse to Jerusalem and eventually to the seven heavens. Surah 17:1 recounts this journey and acknowledges that it was Allah who took "His servant for a journey by night from the Sacred Mosque to the Farthest Mosque."

50. A supernaturalistic worldview is the ontological view about the existence of otherworldly beings beyond the natural realm of human beings yet interacting actively with the latter.

Enhancing the Salience of the *Ayyaana* Model through Creativity

The experiences described above facilitate the kind of mental models of *Ayyaana* that *warra ayyaana* have and that they shared intersubjectively as a religiocultural model of *Ayyaana*. As *warra ayyaana* continue to encounter *ayyaana*, their mental schemas continue to be constructed firmly, and these, in turn, contribute to the way they deal with *ayyaana* as a group. Hence the dynamic relationship between the experiences and the religiocultural model that I mentioned at the commencement of this chapter.

In addition to the experiences that augment the religiocultural model of *Ayyaana*, music and tangible artifacts also enhance the formation of this religiocultural model.[51] Figure 15 below shows this dynamism – that interplay between the lived experiences, the symbolic items, and the religiocultural model of *Ayyaana*.

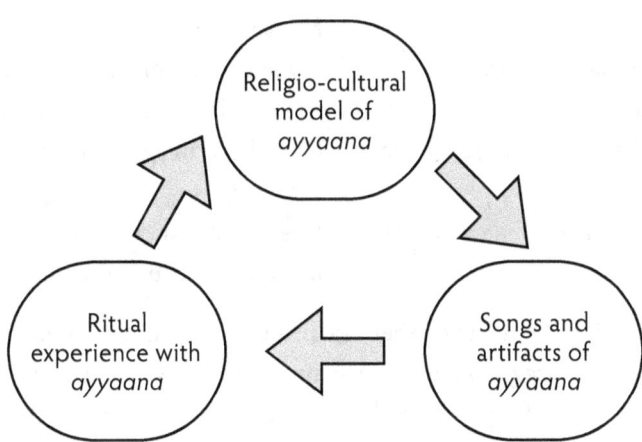

Figure 15: The place of music and artifacts to enhance the *Ayyaana* model

Various ethnomusicologists have examined the relationship between trance and music.[52] It is beyond the scope of this current study to delve into the theories that these scholars have suggested. Pertinent to this chapter is

---

51. The significance of music and cantillation in Sufi brotherhoods is also mentioned by Kirkegaard, who examines the place of music in Sufi popular performances in East Africa. See Kirkegaard, "Music and Transcendence," 29–48.

52. Yarmolinsky, "Music of Jillala"; Jankowsky, "Music, Spirit Possession," 185–208; Rouget, *Music and Trance*; and Becker, *Deep Listeners*.

the place of music in the cognition of *warra ayyaana* in developing the kind of religiocultural model described.

Ayyaana Songs during *Hadhara* Sessions

Rhythmic drumming and clapping accompanied the songs chanted during the *hadhara* sessions I attended. The practitioners led the songs, which were echoed by the participants. Some of the words used in the songs were not comprehensible even to the practitioners. Fatuma, a keen participant, confessed that she does not understand the meanings of some words they frequently sing. In one of the sessions that I observed, the practitioner began by invoking the presence of Sheikh Hussein in the following song:

Ooo mayoo Sheikh Hussein hooo	Ooo, come Sheikh Hussein, hoo
Oooo mayoo Sheikh Hussein hoo	Ooo, come Sheikh Hussein, hoo
An gar kee dufaara, Sheikh Hussien hoo	I am coming to you today, Sheikh Hussein, hoo
Darbate woon damne, Sheikh Hussein hoo	If you throw [something] you cannot miss the target, Sheikh Hussein, hoo
Artha inbota, chaati aboon game	Outside crying grass my father spread.[53]
Ibid asida, ule it gamnaan d'ame	Fire of jealousy, you pointed a stick at it and it was extinguished.

Mentioning the name of Sheikh Hussein and summoning his presence shows that *warra ayyaana* recognize him as a man who was endowed with unusual power.[54] They believe that he still has the *karama* (Kiswahili for "power") to perform miracles. Konso asserted that Sheikh Hussein was "the leader of *ayyaana*."[55] Other practitioners echoed this assertion through the songs and the way they referred to him during the interviews. It was therefore necessary to invoke his presence in dealing with the *ayyaana*.

There were other songs during the *hadhara* sessions. Some of them mentioned the specific names of the *ayyaana* especially after they had identified

---

53. This sentence is not clear in contemporary *afan Borana*.

54. It has been noted before that this Sheikh Hussein should not be confused with Hussein, the grandson of Prophet Muhammad, who is revered by Shia Muslims.

55. Konso, August 26, 2016.

themselves. The song for Odha, for instance, commenced with customary respectful greetings (*yooyah* in *afan Borana*) that are used by a younger person greeting an older one in Borana fraternity.

Odha yooyah, Odha kiya yooo	Odha greetings, my Odha greetings
Odha bobaa yooya	Odha the eagle, greetings
Molu bora yooya	Molu bora, greetings
Uleen diri yooya	Staff of twigs, greetings
Odha boba yooya	Odha the eagle, greetings

The practitioner chanted this song as the participants responded with "*woyo*" (not a Borana word). It was apparent, from their use of the Borana greeting *yooya*, that the practitioners acknowledged the superiority of *ayyaana*. This subservience is also noted in the following song:

Odha kiya waqole yooya	My Odha my god, greetings
Odha boba abole yooya	Odha (Boba) my father, greetings
Taka dufte yooya	You came in unity
Uleen diri, kalchaan siri	Your staff is a silent supporter
Kara gara, abole yooya	Upon the mountains, my father greetings
Konsoon raga abole yooya	Konso prophet, my father greetings
Dalti dacha, abole yooya	Multiply many, my father greetings

Odha is said to be the "oldest" of all *ayyaana* since he was "there from the beginning," according to practitioner Jillo. Other interviewees confirmed this when they referred to Odha as *abba maati* (father of many), hence the words of the song above that refer to Odha as lord and father.

Songs convey the participants' awareness and cognition of spiritual creatures. It is therefore appropriate to consider the role of music in possession rituals. Richard Jankowsky asserts that it is not the music itself that produces healing during therapeutical sessions.[56] *Ayyaana* adepts believe that

---

56. Jankowski, "Music, Spirit Possession," 187; and Rouget, *Music and Trance*, 175. Jankowsky did an ethnomusicological inquiry into the relation between music and possession trance in the stambeli healing rituals in Tunisia. He begins his article by listing a number of anthropologists who have attempted to explain the relation between music and possession trance since the 1960's. One interesting suggestion was that loud and repetitive drumming

the *Ayyaana* music is only a channel through which a particular *ayyaana* is appeased so that it stops troubling the patient. Apart from this placating role, the songs enhance the salience of the religiocultural model of *Ayyaana* in the minds of participants. I have shown above how the songs invoke the name of Sheikh Hussein of Bale, a key figure in the *Ayyaana* possession cult. The prophet Muhammad is also mentioned in the songs. Constant reference to the names of specific *ayyaana* further engrains their reality in the minds of participants. All these contribute to the conceptual knowledge of *ayyaana* and hence foreground the schemas or mental models of *Ayyaana* in individual minds. When the participants join together in the sessions, their collective participation then gives more significance to the religiocultural model of *Ayyaana* than to a cultural model of jinn. The memorability of this model is further enhanced through various artifacts used during the cultic sessions.

Items of *Ayyaana*

Diid, the *Ayyaana* practitioner from Moyale said, "The identity card of *warra Sheikh Hussein* [people of Sheikh Hussein] is the *ule ayyaana* [*ayyaana* stick/staff].[57] It is the thing that helps to make an *ayyaana* that does not talk to speak. It is a gift from the Lord [*khenamti rabbi*]."[58] The *ule ayyaana* is a bifurcated staff that is used to identify the leaders of the *Ayyaana* cult. They carry it everywhere they go. It is valued and is not to be placed flat on the ground; it should only be stuck into the ground with its pointed end.[59] Aisha is a female *Ayyaana* practitioner from Saku Subcounty. Her staff gives her a sense of authority, even over men, as she takes charge of the sessions. Her *ule* has three branches (see picture 2 below).[60]

---

always led to trance. This elicited Gilbert Rouget's famous statement that if this was true, then "half of Africa would be in a trance from the beginning of the year to the end."

57. *Warra oblia* and *warra ayyaana* are sometimes referred to as *warra Sheikh Hussein*.

58. Diid, Personal Interview by author.

59. The *Ule ayyaana* is also well preserved by smearing it with oil. It is decorated, as well, with beads (see picture 2).

60. *Ule* is the general word for a stick or a staff in *afan Borana*. Staffs have great significance in traditional Borana customs and are used for different purposes. Hassan Arero gives a detailed discussion of the use of various types of *ule*, which includes a brief mention of the *ule ayyaana*. See Arero, "Keeping the Peace," 1.

Picture 2: Picture of *ule* carried by *Ayyaana* practitioners (Original photo: Marsabit County, 2017)

Apart from identifying the *Ayyaana* practitioners, the *ule* is also perceived as a sign of leadership and authority similar to Moses's staff. It is believed that the *ule* traced its origin from Prophet Moses and that it passed through Moses and then to Sheikh Hussein. This shows the spirituality associated with the staff and thus the justification for according to it rightful respect. It is believed to derive its power from Sheikh Hussein. It is used to bless or to curse people through its derivative power. It should always be present during the *Ayyaana* healing sessions. Practitioner Dabasso assured one *ayyaana* that the patient had given the edible things demanded as well as the items required including the *ule*. Their conversation went as follows:

> Dabasso: "*Qaal (chale), kha maarite, shibo kha Odha kan sii tolchani?*" (The demands of beads for maarite, the chain of Odha, are all for you.[61] Is this what should be done for you?)
>
> Ayyaana: "*Nama tan naa tolche inebisa, an tokum arge?*" (I will bless the one who will do this for me. But can I see one who can do this for me?)

---

61. Maarite is a type of *ayyaana* that is Habash.

Dabasso: "*Wonti maariteleen tana, garta, shiboon woraana, sii kenne garta? Aqayaan baka bargama ingarti.*" (The Maarite things are here: shibo, which is like a spear for Odha are also here. The family from waters can see.)⁶²

There are different types of *ule ayyaana* designated to show both the rank and the gender of the practitioners. My interviewees kept mentioning the *shibo* and compared it to a "spear that does not miss its target." The implication is that when it is used to deal with *ayyaana*, success is assured. *Ayyaana* acknowledge the authority of the *ule* and comply when told to release a patient, according to Diid, a practitioner, who said, "Even the *ayyaana* respect the staff and release anyone they have caught. The staff is respected."

The picture of the *ule ayyaana* above shows a set of chains and beads hanging from it. These items are also important during the *Ayyaana* sessions. They have a protective function and are considered to be the weapons that *ayyaana* use against offensive entities, like the jinn. Patients under treatment wear a long silver chain across the chest to ward off any attacks from malevolent jinn. Some *warra oblia* had the chains as they performed the *salawat* sessions. Fatuma explained that the silver chain had "some powers to rebuke the devil." A practitioner uses the chain to hit the person with such a devil or a jinni and he or she "would not feel pain because it is the jinn that is being hit and not the person."⁶³

Essentially, like the music of *Ayyaana*, the tangible items described above enhance deeper internalization of the religiocultural model of *Ayyaana* by the ordinary Borana Muslims interviewed. Reference to and usage of the items of *Ayyaana* is congruent with the metaphor of *ayyaana* as an army. Moreover, participants of the *Ayyaana* cult anthropomorphize *ayyaana* as created beings that are stronger than men and that have the propensity to be annoyed. Such anger can only be quelled by using appropriate items of warfare. The tangibility of these items then gives more confidence and an inclination to the *Ayyaana* cult.

---

62. Dabasso, August 1, 2016.
63. Hussein, July 19, 2016.

Enhancing the Salience of the *Ayyaana* Model through Creative Cognition

The foregrounding of the religiocultural model of *Ayyaana* by *warra ayyaana* shows that it is a salient model within their context. The detailed accounts of their experiences with *ayyaana* illustrate the significance they place in the concept. A fundamental premise of this study is that this salience is enhanced through the creativity of the *warra ayyaana* as they seek to find solutions to their problems.

The *Ayyaana* cult has elements that have been borrowed from other traditions. I interpret this as creativity that produces something from amalgamating elements. Similarly, as *warra ayyaana* attribute human characteristics to *ayyaana*, it is also an act of creativity that helps them relate with *ayyaana* on a daily basis. In this final section of the chapter, I present this aspect of creativity in the conceptual framework of *warra ayyaana*.

Creative Borrowing by *Warra Ayyaana*

One of the factors that give salience to the religiocultural model of *Ayyaana* is its congruence with the concept of *nagaa*. It has been mentioned before how *warra ayyaana* pray for *nagaa* during their *salawat* prayers. They also seek for *nagaa* with *ayyaana* during the pacification sessions. To sustain the relevance of the model of *Ayyaana* in maintaining *nagaa*, *warra ayyaana* have had to be creative within a contested environment.

The creativity trait is quite evident in the *Ayyaana* cult. The ability of *warra ayyaana* to appropriate different aspects of their religiocultural context into the cult is notable. Such creativity is apparent from the way they have borrowed some elements from Islam, Sufism, and traditional Borana beliefs and customs.[64]

---

64. I use Sternberg's definition for the term *creativity*, set forth in 1999, "As the ability to construct something new (typically useful) out of existing elements," as quoted by Rosa E. Vega Moreno.. See Moreno, *Creativity and Convention*, 5.

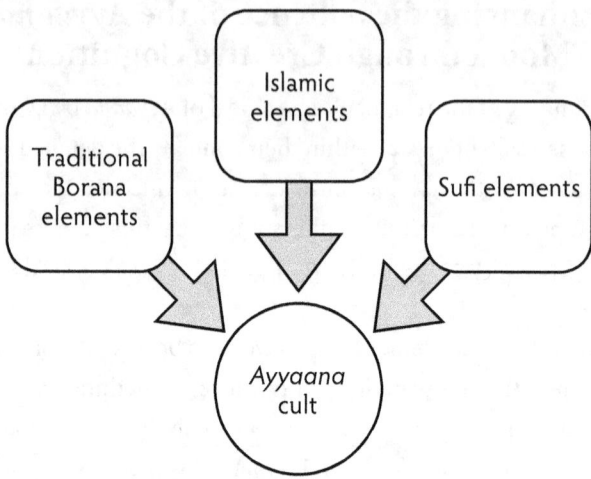

Figure 16: Creative borrowing of elements

There are two main Islamic elements that have been borrowed by *warra ayyaana*, namely, the concept of jinn and the respect for Prophet Muhammad. As Muslims, *warra ayyaana* are expected to believe in the existence of jinn. They believe that jinn are part of the Islamic categorization of spirits.

Another element borrowed from Islam is the respect for Prophet Muhammad. This is required for all Muslims including *warra ayyaana*. However, they also revere Sheikh Hussein of Bale as evident from the *hadhara* songs mentioned above. Reverence for Sheikh Hussein also reveals the other elements that have been borrowed from Sufism by *warra ayyaana*. *Salawat* prayers take the form of *dhikr*, which is a common expression of Sufism. *Warra ayyaana* go further than mere *dhikr* and they add *hadhara* sessions to pacify the *ayyaana*. The appeasing *jilla* (*afan Borana* for "ceremony") similarly involves other elements that have been borrowed from the traditional Borana customs. *Bunna qala* (the coffee "sacrificing" ceremony) is an important Borana ceremony. It has been borrowed and has become a constitutive part of all *Ayyaana* sessions.

Creative Anthropomorphism by *Warra Ayyaana*

The aspect of borrowing from the three traditions discussed above and the addition of other elements is evidence of the creative cognition of *warra ayyaana*. This creativity is further illustrated in the way they construct metaphors and use metonymy to describe *ayyaana* (see chapter 5). Likewise, the use of anthropomorphism illustrates their creativity in constructing a model that seeks to answer their daily concerns. There is a theory that states that one of the reasons that people anthropomorphize is because they lack "a sense of social connection to other humans."[65] This cannot be the case with *warra ayyaana* when they attribute human features to *ayyaana*.

The reason behind anthropomorphism by *warra ayyaana* is the need to relate with *ayyaana* that are deemed to be stronger than humans. Like other ordinary Muslims, *warra ayyaana* seek for practical ways of dealing with their everyday encounters, which include spiritual encounters. They are taught, in the *madrassas* (Islamic schools), about the official Islamic way of dealing with spirits, but this does not become a salient model for them. My proposition is that the religiocultural model of *Ayyaana* is foregrounded in the minds of *warra ayyaana* because it involves creative features. These features offer more practical solutions that enable people to deal with crucial aspects of their context.

The Creative Cognition of *Warra Ayyaana*

Warra ayyaana employ their cognitive abilities to come up with solutions. They realize that there are elements that they can creatively borrow from other religious traditions that they are aware of. They also find a way of relating with the causative agents of their problems. *Warra ayyaana* further anthropomorphize these agents, which they call *ayyaana*, in order to communicate with them. They use conceptual metaphors to refer to *ayyaana*.

When these aspects of creative borrowing (namely, anthropomorphism and the use of metaphors to describe *ayyaana*) are placed together, they signify the creative cognition of ordinary Borana Muslims in their quest for solutions.[66] This creative thinking is shared among the participants of the cult as they experience *ayyaana* both individually and collectively.

---

65. Epley, Waytz, and Cacioppo, "On Seeing Human," 864.

66. Creative cognition is a broad approach that involves the study of processes and structures in creative thinking to produce novel and relevant products. I did not delve into the technicalities of the approach. I use the terminology here in line with the cognitive anthropological framework that I employ for analyzing the *Ayyaana* cult.

The Minimal Counterintuitiveness of the *Ayyaana* Concept

The salience of the *Ayyaana* model by *warra ayyaana* can also be explained by the theory of minimally counterintuitive agency. This theory was developed by Pascal Boyer and advanced by other scholars in CSR like Barret, Whitehouse, Cohen, Atran, McCauley & Cohen, and others.[67] Chapter 7 discusses this in more detail as I give a comparative analysis of the *Ayyaana* religiocultural model and the Islamic model of jinn. Suffice it to say that the minimally counterintuitive (MCI) theory postulates that the minimally counterintuitive cognitive concepts are more memorable than others.[68] I suggest that anthropomorphic conceptualization and experiences with *ayyaana* by *warra ayyaana* makes the concept of *ayyaana* to be minimally counterintuitive.[69] This gives the model of *ayyaana* a transmission advantage over the Islamic model of jinn.

Summary

In this chapter, I have discussed how the religiocultural model of *Ayyaana* is instantiated through the lived experiences of the ordinary Borana Muslims with *ayyaana*. I have mentioned how the religiocultural model of *Ayyaana* is constructed by individual experiences, which consequently become intersubjectively shared within the cultic context. There ensues a dynamic relationship between the religiocultural model and the experiences with *ayyaana* as the model continues to be constructed to give meaning to the daily life.

I have also illustrated how the symbolism involved in the items and songs for *ayyaana* can enhance cognition, which subsequently foregrounds the model of *Ayyaana*. Further, I have highlighted the creative cognition of *warra ayyaana* in the way they borrow elements from Islam, Sufism, and the traditional Borana religion. This creativity is also seen in their usage of metaphors and metonyms as part of the way they anthropomorphize *ayyaana*. And thus, I have concluded that the model of *Ayyaana* is foregrounded because of the creative cognition it entails.

---

67. Boyer, *Naturalness of Religious Ideas*; Barrett, "Coding and Quantifying Counterintuitiveness," 308–38; Whitehouse, *Modes of Religiosity*; Atran, *In Gods We Trust*; and McCauley and Cohen, "Cognitive Science," 779–92. Other writings of Boyer include *Religion Explained: The Evolutionary Origins of Religious Thought*.

68. Justin Barrett, "Cognitive Science of Religion: What Is It and Why Is It?," *Religion Compass* 1, no. 6 (2007): 771.

69. Minimally counterintuitive concepts are contrasted with bizarre concepts that are not as memorable as the former.

CHAPTER 7

Comparative Interdisciplinary Analysis and Theory Formulation

Introduction

In chapters 4, 5, and 6 of this dissertation, I provided a descriptive analysis of the different models of the spirit world as perceived by the Muslim teachers and the ordinary Borana Muslims in Marsabit County. Chapter 4 presented the Islamic model of the spirit world as understood by the Muslim teachers who are the custodians of the official expression of Islam. Chapters 5 and 6 discussed the religiocultural model of *Ayyaana* as perceived by the ordinary Borana Muslims in the two subcounties of Moyale and Saku.

The aim of chapter 7 is to bring these three chapters together in a comparative analytical discussion. Such an analysis is in line with the overall objective of this research, which seeks to understand the ordinary Borana Muslims' participation in the *Ayyaana* cult using a cognitive anthropological perspective. These lived experiences are herein analyzed according to the Islamic model of the spirit world as narrated by the Muslim teachers.

Chapter 6 of this study examined the lived experiences of the ordinary Borana Muslims with *ayyaana*. The chapter discussed how the religiocultural model of *Ayyaana* is instantiated within the people's supernaturalistic context. There is a dynamic relationship between the lived experiences and the model of *Ayyaana*, where they mutually influence each other. Now, chapter 7 examines the resultant model and its instantiation in light of the official Islamic requirements.

An interdisciplinary approach is used to give a comprehensive analytical description of the two models under study. It has been outlined in the preceding chapters that this research uses a cognitive anthropological framework. The advantage of such a framework is that it integrates anthropology with cognitive theories. I also add a psychological dimension that I found valuable in understanding why *warra ayyaana* are inclined to the *Ayyaana* cult. I will discuss these theoretical inferences in a later section of this chapter. The immediate subsequent section compares the Islamic model of jinn and the *warra ayyaana* religiocultural model of *Ayyaana*.

Congruence of the Islamic and *Ayyaana* Models

The supernaturalistic orientation of both the Muslim teachers and *warra ayyaana* allows for significant congruency between the two models of the spirit world. The Islamic texts attest to the the existence of jinn as unseen beings that were in existence before the advent of Muhammad's message. Chapter 2 of this dissertation illustrates how different scholars have interpreted the Qur'anic *ayahs* on jinn as well as other aspects of the concept. Suffice it to say that belief in the spirit world is expedient for all Muslims, including *warra ayyaana*. It is significant to note that this forms a strong foundation for all their practices as well as what they are taught by their teachers.

The ontological understanding of spirits by both the *warra ayyaana* and the Muslim teachers includes the notion that they are found in the unseen world (*al-ghaib*), yet they impinge on the human world. It is also perceived that God created spirits for reasons that will be discussed in the next sections on variations between the Islamic model of spirits and the *Ayyaana* model.

Table 13 below summarizes significant similarities between jinn and *ayyaana* according to the models held by Muslim teachers and *warra ayyaana*. Both jinn and *ayyaana* are attributed with anthropomorphic characteristics. Thus, they also have religious inclinations. Jinn that have accepted Muhammad are considered to be Muslim jinn. *Warra ayyaana*, on the other hand, believe that there are Muslim *ayyaana*, which are consequently given Muslim names like Hajj Hussein, Hajji Sharif, and others. They also assert that *ayyaana* were sent by *Waaqa* to Islamize Borana people.

Table 13: Similarities between the Nature of Jinn and *Ayyaana*

Aspects of similarity between Jinn and *Ayyaana*	Islamic Model	*Ayyaana* Model
Creation	Allah created *jinn*.	*Ayyaana* created by *Waaqa*.[1]
Invisibility	Jinn are invisible.	*Ayyaana* are invisible (*Qileesa Waaqa*).
Anthropomorphism	Jinn have some human characteristics (seeing, hearing, eating, etc.)	*Ayyaana* have human characteristics (seeing, hearing, eating, drinking, etc.).
Religiosity	Good jinn submit to Allah and accept Muhammad's message; they are Muslims.	There are Muslim *ayyaana*. *Ayyaana* are also religious because they were basically sent to Islamize Borana people.
Habitation	Jinn live in *al-ghaib* but interact with human beings.	*Ayyaana* live in *al-ghaib* but also interact with human beings.
Interaction with human beings	Jinn interacted with Muhammad and Suleiman. They also interact with people, today.	*Ayyaana* interact with people on a daily basis.
Ability to "possess" people	Jinn can "catch" people	*Ayyaana* can "catch" people
Pathogenicity	Jinn cause madness and other ailments.	*Ayyaana* cause madness and other ailments.

The habitation of both jinn and *ayyaana* is in the unseen realm, yet they constantly interact with human beings. The Muslim teachers acknowledged that the prophet Muhammad interacted with jinn. They heard him recite the Qur'an since he was sent to preach to the jinn as well.[2] Muhammad's

---

1. I have discussed the concept of God as Allah and as *Waaqa* among the Borana Muslims in Chapter 1.. On the theme of creation, the supremacy of God as Allah and as *Waaqa* is evident as the creator of all things.
2. Sheikh Amr, May 17, 2017.

ability to see jinn was taken as proof of his prophethood. Likewise, *warra ayyaana* believe that Sheikh Hussein of Bale had the ability to interact physically with *ayyaana*. His followers today also interact with *ayyaana* – but not on the same level as Sheikh Hussein. Hence, for both the Muslim teachers and *warra ayyaana*, the closer interaction with jinn and *ayyaana* by Prophet Muhammad and Sheikh Hussein respectively is an indication of their spiritual ability endowed by God for special religious purposes.

Jinn and *ayyaana* are capable of possessing people, especially Muslims. Both the Muslim teachers and *warra ayyaana* mentioned that jinn and *ayyaana* "catch" people and enter their bodies. Loss of sanity is a major symptom of somebody being "caught" by jinn or *ayyaana*. Both are pathogenic as they are said to cause other ailments that are medically undiagnosed.

Variations: The Islamic Model versus the *Ayyaana* Model

Two major differences between the Islamic model of spirits and the *Ayyaana* model are categorization and how to deal with spirits. These two variations are significant and intertwined. The way people categorize spirits determines how they deal with them.

Categorization of *Ayyaana*

The categorization systems used by the Muslim teachers and *warra ayyaana* depict how each group experiences the spirits and the kind of cultural model they have. The Muslim teachers in Marsabit County categorize *ayyaana* as bad jinn, while *warra ayyaana* refute this. The latter classify jinn and *ayyaana* as separate categories of spirits as discussed in chapter 5 of this dissertation.

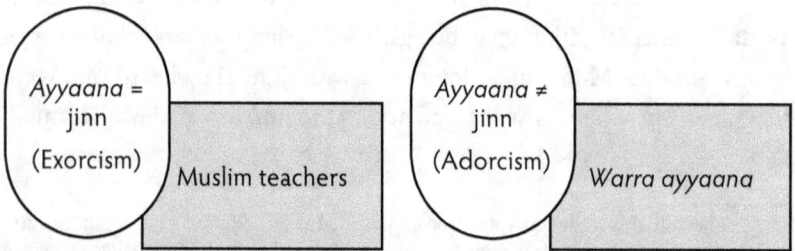

Figure 17: Different categorizations of *ayyaana*

Warra ayyaana classify jinn and *ayyaana* as separate categories of spirits (see chapter 5). They believe that *ayyaana* are superior to jinn since *ayyaana* remove jinn that "catch" people. This contradicts what the Muslim teachers teach as the official understanding of the jinn concept. Jinn are sanctioned in the Qur'an, especially the ones that submit to Muhammad's message and become Muslims. This difference in categorization of *ayyaana* by the Muslim teachers and the *warra ayyaana* shows the variance in cognition between the two. This is further illustrated in the way each group relates to *ayyaana*. For the *warra ayyaana*, *ayyaana* are more relational than jinn. *Ayyaana* have a closer relationship with the people than jinn do according to the way they are depicted by the teachers. *Warra ayyaana* reiterated that Prophet Suleiman had jinn that worked for him. Such a servile nature then makes *warra ayyaana* to conceptualize jinn as servants of *ayyaana*. *Ayyaana*, on the other hand, interact with people on an unservile basis, according to *warra ayyaana*. They relate to human beings in a superior way. This superiority is evident from the metaphors used regarding *ayyaana* as *qileensa Waaqa* and as an army. Such metaphorical reference is minimal among the Muslim teachers even though they still anthropomorphize jinn.

Evidently, *warra ayyaana* have more relational experiences with *ayyaana* than the Muslim teachers have with jinn. These experiences are illustrated in the ways they both deal with *ayyaana* or jinn. Such experiences demonstrate the creativity involved therein vis-à-vis a rigidity that sticks to the stipulated orthodox requirements on how to deal with the spiritual beings.

Variations in Dealing with Spirits

The Muslim teachers and *warra ayyaana* conceded that both jinn and *ayyaana* "catch" people and can cause havoc when annoyed. It is essential, then, to know how to deal with the exasperated jinn or *ayyaana* in order to bring relief to a troubled person. There was clear variance between what the teachers advised and the way *warra ayyaana* dealt with *ayyaana*.

Muslim teachers insist that *ayyaana* should be "burnt with the Qur'an" since they are classified as bad jinn. *Warra ayyaana* defy this because their classification of *ayyaana* differs considerably from that of their Muslim teachers, as mentioned above. The relational aspect between *ayyaana* and the people they "catch" makes it expedient to deal with the former in a mollifying way in order to make peace. *Nagaa* is a crucial element in the religiocultural model of *warra ayyaana*.³ This is seen in the way they conduct the *salawat* prayers as they seek peace from *Waaqa* and with *ayyaana* during the *hadhara* sessions.

Warra ayyaana pacify *ayyaana* by singing in the *hadhara* sessions and giving the *ayyaana* what they demand. This is the concept of adorcism where the relationship between the *ayyaana* and the people is seen to be positive. Adorcism differs from exorcism, which involves expulsion of jinn or *ayyaana* according to the official teachings. Exorcism has a negative relational connotation that does not fit well with the *warra ayyaana*'s cognition. This understanding enhances the predominance and transmission of the *Ayyaana* model among the ordinary Borana Muslims, hence the salience of the model.

Saliency of the *Ayyaana* Model vis-à-vis the Islamic Model

Foregrounding of the model of *Ayyaana* by *warra ayyaana* implies that it is more salient than the Islamic model of the jinn (see figure 18 below).⁴ This increased salience is reflected in the continued participation in the *Ayyaana* cult.

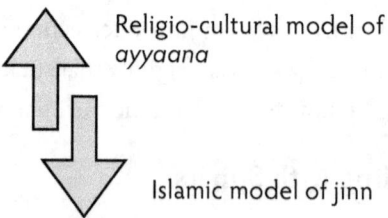

Figure 18: Increased salience of the *Ayyaana* model

---

3. Watson and Kochore include peace as a crucial aspect in the religious cosmology of the Borana people when they assert, "peace, ritual, rain, human welfare, animal health, and environmental well-being are closely linked." See Watson and Kochore, "Religion and Climate Change," 321.

4. Usage of the term *salience* in this section denotes the quality of one cultural model being predominant over the other. I did not undertake a quantitative or statistical examination to measure the level of saliency in order to determine the quantifiable observations that places the salience of the *ayyaana* model above that of the Islamic model. The findings of this study demonstrate that the *ayyaana* model is assigned higher relevance than the Islamic model, hence the increased participation in the *Ayyaana* cult in spite of the prohibitions by the Muslim teachers in Marsabit County.

The significance of the *Ayyaana* model is demonstrated by the fact that it is through this model that the *warra ayyaana* are able to interpret and respond to the impingement by the inhabitants of *al-ghaib*. The essence of cultural models is that they represent the world in people's minds, as well as giving explanations about the issues pertaining to the world around them.[5] Actions are planned and behavior is performed according to the salience of models, especially in cases where there are contesting models. Thus, the *Ayyaana* model predominates in the cognition of *warra ayyaana* because it acts as a motivational force that drives them to participate continually in the *Ayyaana* cult. Their lived experiences have been discussed in chapter 6.

The salience of the *Ayyaana* model is further enhanced by the constant experiences that *warra ayyaana* have with *ayyaana*. Since *ayyaana* are perceived to be relational, it is easier to interact with them than with the jinn. This interaction further enhances the relevance of the concept of *ayyaana* to *warra ayyaana*. The increased number of experiences is directly proportional to the salience of the *Ayyaana* model. *Warra ayyaana* assign higher salience to the model as they continue to interact with *ayyaana* in their daily lives.

The salience of a model is also boosted by its flexibility and adaptability. Bennardo and de Munck state that cultural models are inherently flexible.[6] Cultural knowledge is not a monolithic unit.[7] This permits the cultural model to be flexible and to adapt to the dynamism inherent in them. The *Ayyaana* model is therefore considered to be more salient because it is flexible and not rigid. Its flexibility is apparent in the way it has been able to accommodate different elements from Sufism, Borana customs, and Islam. The *warra ayyaana* find significance in borrowing these elements and including them in the *Ayyaana* cult, and consequently they form part of their mental constructions. A crucial aspect of the *Ayyaana* cult in borrowing these elements is the concept of *nagaa*.

The Salience of the *Ayyaana* Model in Promoting *Nagaa*

David Maranz's assessment of "peace is everything" in his study of the worldview of Wolof Muslims in Senegambia resonates with the *nagaa* concept of the

---

5. Bennardo and de Munck, *Cultural Models*, 59.
6. Bennardo and de Munck, 3.
7. Quinn and Holland, "Culture and Cognition," 10.

ordinary Borana Muslims in Marsabit County.[8] This section analyzes how the *Ayyaana* model promotes *nagaa* vis-à-vis the Islamic model of jinn. I will compare the roles of the two models, *Ayyaana* and Islamic model, promote peace with God, *ayyaana* spirits, and among Borana people.

From my research findings, I concur with Hassan G.W. Arero, who examined the concept of *nagaa Borana* (peace of Borana) among the Borana and Gabra pastoralists in northern Kenya.[9] Arero perceives *nagaa* as an important concept that has a wider meaning than just the absence of war.[10] I have noted, in chapter 6, that the concept of *nagaa* is pertinent to *warra ayyaana*. *Nagaa* is a major theme in their *salawat* prayer. The *hadhara* sessions are basically about making *nagaa* with *ayyaana*. Thus, *warra ayyaana* find their model of *Ayyaana* to answer their quest for peace, unlike the Islamic model, which does not emphasize peace with the spirits.

Peace is about relating with both human and non-human entities among the Borana people. This value of relationship is prominent among the *warra ayyaana* as they relate closely with *ayyaana* and with one another. Aguilar Mario agrees that the concept of *nagaa* is a "foundational principle, which stems from the right relation between the Waso Borana (and every Boorana) with God and with the world. Every ritual moment and every ritual practice ... contributes to realizing that Peace."[11] The Islamic model of the spirit world prohibits any relationship with the transcendental Allah, with the jinn, or with any other spirits, like *ayyaana*. Any close association with any of these is tantamount to the sin of *shirk* according to the Muslim teachers. Yet, this explains why *warra ayyaana* tend to background the Islamic model because it does not contribute to the aspect of peace with *ayyaana*. It may serve to point to peace as popularly indicated by the meaning of the word "Islam" as one who submits to Allah. It still lacks the practical notion akin to what *warra ayyaana* experience as they chant their *salawat* prayers together.

---

8. David. E Maranz, *Peace Is Everything*.

9. Arero, "Keeping the Peace."

10. I note that Hassan Arero uses the spelling *naga*, while I prefer to use *nagaa*. His broad sense of the concept includes "fertility, social co-operation, good health and continuity." Arero, "Keeping the Peace," 6. Mario Aguilar also mentions the significance of *nagaa Borana*, which is maintained through the prayers, blessings, and customary greetings of Borana people. See Aguilar, "Current Religious Practices," 51.

11. Aguilar, "Nagaa," 183–287.

The *jamaat* (brotherhood) association within the *Ayyaana* cult is comparable to the concept of *umma* as described in Islam in the maintenance of peace. *Umma* revolves around the mosque and excludes Muslim women especially during their menses. Women are also not allowed to mingle with men during the prayer sessions. This contrasts with the *jamaat* in the *Ayyaana* cult, which allows both genders to pray together. This mixing enhances a sense of belonging for the women, who are given ample space to express their religious activities. It increases the relevance of the concept in the cognition of the women and may contribute to their increased number in the *Ayyaana* cult.

Increased Salience through Counterintuitive Properties

Barrett and Nyhof assert that counterintuitive features of a religious concept make it salient.[12] *Ayyaana* have counterintuitive features as discussed in chapter 5. These are characteristics that "violate intuitive expectations that are regularly acquired."[13] Such features include the ability to "enter" people and make them perform counterintuitive actions such as licking a red-hot machete without burning. They cannot do this without *ayyaana*; hence it is a counterintuitive feature of *Ayyaana* that makes the model constructed in the minds of *warra ayyaana* to be more salient.

The Qur'an also mentions some counterintuitive features of the jinn. In Surah 2 and Surah 27, jinn are said to have worked for Solomon. Sheikh Amr admitted that there was a jinni that carried a throne within a very short time (see chapter 4). Such features of the jinn can also be said to be counterintuitive. Thus, a germane question is why the jinn concept is less salient than the *ayyaana* concept according to *warra ayyaana*.

Pascal Boyer's theory of minimal counterintuitive (MCI) is helpful to explain the difference between the salience of the concepts of *ayyaana* and jinn. The concepts that are more salient are the ones that are transmitted more within a cultural group. Boyer suggests that concepts which "slightly deviate from the intuitive expectations of our mental tools might be transmitted even more successful."[14] This is the theory of minimal counterintuitive that

---

12. Barrett and Nyhof, "Spreading Non-Natural Concepts," 72.
13. Barrett and Nyhof, 72.
14. Barrett, "Cognitive Science of Religion," 771.

explains why religious concepts are more prevalent than others.[15] Cohen also used this theory in her study of an Afro-Brazilain spirit possession cult.[16] For this study, I use the MCI theory to inquire which of the two models – *Ayyaana* or Islamic – is minimally counterintuitive and hence more transmittable by the *warra ayyaana* in Marsabit.

The manner in which *warra ayyaana* anthropomorphize *ayyaana* makes them less counterintuitive than jinn.[17] The latter have some human attributes, like the ability to become Muslims as mentioned in chapter 4. However, these humanlike characteristics are not taken to the relational extent that the *warra ayyaana* give to *ayyaana*. This makes the jinn be more counterintuitive when they seem to interact with people in the way the official texts present them according to the Muslim teachers in Marsabit County. *Ayyaana* are less counterintuitive because of their relational proximity to *warra ayyaana*.

The artifacts, music, and sacred places involved in the *Ayyaana* cult are considered to be "cultural scaffolding" that allows for the minimal counterintuitiveness of *Ayyaana*.[18] This cultural scaffolding offers memory aids to *warra ayyaana*, who are mostly oral learners. Barrett also postulates that written texts (scriptures) and sermons are the "clearest example of cultural scaffolding" that

---

15. There are other scholars of cognitive science of religion who have questioned the MCI theory. Purzycki and Willard assert that the theory does not provide enough of an explanation for the persistence and ubiquity of religious concepts. See Purzycki and Willard, "MCI Theory," 2.

16. Cohen, *Mind Possessed*.

17. Justin Barrett alludes to a debate among cognitive scientists. Some argue that the ideas of spirits/ghosts and God are not minimally counterintuitive, and others say the contrary. I acknowledge Barrett's quantification coding of counterintuitive concepts. According to him, the "counterintuitiveness score for ghosts/spirits is then 1; the epitome of a minimally counterintuitive concept." See Barrett, "Coding and Quantifying Counterintuitiveness," 327. Barrett has developed a metric for quantifying the relative counterintuitiveness of religious concepts. See Barrett and Nyhof, "Spreading Non-Natural Concepts"; and Barrett " Coding and Quantifying Counterintuitiveness." Barrett realized the ambiguity in determining the level of counterintuitiveness according to Boyer's theory. I did not delve into this statistical endeavor, since my study was not based solely on the concept of counterintuitiveness. Rather, I employed it here to give part of the explanation for the predominance of the *ayyaana* model over the Islamic model of jinn among *warra ayyaana*.

18. Barrett asserts that most god concepts are highly counterintuitive and hence most likely not easily transmitted. Such concepts then require "special cultural scaffolding to aid their transmission: special artifacts, institutions, practices, or other devises that help people learn and use these more complex concepts." See Barrett, *Cognitive Science, Religion*, 105. He defines "cultural scaffolding" as the special resources or features within a cultural setting that are used to aid in cognition of highly counterintuitive concepts. See Barrett, 141.

aid in transmitting counterintuitive ideas.[19] The Muslim teachers interviewed for this study admitted that they preach against the belief in *ayyaana* and the cultic activities thereby. Thus, one would expect that *warra ayyaana* would have better understanding of jinn than of *ayyaana*. Yet this is not the case, as this study has established. I suggest, herein, that the creativity that allows for the adaptability of the *ayyaana* model allows it to be more foregrounded in the cognition of *warra ayyaana* than the Islamic model. As noted earlier, most of *warra ayyaana*'s orality makes them incline more to the artifacts, music, and *dargas* as sacred places than to the written texts or sermons from the mosque. The experiences of *warra ayyaana* with *ayyaana* further enhance their cognition and thus they foreground the *Ayyaana* model while backgrounding the Islamic model of jinn.

The element of experience is crucial in this discussion of the religious inclination of people. Yet I find that the cognitive scholars who have examined the religious transmission of concepts have not really highlighted this element of experience. Further, I noted the aspect of creativity by *warra ayyaana*. Creativity as an aspect of human cognition is also not emphasized by the same scholars. It is on this premise that I suggest a theory, which helps to explain the inclination of *warra ayyaana* to the concept of *ayyaana* and not to jinn.

Formulating the Theory of Experiential Creative Cognition

This section proposes a theory that seeks to rationalize the discrepancy between the *Ayyaana* and Islamic models as discussed in the sections above. I suggest that this variance is based on an aspect of experiential creativity by *warra ayyaana* in seeking to deal with their contextual realities. This section will therefore discuss this aspect of creativity in order to explain further the apparent discrepancy in the kind of Islam found in Marsabit with regard to the spirit world.

---

19. Barrett, *Cognitive Science, Religion*.

The *Ayyaana* Cult as a Creative Product

The *Ayyaana* cult is a creative product of the cognition of *warra ayyaana*. This cognition is augmented by the ritual experiences during the cultic activities as discussed in chapter 6. The continual individual and collective experiences by *warra ayyaana* are instantiated first as individual mental representations and then shared intersubjectively as a religiocultural model of *Ayyaana* as discussed in chapter 5. The relevance of the *Ayyaana* model was based on the fact that it explains what happens in their contextual environment and also offers solutions to their problems in accordance with their supernaturalistic worldview.

Continual transmission of the model of *Ayyaana* depends on how the *warra ayyaana* routinize the cultic activities. Yet routine can be monotonous and may demotivate participation. To avoid this tedium, *warra ayyaana* have had to be creative and take initiative in dealing with *ayyaana*. The flexibility of the *Ayyaana* model in their cognition allows them to borrow elements from other religiocultural traditions.

Creativity and innovation are conceptual processes that human beings use to solve problems. The ability to be creative is not limited to a few intellectual persons. Creativity is endowed to all human beings, as Moreno asserts, "The human mind is exceptionally creative."[20] In Islam, the prophet Muhammad has been presented as the epitome of creative thinking.[21] Ordinary human beings, as well, are endowed with a propensity to be creative. *Warra ayyaana* thus use their creativity to deal with *ayyaana*.

Creativity is not only apparent in the use of material things. It is essentially about making use of both physical and ethereal things to solve pertinent human problems. Thus, the *warra ayyaana* believe that *Waaqa* has endowed them with *ayyaana* to help them solve germane religiocultural issues relating to their supernaturalistic world. Last, their environment is conducive for creative cognition in spite of their opposing Muslim teachers. There are many non-participant sympathizers who acknowledge that the *Ayyaana* cult solves

---

20. Moreno, *Creativity and Convention*, 5.

21. Muslim scholars have examined the concept of creativity from an Islamic perspective. Examples include Nizah et al., "Preliminary Study"; Zafir et al., "Creating Creative and Innovative"; Adibah et al., "Creativity and Innovation"; Yousif, "Creativity in Islamic Thought"; Al-Ajeen and Al-Khateed, "Islamic Legislation for Creativity"; Al-karasneh and Saleh, "Islamic Perspective of Creativity"; and others.

colossal problems of life. This is the reason why many of the eyewitnesses interviewed for this research gave a positive report even though they were not directly involved in the cultic activities.

Al-Ajeen and Al-Khateed restrict the Islamic creativity to whatever will actualize the main goal of man's creation, namely, worship of Allah.[22] They prohibit *bid'ah* (heretical innovation) and advocate for *ibtidā'* (creativity).[23] Hence, a pertinent issue, as I advance the theory of experiential creative cognition, may have to do with whether the *Ayyaana* cult is *ibtidā'* or *bid'ah*. However, dealing with the question of *ibtidā'* or *bid'ah* is beyond the scope of this research since it falls in the category of Islamic theology.

In their quest for religious piety and societal *nagaa* as Borana Muslims, *warra ayyaana* experience a spiritual and psychological void that frustrates them. Kim realizes that a sense of "spiritual frustration" is found in societies that have a supernaturalistic worldview. This is true especially in societies that subscribe to a strict monotheistic religion that adheres to unrealistic doctrinal demands.[24] Ordinary Borana Muslims like *warra ayyaana* find the doctrinal requirements of dealing with spirits to be insufficient. This makes them employ their cognitive abilities and creatively search for alternative ways to deal with the spirit world. They achieve this by exploiting different elements from their religiocultural setting. That is why they integrate elements from Islam, from traditional Borana, and from Sufi traditions to form the *Ayyaana* cult.

The findings of this research have shown that the religiocultural model of *Ayyaana* is more salient than the Islamic model of jinn. The latter is seen to be more practical in dealing with the spirit world than the former. The Islamic doctrinal standards are considered to be too rigid to offer pragmatic solutions that fill the spiritual and psychological gap experienced by ordinary Borana Muslims.

Like all human beings who seek to live a better life each day, *warra ayyaana* then apply their cognition. They participate in the *Ayyaana* cult to try and alleviate their frustrations. The *salawat* prayer and the *hadhara* healing sessions offer creative ways of upholding *nagaa* with *Waaqa*, with *ayyaana*,

---

22. Al-Ajeen and Al-Khateeb, "Islamic Legislation for Creativity."

23. *Ibda't* in Arabic is to "create in the sense of creating a masterpiece." It is used in a positive sense unlike *bida'*, which is translated as "blameworthy innovation." See Christelow, *Muslim Law Courts*, 113.

24. Kim, "Supernaturalism in Swahili Islam," 97.

and with fellow Borana kinsmen. They are able to appeal to God through the *salawat* prayer sessions as they intercede for different issues. They encounter the spirit world in a way that seems to relieve their insecurity. And last, they maintain the *umma* when they meet as members of the *jamaat* group. All these are activities that are shared intersubjectively among the *warra ayyaana* and contribute to the relevance of the *Ayyaana* model.

The Experiential Creative Cognition of *Warra Ayyaana*

Chapter 6 of this study demonstrated how the lived experiences of *warra ayyaana* enhance their mental representation of *ayyaana*. Experience enhances cognition, which in turn improves the memorability of the mental contents of a significant religiocultural feature. Experiential knowledge is therefore a key aspect that explains the inclination of *warra ayyaana* to the *Ayyaana* cult. Such knowledge contests with the abstract knowledge provided by the Muslim teachers concerning the spirit world. The significance of experiential knowledge in foregrounding the *Ayyaana* model, then, makes it expedient to formulate the theory of experiential creative cognition.

This theory does not delve into the cognitive mechanisms involved within the study area of creative cognition.[25] The essence of the theory is to recognize the significance of the experiences of people in formulating their creative thinking, and consequently the kind of mental models that motivate them to the activities they engage in.

---

25. The term "creative cognition" was coined by Finke, Ward, and Smith. See Smith, Finke, and Ward, *The Creative Cognition Approach*. It is the area of study that investigates both the "cognitive processes that lead to the emergence of novel cognitive structures and the role of existing cognitive structures in this emergence." See Moreno, *Creativity and Convention*, 6. The technical processes and mechanisms include aspects of "analogical transfer, imagination, incubation, and fixation." See Christensen, "Creative Cognition," 6. I did not delve into these mechanisms.

Comparative Interdisciplinary Analysis and Theory Formulation 215

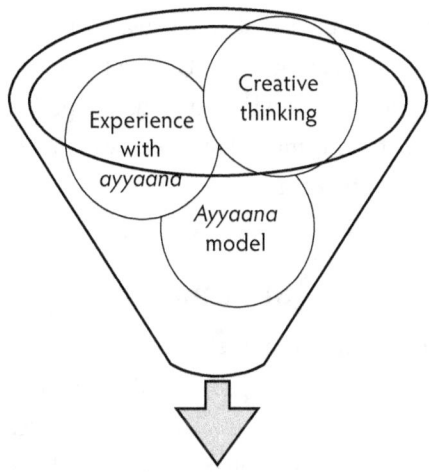

Figure 19: Formulating the theory of experiential creative cognition

The theory of experiential creative cognition explains why a particular religiocultural model is foregrounded and not another.[26] Thus it rationalizes the proclivity of people toward a particular religiocultural phenomenon like spirit possession. The advantage that this theory brings to the discussion is its non-reductionist perspective. It explores the cognition that motivates behavior. This theory thus delves into a deeper understanding of a religiocultural phenomenon than the surface level that only maps the behavioral dimension.

From figure 19, I have illustrated how the various aspects of *warra ayyaana* cognition facilitated the formulation of the theory of experiential creative cognition. The experiences that the participants of the *Ayyaana* cult continue to have with *ayyaana* make them filter and categorize any new information they receive. Their selective and creative minds consequently enable them to choose relevant information that will address these daily concerns. Their creative minds lead them to come up with beliefs and practices that they deem salient in providing solutions to these concerns. Chapter 6 has shown how they anthropomorphize *ayyaana*, and also borrow different elements to make up their unique cultic practices. Their creative thinking is also evident in the way they use metaphors to refer to *ayyaana*. Thus, the conclusion I make

---

26. The position of the words included in this theory is significant. The term "experiential" is placed first as people interact with causative agents. It is from these experiences that they apply their cognitive abilities to come up with creative solutions to their religiocultural issues.

concerning the *Ayyaana* cult is that it is a creative product that is based on the *Ayyaana* religiocultural model shared intersubjectively by *warra ayyaana*. Since they find this model useful in answering the problems that pertain to the spirit world, then it is transmitted more easily than the traditional Islamic model held by the Muslim leaders.

Summary

The overall goal of cultural model research is to provide a description of how knowledge is organized in people's minds. I have used the theory of cultural model to examine how the *warra ayyaana* organize their knowledge of the spirit world. In this comparative chapter, I have shown how they foreground the religiocultural model of *Ayyaana*, while they background the Islamic model of spirits as required by their Muslim teachers. The *Ayyaana* model is more salient than the Islamic model according to the cognition of the ordinary Borana Muslims. I have shown that this saliency is based on how adequate a model is to direct behavior that mitigates the daily issues pertaining to the spirit world.

I have also used the cognitive science theory of minimal counterintuitiveness propounded by Justin Barrett. Based on this theory, I have discovered that the more a spirit is anthropomorphized, the more minimal counterintuitive it becomes, and thus is easily transmitted within a cultural group. Music and artifacts help promote memorability and transmission. The Islamic model of spirits lacks the mnemonic attribute found in the music and artifacts that the *Ayyaana* cult thrives on. When I have combined the idea of anthropomorphism and the art of music and artifacts, I have been able to deduce a creative cognition that is displayed in the *Ayyaana* model by *warra ayyaana*. I then formulated the theory of experiential creative cognition that explains why the *warra ayyaana* are more inclined to the *Ayyaana* model than to the Islamic model. This theory has highlighted the need to consider people's lived experiences as crucial elements that determine their cognition and consequently the kind of cultural models they construct.

CHAPTER 8

Summary of Findings and Recommendations

Introduction

This chapter serves a threefold purpose: first, it offers a concise summary of the central research issue and the findings that I have derived as discussed in the foregoing chapters. Second, it gives significant implications arising from the findings that are deemed useful, specifically in anthropological and Islamic studies. Last, it suggests pertinent areas that I would recommend for further studies. These are some interesting issues that I encountered during the research and writing stages and yet were beyond the scope of this study.

Essence and Findings of the Research

This research was framed in a cognitive anthropological perspective. I have endeavored to describe the Islamic and religiocultural models of the spirit world according to the cognition of the Muslim teachers and of the ordinary Borana Muslims in Marsabit County, respectively. I have also described the self-identity of *warra ayyaana* as Muslims despite the criticism from their Muslim teachers. The essence of this task was to understand the lived experiences of the ordinary Borana Muslims as they participate in the *Ayyaana* cult. This has been done by analyzing their religiocultural model of *Ayyaana* in light of the Islamic model of spirits as constructed by the custodians of official Islam in the county. From this analysis, a theory has been formulated to explain the cognitive experiences of *warra ayyaana*'s participation in the *Ayyaana* cult in spite of the prohibitions from the Muslim teachers.

The Islamic and *Ayyaana* models have been realized using ethnographic interviews and participant observation. Using a qualitative design, these research tools have enabled me to interact closely with the interviewees as I listened to their discourses about the *ayyaana* and jinn. I was able to observe the ritual activities of the *warra ayyaana*, who are the adepts of the *Ayyaana* cult. The ability to intermingle with my interviewees was very appropriate for the phenomenological disposition that focuses on the people as the main sources of information.

The people factor has been a key aspect of this study. This made the study tilt toward anthropology as an essential element in studying Muslims. Most conventional Islamic studies programs have tended to incline toward the ideological side of Islam. The findings of this research have demonstrated that leaning toward the ideological or doctrinal side of Islam does not present a comprehensive or eclectic understanding of Muslims as the adherents of Islam. A germane inquiry is whether ordinary Muslims adhere to the tenets of Islam as stipulated in their official texts, or as taught by their *madrasa* teachers. In other words, do the lived experiences of ordinary Muslims reflect the teachings of official Islam? The findings of this research have shown that there is a disparity between what the Muslim teachers teach and what is practiced by the ordinary Borana Muslims in Marsabit County. This is illustrated from the summary of findings that I discuss below, following the research questions that guided my study.

Summary of Findings for Research Questions (RQs)

RQ 1: How can the Islamic model of the spirit world according to the Muslim teachers in Marsabit County be best described?

i. What knowledge do the Muslim teachers have about the spirit world in Marsabit County?

The Muslim teachers in Marsabit adhere to the official requirement that all Muslims must believe in the existence of a trans-empirical world (*al-ghaib*). They acknowledge that some of the inhabitants of this world are jinn, which

Summary of Findings and Recommendations

interact with the human world. All these spirit beings were created by Allah to worship him.

ii. What is the official position on jinn and possession as known and taught by the Muslim teachers?

The Muslim teachers conceptualize and categorize jinn as beings that are "exalted" by Allah together with man and angels. There are good and bad jinn. The former are the ones that believe the message of Muhammad and become Muslims. Such a position is derived from Qur'anic references mentioned by the Muslim teachers during the interviews. They further anthropomorphize jinn as endowed with somatic, spiritual, and emotional characteristics. These features allow jinn to interact with man on a subservient level. All the Muslim teachers interviewed consented that there are jinn that "enter" or "catch" people. These are the bad ones that "possess" people and cause trouble.

iii. What is the official Islamic position on dealing with spirits in Marsabit County?

The Muslim teachers, as custodians of official Islam, advocate for a non-relational approach in dealing with malevolent jinn. This involves exorcism and not accommodation or adorcism. One popular method is burning the jinn with the Qur'an. Appeasing them in cultic séances is considered to be *shirk* and should be avoided.

iv. What is the perception of *ayyaana* and participants of the *Ayyaana* cult by the Muslim teachers?

The Muslim teachers agree that *ayyaana* are real spiritual beings created by Allah. They categorize them as bad jinn that mislead Muslims. All the *warra ayyaana* who participate in the *Ayyaana* cult are committing the sin of *shirk*. The rituals involved in the cult are considered to be religious innovations (*bid'ah*). Hence, the Muslim-ness of *warra ayyaana* is questionable, according to the Muslim teachers.

RQ 2: What is the religiocultural model of the *Ayyaana* according to Borana Muslims who participate in the *Ayyaana* cult?

This research question has been addressed in chapters 5 and 6, whose aim was to describe the religiocultural model of *Ayyaana* and how it is instantiated by the *warra ayyaana*. The sub-questions (i–iii) below were useful in discovering this model as they provided the guiding questions for the ethnographic interviews as well as a trajectory for the participant observation exercise.

i. What do the adepts and practitioners of the *Ayyaana* "possession" cult believe about *ayyaana*?

Warra ayyaana conceptualize the term *ayyaana* in a polysemous way. The religiocultural model of *Ayyaana* as a spirit was unconsciously constructed from the repeated experiential contact that the *warra ayyaana* had with *ayyaana*, first individually and then intersubjectively. The metaphors used to refer to *ayyaana* as *qileensa Waaqa* (wind of God) and as a *jeshi* (an army) contribute to the development of the religiocultural model of *Ayyaana*. Chapter 5 illustrated how *ayyaana* have been anthropomorphized with human attributes like being religious, having the ability to do certain things, like eat, speak, hear, and relate with people closely.

ii. What are the rituals involved in the *Ayyaana* "possession" cult?

One crucial component of the religiocultural model of *Ayyaana* is the perception that *ayyaana* are not jinn. This conceptualization determined the approach to use in dealing with *ayyaana* that "caught" people. Chapter 6 showed how the religiocultural model is instantiated by the *warra ayyaana* as they participate in the *Ayyaana* cult. Essentially, the ritual practices allude to an accommodative relationship between *ayyaana* and the *warra ayyaana*. The latter do not consider this as *shirk*, as the Muslim teachers allude. *Warra ayyaana* believe that *ayyaana* came to Islamize them, and hence they consider themselves to be true Muslims as they perform the *hadhara* healing and *salawat* prayer sessions. They find that such cultic practices help to provide pragmatic solutions to their daily experiences with the spirit world.

iii. What are the lived experiences and perceptions of Borana Muslims who participate in the *Ayyaana* cult?

There is dynamism between the religiocultural model of *Ayyaana* and the lived experiences of *warra ayyaana* as they participate in the cult. Chapter 6 illustrated this dynamism and showed how the interplay is further heightened through the music and tangible artifacts used during the sessions. The vignettes recounting the lived experiences of ordinary Borana Muslims with *ayyaana* illustrate the positivity they have as they participate in the *Ayyaana* cult.

The positivity that *warra ayyaana* derive from the *ayyaana* made me conclude that the religiocultural model of *Ayyaana* is salient. This salience is evident in the way the participants borrow elements from their traditional Borana customs, from Islam, and from Sufism as practiced among the Borana Muslims.

RQ 3: How can the religiocultural model of *Ayyaana* be assessed in light of the Islamic model of spirits in Marsabit County among the Borana Muslims using cognitive theories?

Chapter 7 answered this question. It offered a comparative analysis of the religiocultural model of *Ayyaana* as examined in light of the Islamic model of spirits represented by the Muslim teachers in Marsabit County. The sub-questions (i–iv) below enabled me to compare the two models and then offer an explanation of the ensuing comparative analysis.

i. What are the similarities between the official Islamic model of the spirit world by the Muslim teachers in Marsabit County and the religiocultural model of *Ayyaana*?

A pertinent similarity between the *ayyaana* and Islamic models is the explicit orientation toward a supernaturalistic worldview. In both models, the belief in the existence of spirits created by God is notable. Both the Muslim teachers and *warra ayyaana* apply their cognitive abilities to classify the spirits accordingly. They also anthropomorphize these non-human beings.

ii. What distinctive features of the *Ayyaana* cult tend to make Borana Muslims deviate from the official path concerning spirits and "possession"?

The *Ayyaana* religiocultural model varies from the Islamic models of the spirit world in two distinctive ways: first, in the categorization of *ayyaana*, and second, in the approach used to deal with *ayyaana*. The Muslim teachers exorcise *ayyaana* because they classify them as jinn. The *warra ayyaana*, on the other hand, do not categorize *ayyaana* as jinn; hence they accommodate *ayyaana* instead of exorcising them.

The Muslim-ness of *warra ayyaana* is also a distinctive feature that has been examined in light of the Muslim teachers' perception. The teachers question the self-identity of *warra ayyaana* as Muslims. The phenomenological disposition of this study entailed that I describe the self-identity of *warra ayyaana* as they narrated to me. I analyzed this identity in light of the official Islamic position regarding the beliefs and practices concerning the spirit world. I concluded that the *warra ayyaana* are ordinary people with felt needs that solicit pragmatic solutions. Their beliefs and experiences drive them to participate in the *Ayyaana* cult amid prohibitions from their Muslim teachers. This cult seems to offer solutions to their frequent encounters with the spirit world beyond what the Muslim teachers recommend for them. Hence, the *Ayyaana* model becomes foregrounded while the Islamic model of spirits is backgrounded.

iii. What suitable theory or theories explain the relationship between the *Ayyaana* and Islamic models?
This study has shown that the salience of the *Ayyaana* model is higher than that of the Islamic model of the spirit world. This implies that the *warra ayyaana* find the *Ayyaana* model more relevant in addressing germane issues that they encounter in their daily lives. Significantly, this study has shown that the *Ayyaana* model is significant as it promotes *nagaa* (peace), an essential element in the lives of Borana Muslims.

The salience of the *Ayyaana* model over the Islamic model of spirits is further expounded by the cognitive theory of minimal counterintuitiveness. This theory helps to explain why the *warra ayyaana* cognitively select the *Ayyaana* model. This model is considered to be minimally counterintuitive and hence is easily remembered and selected instead of the Islamic model of spirits as taught by the Muslim teachers.

Examining the religiocultural model of *Ayyaana* has stimulated the need to offer an explanation for the disparity evident between the ideological stipulations of Islam and the lived experiences of ordinary Muslims. Chapter 2 of this dissertation presented the various attempts by scholars to examine and explain the phenomenon of spirit possession among Muslims. A number of these scholars used an anthropological perspective that formulated pertinent theories. The theory of domain of total synthesis by Kim was helpful in realizing that African Islam is contextual as it merges with specific African religiocultural contexts.[1] I. M. Lewis's famous deprivation theory explains why spirit possession is rampant among women as the most socially deprived people. Based on a functionalist approach, I found Lewis's theory slightly

---

1. Kim, "Supernaturalism in Swahili Islam"; and Kim, *Islam among the Swahili*.

reductionist in explaining the inclination of adepts to cultic activities. There was need for a more comprehensive approach to the study of the phenomenon. Emma Cohen's cognitive anthropological inclination was useful in showing the possibility of examining the phenomenon using such a framework.[2]

All these theories and others have contributed significantly toward a greater understanding of possession cults and their adherents. Yet, I realized the paucity of studies that use a cognitive anthropological perspective. Cohen, mentioned above, is one of the few anthropologists who examined the phenomenon of spirit possession from a cognitive anthropological perspective. I used the minimal counterintuitive theory as she did. I combined this with the cultural model theory as expounded by Bennardo and de Munck in order to offer a more comprehensive explanation of the *Ayyaana* cult.[3]

As I listened, observed, and analyzed the *Ayyaana* model, I realized there was a type of religiosity that transcends the behavioral aspects. It was therefore expedient to formulate a theory that went beyond the functionalistic approach used in Lewis's deprivation theory. It was also needful to get a perspective that would be phenomenological in listening to the discourses from the people themselves as they narrated them in their language. These discourses further highlighted the place of experience in the creative cognition of people. The aspect of experience has not been adequately acknowledged in the cognitive theories that I used to explain the disparity in Borana Islam. There was need to formulate a more comprehensive theory.

I have submitted the theory of experiential creative cognition. This stemmed from the creativity I noted in the way the *Ayyaana* religiocultural model is instantiated by *warra ayyaana*, as well as their experiences with *ayyaana*. The *Ayyaana* cult is a creative product that is an amalgamation of borrowed elements that are put together in a creative way. *Warra ayyaana* employ their cognition in a bid to come up with a way of solving their pertinent issues that they find are not addressed adequately by the official Islamic stipulations.

---

2. Cohen, *Mind Possessed*, and Cohen, *The Mind Possessed*.
3. Bennardo and de Munck, *Cultural Models*.

The *Ayyaana* Model as a Feature of Borana Islam

One pertinent aim of this study has been to describe the lived experiences of *warra ayyaana* and present their self-identity as Muslims despite the criticism from their teachers. Their participation in the *Ayyaana* cult stems from their intersubjective mental representations of *ayyaana*. This therefore forms a significant feature of the kind of Islam practiced among the Borana people in Marsabit County.

Scholars who have examined Islam or Muslims in Africa have realized a common thread of syncretism that runs across most, if not all, African Muslims. I have cited Kim, who formulated his theory of domain of total synthesis based on the syncretistic nature expressed by the Swahili Islam in Zanzibar. David Shenk also found that the Somali Muslims' quest for *baraka* (blessings) integrates Sufism and African traditional religious practices with Islam to come up with a localized Islam in Somalia.[4] This current study has discovered a similar trend displayed by the Borana Muslims in Marsabit County.

The religiocultural model of *Ayyaana* discussed herein presents a significant aspect of the kind of Islam practiced in Marsabit County by ordinary Muslims. At the core of their Islamic identity is their identity as Borana who stand in solidarity with their fellow tribesmen and tribeswomen. One of the ways they have displayed this identity has been indicated in chapters 5 and 6. It was shown how they integrated key traditional Borana elements into their cultic beliefs and practices that revolve around *ayyaana*. The ordinary Borana Muslims have a distinct causal understanding regarding *ayyaana*. The saliency and transmission of the religiocultural model of *Ayyaana* helps to buttress this cognition in a way that most ordinary Borana Muslims are likely to seek redress from *Ayyaana* practitioners in order to live peaceful lives.

Generally, peace is a fundamental element in African religiocultural contexts. The means to attain this peace are specific for different African settings. Traditionally, Africans yearn for *baraka*. Peace is an inherent virtue encompassed in the concept of *baraka*. This *baraka* is both tangible and intangible, and it deals with both human and non-human beings that are part of the human world.

---

4. Shenk, "African Christian and Islamic Mysticism." See also Marranci, *Anthropology of Islam*, 4.

Nagaa (peace) is a central domain of the religiocultural model of *Ayyaana*. The findings of this study have shown that Borana Muslims pursue peace with *Waaqa*, *ayyaana*, and fellow Borana people. Thus, they recognize the importance of *nagaa*, not only with Allah, as stipulated in official Islam. They also seek to be at peace with *ayyaana*, hence the *hadhara* (singing) sessions performed during the *salawat* (prayer) and healing gatherings (see figure 20 below).

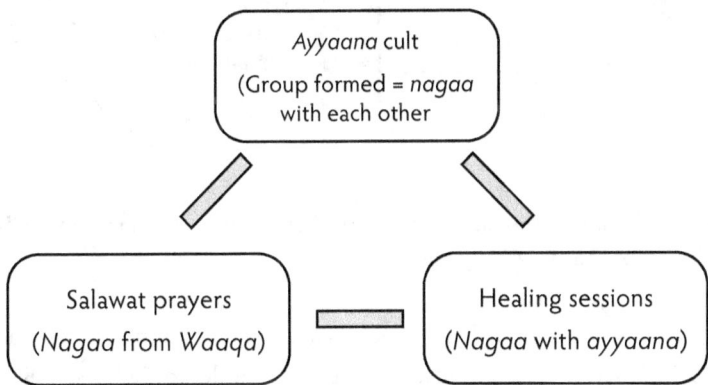

Figure 20: Centrality of *nagaa* in the *Ayyaana* cult

The quest for *nagaa* is central among Borana Muslims. The domain of *nagaa* is intertwined with that of *baraka* that is derived from *Waaqa* through the *Ayyaana* practitioners. The mention of Sheikh Hussein's name also brings *baraka*, which is a significant component of the *Ayyaana* cultic sessions. Hence, the quest for *nagaa* makes the *Ayyaana* model a key component of Borana Islam. Understanding this pursuit for peace and how it has been creatively undertaken then yields essential implications for the studies of Islam and anthropology.

Implications for Islamic Studies

This study has unraveled an aspect of ordinary Borana Muslims that appeals for greater understanding. The disparity between their daily lives and the ideological requirements has shown that focusing on the latter obfuscates the real-life experiences of these Muslims. Furthermore, such a skewed focus fails to demonstrate the existence of a tension between the ideological expression of Islam and the lived experiences of ordinary Muslims as illustrated in figure 21 below.

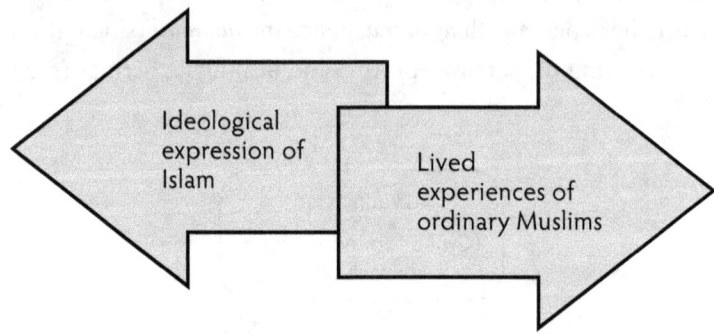

Figure 21: Tension between the ideological expression of Islam and the lived experiences of ordinary Muslims

It is essential to acknowledge that this tension exists and to investigate the interaction therein. The significance of such an endeavor helps stakeholders of Islamic studies to understand where the ordinary Muslims place their cognition and efforts. This calls for the need to study their lived experiences and how they relate or interact with the ideological expression of Islam.

It is imperative to acknowledge the existence of the lacunae in the different expressions of Islam. This realization will enable those engaged in Islamic studies to broaden their focus beyond the ideological emphasis that has been prevalent. It is recommended that scholars and researchers endeavoring to understand Muslims better would seek to find out if the lived experiences of Muslims are congruent with the tenets of Islam. It is also recommended that such anthropological research should creatively come up with novel methodologies and methods that are also compliant with the cultural systems of particular people. Bennardo and de Munck, for instance, have offered a research method that aims at discovering cultural models. I found this quite useful for this study even though I could not use every step of their suggested methods. This is because most of my interviewees were semi-illiterate and hence could not list down words and phrases as suggested for the free-listing exercise. I therefore recommend that anyone working among such people with low literacy levels devise an oral free-listing exercise.

Marranci bemoans the isolation experienced by anthropologists who study topics related to Islam. These researchers, with the exception of Geertz, have not been very successful in reaching a wider audience beyond their own disciplines.[5] To try and mitigate this, there is a need for an ongoing conversation between scholars from different disciplines. A multidisciplinary effort would include sociologists, anthropologists, cognitive psychologists, and others. This current study has shown the possibility of such inter-disciplinary efforts where theories from different disciplines have been employed to understand Muslims' lived experiences.

The information in this dissertation is available to anyone interested in understanding the *warra ayyaana*'s cultic participation in a deeper way. Such an understanding would pave the way to an appropriate approach that seeks to address the felt needs of ordinary Muslims. It would most likely point out any deficiency that may be inherent in the ideological requirements that do not tackle the immediate needs of the people. This would consequently allow for the creative and contextual articulation of the official tenets.

My assertion about the creativity of *warra ayyaana* also points to another pertinent issue in Islamic studies. There has been a debate concerning the diverse representations of Islam globally. The question is whether there are many Islams or one Islam with different expressions. I acknowledge Talal Asad's concept of discursive tradition in understanding the diversity in Islam.[6] Asad disagrees with the notion of Islams as I have done according to my findings herein. *Warra ayyaana* are not practicing a different kind of Islam. They practice an expression of Islam that is creative in providing answers to issues they deem are beyond them.

Such endeavors ensure that the focal point of studying Islamic religiosity is not the textual ideals but the people who attempt to live out the precepts. The importance of studying Muslims as people cannot be understated as evident from this current study. This focus has continued to raise an interest among anthropologists who study Islam.

---

5. Marranci, *Anthropology of Islam*, 4.

6. Asad, "Idea of an Anthropology," 10. The discursive nature of Islam is interpreted to mean that Islam is flexible in allowing local decisions that determine what is *halal* (allowed) and what is *haram* (forbidden) in line with the official texts. See Lukens-Bull, "Between Text and Practice," 9. This discursive aspect respects the self-identification of Muslims within their local settings. See Lukens-Bull, 11.

Implications for the Anthropology of Islam

A germane religiocultural question that could be raised from this current study is whether I have been dealing with Borana "invented traditions" that have only been Islamized or whether I have been studying Islam that has been influenced by Borana traditions.[7] Essentially, at the core of this question is the anthropological definition of *Islam*; in other words, who defines what Islam is?

This study sought to understand the *warra ayyaana* as ordinary Muslims who participate in the *Ayyaana* cult. It was apparent that their cognition of *ayyaana* is incongruent with what their Muslim teachers teach them. Then the question of defining Islam anthropologically is valid and relevant. I have discussed the self-awareness of *warra ayyaana* as Muslims who participate in the *Ayyaana* cult. I have also shown how the Muslim teachers dispute their "Muslim-ness." Since I am a non-Muslim, I cannot place my verdict on who is correct in this issue of "Muslim-ness." The apparent disparity begs for a deeper anthropological understanding of the ordinary Muslims like the *warra ayyaana*.

This study augments the appeal by anthropologists of Islam to take the "people factor" more earnestly in order to understand Muslims as people. Chapter 4 mentioned some scholars who have delved into the area of the anthropology of Islam. Most of these scholars, however, have studied Muslims from non-African contexts. A few, like Kim, have endeavored to examine African Muslims anthropologically. This study on the phenomenon of *ayyaana* among the ordinary Borana Muslims is significant as it contributes to the anthropological research on African Muslims south of Sahara. The anthropological significance of this study is further shown by the interaction between culture and the mind. This interface is displayed by the dynamism portrayed between the lived experiences of *warra ayyaana* and their religiocultural model of *Ayyaana*. Before the area of cognitive anthropology was founded, there was a conspicuous dichotomy between culture and cognition. Such a divide seems to result in a reductionist understanding of the people or phenomenon under empirical study. The popular Lewisian deprivation theory is an example of a reductionist reading of the phenomenon of spirit

---

7. In other words, I ask a reflective question: whether I have been studying Islam or Borana traditions that have been Islamized. Regarding use of the term *islamized*, see Lukens-Bull, "Between Text and Practice," 1.

possession. The functionalistic framework that guided I. M. Lewis's study and eventual theoretical formulation lacks a deeper view of the underlying factors that contribute to participation in possession cults. This current study showed the importance of going beyond the superficial behavioral episodes. It highlights the necessity of investigating the underlying cognitive factors that make people behave the way they do.

This study has also highlighted the importance of listening to the ordinary Muslims, not only to their voices, but also to their emotions and feelings. A clarion call was sounded by Marranci, who suggests that the emotions and feelings of Muslims "should be at the center of our studies of Islam."[8] I have already noted that the *warra ayyaana* consider themselves to be true Muslims in spite the objections from their teachers. The cognitive anthropological approach used in this study recognized the authenticity of the feelings of ordinary Muslims.

Propositions for Further Studies

This study has triggered fundamental empirical questions that are worth highlighting as recommendations for further inquiry. The phenomenon of spirit possession is very comprehensive and eclectic. This encourages more research in various cultural settings and specifically among Muslims. The first area that I would recommend for further studies is the music of the spirits examined using an ethnomusicological approach. I found the *Ayyaana* songs quite intriguing, but I could not delve deeper or move beyond tracing their general themes. I would recommend that more in-depth studies be done that would consider the genre, syntax, phonetics, grammar, language, and other aspects of the songs.

Having read Cohen's investigation of transmission of possession concepts, it would be interesting to explore, in more detail, what the Borana Muslims / *warra ayyaana* think about the possession of human bodies by spirits.[9] The central aim in this regard would be to examine what *warra ayyaana* believe about occupation of the mind by the spirits. It would be fascinating to examine whether they believe that the *ayyaana* displaces the host's mind such that

---

8. Marranci, *Anthropology of Islam*, 6.
9. Cohen, *Mind Possessed*.

any behavior by the possessed person is attributed to the *ayyaana* (principle of displacement), or whether they believe that there is a fusion between the host's body and the spirit and hence one entity (fusion principle). Such a study would be significant in verifying whether the results would be comparable with those of Cohen. According to Cohen, the principle of displacement is easily remembered by people because it is minimally counterintuitive, unlike the fusion principle that is largely counterintuitive and hence less likely to be recalled or transmitted.[10] It would be appropriate to examine the general applicability of this assertion within the *Ayyaana* cult.

There is a need to study the concept of *ayyaana* among other Borana-speaking people groups in Kenya like the Sakuye, the Gabra, the Garre, the Watta, the Orma, and the Munyoyaya. Most of these have a rising number of Muslims. A study of how each of these people groups experiences *ayyaana* within their religiocultural context would be useful. Such a study would unravel any similarities or differences that would be expedient in a deeper understanding of Islam as experienced by different people.

The tension between the ordinary Muslim experiences and the ideological requirements is not restricted only to Islam. Hiebert, Shaw, and Tienou realize that there is a two-tier Christianity, also called "Split-level Christianity."[11] Since there are some churches in Marsabit County, it would be appropriate to examine how Christianity is affected by the *ayyaana* phenomenon. Is there a similar tension between the religious experiences among the few Borana Christians and the doctrinal requirements of Christianity?

More collaborative studies should be attempted in order to understand Muslims in a comprehensive way. The cognitive anthropological perspective that I used for this dissertation shows that it is possible to do a collaborative study. I would recommend that further studies be done that are framed in a historical, anthropological, and cognitive perspective. It would be interesting to trace the historical development of the *ayyaana* phenomenon right from Ethiopia and what people say about its progressive expansion into southern Ethiopia and northern Kenya. Furthermore, such a study would also elucidate the contribution of the phenomenon to the expansion of Islam in the respective regions as popularly asserted.

---

10. Cohen and Barrett, "When Minds Migrate," 44.
11. Hiebert, Shaw, and Tienou, *Understanding Folk Religion*, 15.

Both the official and popular Islamic phenomena have a general supernaturalistic worldview that guides the textual narratives as well as the lived experiences of Muslims. Thus, studying the concept of spirits and possession would illuminate more about the essence of Islam and enhance a deeper understanding of the spirit world in Islam. This implication concurs with El-Zein's suggestion that examining the concept of jinn in Islam clarifies the "particularity of Islam."[12] It would be helpful to examine how different communities appropriate or experience the jinn phenomenon in their localized Islam. I appreciate the extensive focus on Zanzibar/Swahili Muslims' participation in jinn possession cults by various outstanding scholars. This should motivate more empirical investigations on how the spirit world is understood by other African Muslims. It would also be fascinating to know if the supernatural worldview of African Muslims who live in the diaspora could prompt them to concerted efforts in dealing with jinn or *ayyaana*.

Summary

This chapter offers a summary of the findings of this research as well as appropriate recommendations especially for further studies. Steeping this research within a cognitive anthropological framework has elicited exciting findings that are significant to the discipline of anthropology and inter-religious studies. The findings have realized the importance of going beyond the surface level if one is to gain an indepth understanding of a religious phenomenon. Furthermore, this study has shown the need of examining the lived experiences of ordinary people as they go about their lives. The analysis of data collected from the field of study elicited two broad cultural models: the Islamic model of the world of spirits, and the religio-cultural model of *ayyaana*. The findings showed the contrast between the two mental representations, which made the ordinary Borana Muslims engage the *ayyaana* spirits in a different way from what was taught by the Muslim teachers. Essentially, this study has shown that there is tension between the ideological expressions of Islam and the lived experiences of the ordinary Muslims. Therefore, focusing only on the classical studies of Islam misses out on a crucial dimension of how Islam is lived out by ordinary Muslims.

---

12. El-Zein, "Evolution of the Concept," vii.

CHAPTER 9

Some Missiological Implications for Christian-Muslim Interactions

Introduction

I entered an office excited that I would eventually meet one of my favorite authors, who has researched and published on spirit possession from a cognitive anthropological perspective. I left that office disheartened after a very brief chat in which I was told that this author has stopped working on the topic of spirit possession and is concentrating on other "more important things." I went away contemplating and asking myself: "Spirit possession? Not an important topic?"

The previous chapter, chapter 8, has elucidated the importance of studying the phenomenon of spirit possession vis-à-vis the conventional focus on classical issues in Islam. The chapter also expounded on what this dissertation has achieved in the objectives set out in chapter 1. The study sought to understand the Borana Muslims who live in Marsabit County, Kenya. It focused particularly on seeking to understand their lived experiences as they participate in the *Ayyaana* possession cult that is prevalent in the region. These experiences were compared with the official tenets of Islam concerning the spirit world, thereafter an analytical discussion was provided that is in line with the methodological guideline STA, which framed the whole study. Without repeating the implications that have already been discussed in the preceding chapter, this current chapter will focus on the missiological implications that are deemed relevant for Christians who want to interact with Muslims more effectively. A sequence to this study is ongoing that will provide an expanded discussion on the issues of deliverance and inner healing for those tormented by malevolent spiritual beings and forces. Suffice it, for now, to highlight some key implications that arise from the discussion brought forth in this study. For each subsequent section, a biblical response will be provided so that it is evident to anyone reading this book that the Bible also addresses the issue of the spirit world.

No Longer the Excluded Middle

Paul Hiebert's 1982 article, "The Flaw of the Excluded Middle," has continued to elicit responses from both the Western and non-Western contexts. In the article, Hiebert begins by recounting his sense of uneasiness when he encountered the phenomenon of spirit possession and the world of spirits both in the Bible and among the people he served as a missionary. His uneasiness originated from his worldview orientation that had "excluded the middle level of supernatural but this-worldly beings and forces."[1] The same discomfort would be inevitable for people from the Western Hemisphere who have been enculturated in a two-tiered view of reality (the "Two-Tier worldview") that excludes the middle level of supernatural beings and forces.

The Two-Tier worldview orientation consists of the transcedental world that is considered to be the realm of religion, and the natural world that is explained by scientific theories. Religious beliefs and practices are basically explained using organic analogies, while scientific explanations are given using mechanical analogies. Explanations that were based on supernaturalistic descriptions were conspicoulsy absent. Pioneer missionaries from Western countries were therefore not able to fathom the supernaturalistic beliefs and practices that pervaded the minds of Africans. The latter asked questions about their daily lives, which included issues concerning the malevolent spirits that were oppressing them. The cause-effect dimension was based on personal causality where every misfortune, accident, barreness, etc., was attributed to supernaturalistic beings and forces, which needed appropriate remedies. Such remedies were not explained using organic or mechanical analogies, which baffled the minds of those inclined to the Two-Tier worldview orientation. As

---

1. Hiebert, "Flaw of the Excluded Middle," 35–47.

such minds continued to interact with non-Two-Tier people, they also have slowly continued to accept that the reality of most non-Westerners should be respected and appreciated if one is to interact with them appropriately.

Chapter 2 of this book has illustrated that many scholars from the Western Hemisphere have continued to delve into the study of spirit possession and the spirit world. The anthropogical perspective has been particularly popular as Westerners have sought to understand people from other worldview orientations, including Africans. My assessment is that the contemporary Western missionaries, missiologists, and Christian anthropologists have come to the point of accepting that the supernaturalistic worldview portrayed in the Bible resembles that of most non-Westerners whom they encounter whether in research or Christian witness. Furthermore, some Westerners have gone to the other extreme of wholesale adoption of the "assumptions of the spiritual warfare paradigm popularized by the so-called Third Wave movement."[2]

When I entitled this section "No longer the Exlcuded Middle," I had in mind the pentecostal/charismatic movement that has been characterised by the "Third Wave movement" and that originated in the Western Hemisphere. Key advocates include John Wimber, Peter Wagner, and Charles Kraft. The term *Third Wave* was coined by Peter Wagner in the 1980s to describe a pentecostal movement characterised by manifestations of spiritual phenomena including healings and other miraculous maifestations. Wonsuk Ma explains that "one of the most characteristic concepts identified with this movement is the 'power encounter.'"[3] I will come back to the topic of the power encounter when discussing practical suggestions for dealing with the spirit world in African contexts. Prior to that, it is expedient to turn to the Bible and find out if there is any provision for excluding the middle level.

Biblical Intepretation of the Spirit World: Included Middle

Both the Old and the New Testaments attest to the fact that there is no suggestion for excluding the middle level. The Bible is replete with references to the supernaturalistic orientation of the Hebrew people. The German Lutheran

---

2. Gilbert, "Further Reflections," 206–18.
3. Ma, "'First Waver' Looks," 190.

theologian and professor of the New Testament, Rudolf Bultman, attests to the existence of the other-worldly supernatural powers that impinge on the this-worldly realm inhabited by human beings. He refers to the earth as not only a "scene of natural day-to-day occurrences [. . .] it, too, is a theater for the working of supernatural powers, God and his angels, Satan and his demons."[4] Bultmann further asks a pertinent question and offers an answer:

> Can Christians proclamation today expect men and women to acknowledge the mythical world picture as true? It woul be pointless because there is nothing specifically Christian about the mythical world picture, which is simply the world picture of a time now past that was not yet formed by scientific thinking.[5]

Bultmann represents a crop of theologians who were influenced by the philosophical assumptions prevalent during the Enlightenment Era, which placed rationalism at the fore. Missionaries who were taught by and who read the books penned by such famous theologians went to non-Western regions with such notions and relegeted the supernaturalistic worldview elements to the periphery or ignored them all together. Fortunately, not all renowned theologians and biblical exegetes follow this trail. Craig Keener, a premier American professor of New Testament, submits his spirit hermeneutics and therein acknowledges that the supernaturalistic worldview dispalyed in the biblical accounts bear striking resemblance to cross-cultural experiences in various contexts in contemporary times.[6]

Keener further alludes to the obliviousness of most NT scholars who are not familiar with the corpus of anthropological documents describing the phenomenon of spirit possession in contemprary era.[7] Keener thus seeks to introduce his fellow NT scholars to these documents to broaden their perspectives on the spirit world in order to offer a more relevant biblical interpretation. I will also add to this discussion by mentioning that this current study on spirit possession among Borana Muslims, is also significant because it provides a detailed account of the lived experiences of the people as they parpticipate in possession séances.

---

4. Bultmann, *New Testament and Mythology*, 1.
5. Bultmann, 3.
6. Keener, "Spirit Possession," 216.
7. Keener, 216.

Imperative of a Missional Response to the Supernaturalistic Worldview in African Islamic Contexts

This current research has explicitly shown that the Borana Muslims have a supernaturalistic worldview that influences their thought pattern and subsequent behavior. Kim, Travis, and Travis's article on the spirit world in Muslims' thought and practice further buttresses the fact that Muslims have an inherent supernaturalistic worldview orientation. The article begins by describing the spirit world of Muslims before offering a "Christ-centered response" that begins with questions about the relevancy of Jesus's message to popular Islam: "Do Jesus and his followers have a response to the Muslim fear of jinn and evil forces, their quests for physical healing, and their hopes to be blessed in this life and the life to come?"[8]

Kim, Travis, and Travis's quest to provide a relevant response to popular Muslim piety is among a rising number of scholars and practitioners who have heeded the imperative to respond to a dire need. I have also joined this bandwagon, which includes several upcoming African scholars interested in studying and offering relevant responses to a pertinent issue in Christian ministry. I have written an article, published by Langham Global Library, which I entitled "A Missional Approach to Suffering Inflicted by Spiritual Powers: A Case Study of Northern Kenya."[9] The article suggests a missional approach that includes three main steps in missional theology: phenomenology, ontology, and missiology. This current book applies the first step, phenomenology, by examining the beliefs and rituals of the lived experiences of the Borana Muslims as they participate in the *Ayyaana* possession cult in the northern part of Kenya. The forementioned article takes this phenomenological step further, to step 2, which is ontology. This second step examines the biblical precepts and events concerning the spirit world, which reinforces the above-mentioned section that there is no excluded middle in the either the Old or the New Testament. Other scholars, like Scott Moreau and Keith Ferdinando in their classic book, *The Triumph of Christ in African Perspective: A Study of Demonology and Redemption in the African Context*, provide an extensive biblical survey of the spirit world as a response to the African supernaturalistic

---

8. Kim, Travis, and Travis, "Relevant Responses," 245.
9. Wang'ombe, "Missional Approach to Suffering," 125–43.

worldview.[10] Ferdinando offers an abridged version, which is shorter and intended for a wider readership.[11]

There are other African scholars who have examined and written about the spirit world in African contexts. This is an encouraging trend as more Africans delve into this important topic. Yet, it is needful that more African scholars examine the Muslim/Islamic spirit world in African contexts. Colin Bearup offers his book, *Clues to Africa, Islam, and the Gospel: Insights for New Workers*. He asserts that one would be mistaken to think that, in a post-modern world with advanced technology, the power-fear dynamic would diminish, even in Africa.[12] The clarion call for more African scholars to engage in the studies of the Muslim spirit world stems from this fact: that in spite the technological advances in Africa, the supernaturalistic worldview orientation is still very foregrounded in the conceptualization of African Muslims. This current research study has indicated the salience of the *Ayyaana* religiocultural model that is enhanced in the creative minds of the Borana Muslims as they participate in the *Ayyaana* possession cult. It has also been shown that the *Ayyaana* model is more salient than the Islamic model of the spirit world in the perceptions of Borana ordinary Muslims. Essentially, the *Ayyaana* model is foregrounded because it seems to "answer" the daily life questions that the ordinary Muslims grapple with. Is this not an indication of the "frustrations" experienced by the ordinary Muslims as they seek for solutions to their spiritual encounters?

The Bible is rife with instances of Jesus dealing with the spirit world. Theologians should desist from the rationalistic approach to the biblical interpretation of the spirit world, which claims that the biblical world was different from any contemporary context. Likewise, as missionaries reach out to African Muslims, they need to reflectively examine their own worldviews that would hinder their understanding of the supernaturalistic worldview orientations of the people they seek to interact with. I agree with Keener's recommendation for an anthropological approach to spirit possession even for the scholars who are reticent about such an approach.[13] Kim also em-

---

10. See Moreau, *World of Spirits*; and Ferdinando, *Triumph of Christ*.
11. Ferdinando, *Battle Is God's*.
12. Bearup, *Clues to Africa*, 65.
13. Keener, "Spirit Possession," 217.

phasizes such an anthropological approach in his call to focus on the people factor ("people thing"), rather than the ideological factor ("ideological thing") in the Islamic studies arena.[14] This current study has also joined this call for more concerted efforts to understand the lived experiences of Muslims in their daily lives' encounters, especially with the spirit world. It is not only needful to understand these experiences; it is also important to know how to deal with the spirits and spirit possession in African Islamic situations.

Dealing with Spirits and Spirit Possession in African Islamic Contexts

Jesus dealt with demonic spirits and gave his disciples the power and authority to overcome all the power of the enemy. This is recorded in Luke 10: 17–20, which includes the report by the seventy-two disciples who excitedly told Jesus that "even the demons submitted to us in your name." The contemporary Pentecostal Christians in Africa have gradually taken up the ministry of deliverance for people who are oppressed by demonic spirits. Wang'ombe has indicated that, in spite of the relevance of the ministry of deliverance, there is need to combine it with inner healing.[15] This concept of inner healing is derived from Charles Kraft's model of "deep-level healing" that seeks to help Christian believers break free from the bondage of demonic oppression.[16]

Kraft uses the rat-dirt analogy to illustrate the significance of inner healing. Deliverance where the expulsion of demons is performed is compared to removing rats in a dirty house. Unless this house is cleaned by removing garbage, the rats will be attracted to the dirty house and come back. Similarly, when deliverance is performed, the demons are supposedly expelled. Yet, if the heart of the delivered person is "dirty" because of the garbage of negative emotions like bitterness, anger, self-doubt, etc., the demons ("rats") will still come back to the house. Inner healing helps oppressed people to deal with this garbage so that total deliverance is attained. I will not get into the details of this crucial ministry of inner healing. A sequence to this study is underway, in which I will discuss the details of the inner healing ministry within

---

14. Kim, *Islam among the Swahili*, 3.
15. Wang'ombe, "Missional Approach to Suffering," 140.
16. Kraft, *Defeating Dark Angels*.

the African context. I will, however, summarize the inner healing approach using the following points:

1. Inner healing deals with past emotional wounds by allowing the Holy Spirit to bring them to the fore in our minds.
2. Inner healing should be included in all discipleship materials as an essential element for spiritual formation.
3. Many Africans who have delved into spiritual issues like spirit possession, witchcraft, etc., tend to have also experienced deep inner hurts that are carried along in life.
4. Inner healing is a process that should involve the following encounters in a Christian's spiritual life: Power encounter, Truth encounter, and Allegiance encounter.

I owe a lot of gratitude to my academic supervisor, Prof. Caleb Kim, who has proficiently developed a module for spiritual warfare. Kim has discussed, in detail, the three different encounters and how they need to be balanced for appropriate spiritual enhancement. In the sequence that will follow this current book, I will apply much of his discussion to the African context.

Final Concluding Remarks

This research has demonstrated the significance of studying the lived experiences of people in order to gain a better understanding of what makes them behave in a certain way. Anthropologically, the "people factor" is important, especially for Christian-Muslim relations whose germane interest is to gain a better understanding of the "Other."

This final chapter has also added value to the missiological conversation, especially in Africa, where supernaturalistic worldview orientation is rife. The conversation can be carried on from a Christian-Muslim relation where Muslims and Christians seek to understand each other's perspectives about the spirit world. This study provides some useful contents for such a forum, which is relevant and needful in this contemporary world where people from different religions continue to intermingle more than before.

APPENDIX 1

The Borana Calendar

The 27 Days of the Borana Calendar

1. Marganati Biriiti
2. Salbaani
3. Salbaani Balla
4. Salbaani Dullacha
5. Gardaaduma
6. Sonsa
7. Ruruma
8. Lumaasa
9. Gidaada
10. Ruunda
11. Areeri
12. Areeri Ballo
13. Adula
14. Adula Balla
15. Garba
16. Garba Balla
17. Garba Dullacha
18. Bita
19. Bita Balla
20. Sorsa
21. Algajima
22. Arba

23. Walla
24. Baasa
25. Baasa Balla
26. Ch'arra
27. Maganati Jaara

The Months of the Borana Calendar (2004–2005)

1. Abraasa (October 15, 2004–November 13)
2. Ammaji (November 14–December 12)
3. Gurand'ala (December 13–January 12, 2005)
4. Bitotteesa (January 13–February 9)
5. Ch'aamsa (February 10–March 10)
6. Buufa (March 11–April 9)
7. Woch'abaji (April 10–May 8)
8. Obora Gudda (May 9–June 7)
9. Obora Diqa (June 8–July 6)
10. Birra (July 7–August 5)
11. Ch'iqa (August 6–September 4)
12. Sadaasa (September 5–October 3)
13. Abraasa (October 4–November 2)
14. Ammaji (November 3–December 2)
15. Gurand'ala (December 3–December 31, 2005)

APPENDIX 2

Excerpt from a Conversation between a Practitioner and *Ayyaana*

The following is an excerpt from a recorded conversation that was carried out in *afan Borana* between a practitioner and an *ayyaana*:

Practitioner: *Asalam alekum, aba kiya* (Peace with you, my father)

Ayyaana: *Aleikum salam*

Practitioner: *Hoja atin saqanya atho dalachi baat ato dubachu baate, a waan duga rabi yo duba'de, yo at bargama dufte, atin ak qaala deemta mo, qaal male deemta, fullan tun fulla qalatiyu? Itani me korm mo, shinchoomho, chnchoon sun oja busan, arthif samii deema, itaani deema? Me duga dubadi, laf kami duft?* (If you are really our family, you were born with us. Even if you don't speak, if I speak the truth, if you came from water [*bargama*], you will walk according to your demands, not without any demands [*qaal*]. This place is for you seeking demands, is it? Not incense, not bull, not burned meat [*chicho*]. If you put meat in fire, its smoke reaches heavens, is it? What about incense burning? Now tell me the truth, where are you from?)

Ayyaana: *Gar rabiti dufte.* (I come from God.)

Practitioner: *Duga indubane duga dubadi.* (Speak the truth, you did not tell me the truth.)

Ayyaana: *Anin maati rabiiti, achi argame.* (I am family of God. I came from there.)

Practitioner: *Nyaadi male inyatani, emari male inemaraan.* (You cannot eat without being given permission and you cannot speak unless you are called.)

Ayyaana: *Naa inkenee kirro baasa.* (If am not given anything, I will kill him.)

Practitioner: *Qaali kooki sirate, kiro baasu kami re yo at nama rabi taate, a qanyaani waan sunu it indiatu, yo at (marthuthanya) esa gad dufte atiin? Itojja rabiiti dufte, wori rabi waan sunuyu afaan inkan qaal kamiin afan keete, qaal kamiin farso dude, yokhan ambasha, yokhaan marite, ayiti. Meeyi yo at gar rabiti dufte, kha qute taate, ato abaan madaba chicho insoratinu sii kenne itaanale ya si kenne, ta bargamatif, ta kookile yo taate?* (There is no demand for something it eats and kills. What tradition is that? The older *ayyaana* even do not mention such bad things, if you came from God. What is that? But if you are a young one [*marthuthanya*] who came just now, where did you come from? If you came from God [*Rabi*], people of God do not mention even such with their mouth, so how come you say such with your mouth?)

Ayyaana: *Kha kooki fakaata?* (Does it look like one under influence?)

Practitioner: *Qaali ke qaal kami kan?* (What are your demands [*qaal*]? What do you want to eat or drink?)

Ayyaana: *Atin naichbini (mardhathunya) afaan narat imbaraatu abaan madaba, gudan odhani beeta, kha ag bari bane dig nara imbane jeda.* (Don't waste time. You are new [*marthathunya*]. You cannot learn to speak today. Not even *odha* [firstborn of all] can cheat, the one which says, "Since we left the waters, we are satisfied with blood.")

Practitioner: *Atharum keenaan nuu dabra?* (Let us just continue with our *hadhara*?)

APPENDIX 3

Ashaka's Experience with *Ayyaana*

Ashaka once travelled to Nairobi from her home in Marsabit County. Since *ayyaana* are not constrained by spatial boundaries, an *ayyaana* called Jaani "caught" her, and she became mad. She said, "I did not know myself. I looked very bad, my hair stood up; I slept in the dust every night. Some people gave up on me and said that I was going to die." A practitioner was called who diagnosed the *ayyaana*-inflicted problem. A *hadhara* session was performed, but the practitioner could not deal with the *ayyaana*. Another practitioner was called in who was deemed to be higher in rank. When Ashaka saw him, "she" rushed toward him with a kitchen knife and had to be restrained from stabbing him. Another *hadhara* session was held, and the *ayyaana* finally made his demands. He wanted a he-goat of a certain color. Since this was still in Nairobi, one man offered to carry the goat on his shoulder and took it to the place of *hadhara*, where Ashaka was. The *abba sera* (litterally: "father of law," meaning an *ayyaana* practitioner) commanded the *ayyaana* to leave Ashaka after offering the he-goat. The *ayyaana* then requested to be consigned to a *kobat* (Borana for "anthill") knowing well that there were no anthills in Nairobi. And so it did not leave. It was a very desperate time for all the people concerned as they watched Ashaka's health deteriorate. All the *abba sera* were "defeated." Then one day when everybody had given up and was tired, the *ayyaana* in Ashaka spoke and asked for a lemon. A *hadhara* session was quickly organized the following day, and the demand was given. Ashaka began the road to recovery. She got healed and went back to her rural home in Marsabit. Since then, the *ayyaana* has not bothered her. She was inducted into the cult, and she had to constantly hold *hadhara* sessions to ensure that "*ayyaana* does not feel neglected or forgotten. He just needs *hadhara* songs and he gets contented and does not affect me in any way." This continued to be Ashaka's lived experience. Everyday she lived with an awareness of the presence of *ayyaana* as part of her life. Such consciousness is shared by the other ordinary Borana Muslims who have been initiated and participated in the *Ayyaana* cult.

APPENDIX 4

References to Jinn in the Hadith (Bukhari and Muslim)

Name of Hadith	Reference Number	Aspects of Jinn	Implications
Bukhari	Vol. 1, book 8, no. 450; vol. 4, book 55, no. 634; vol. 6, book 60, no. 332. (Narrated by Abu Huraira)	A big demon from the *efreet* (jinn) attempts to interrupt Muhammad's prayers; Allah helped him to overcome him.	Muhammad physically encountered jinn.
Bukhari	Vol. 1, book 11, no. 583 (Narrated by Abdul Rahman)	Advice is given when someone is grazing sheep in the wilderness; he or she should pronounce the *adhan* loudly for people and inn to hear.	Jinn have the ability to hear.

Name of Hadith	Reference Number	Aspects of Jinn	Implications
Bukhari	Vol. 1, book 12, no. 740; vol. 6, book 60, no. 443; (Narrated by Ibn Abbas)	While Muhammad and his companions are at Nakhla offering prayer/recitation, some jinn/devils listen and believe. This was the occasion of the revelation of Surah 72.	Muhammad encountered jinn, and they heard the Qur'an and became Muslims.
Bukhari	Vol. 2, book 19, no. 177; vol. 6, book 60, no. 385 (Narrated by Ibn Abbas)	Muhammad prostrated together with jinn	Jinn can also prostrate.
Bukhari	Vol. 4, book 54, no. 517	Jinn will bear witness in favor of the person who says the *adhan* loudly while grazing sheep in the desert.	Jinn will be in paradise and will bear witness.
Bukhari	Vol. 4, book 55, no. 634 (Narrated by Jabir bin Abdullah)	Muhammad told people to cover their water skins, close their doors, and keep children close to them at night since the jinn are present then.	Muhammad acknowledged the presence of jinn especially at night.
Bukhari	Vol. 5, book 58, no. 200 (Narrated by Abu Huraira)	Muhammad said that bones and animal dung are food for jinn.	Jinn also eat food.
Bukhari	Vol. 5, book 58, no. 199	A tree informed the Prophet that jinn heard the Qur'an on a certain night.	Trees know the whereabouts of jinn.
Bukhari	Vol. 6, book 60, no. 238 (Narrated by Abdullah)	Jinn were worshipped by some Arabs but converted to Islam.	Jinn can convert to Islam.

References to Jinn in the Hadith (Bukhari and Muslim)

Name of Hadith	Reference Number	Aspects of Jinn	Implications
Bukhari	Vol. 7, book 71, no. 657	Muhammad says that jinn take the truth about something and tell the fortunetellers, who mix it with lies.	Jinn are able to give information to fortunetellers.
Bukhari	Vol. 9, book 93, nos. 638 and 650 (Narrated by Aisha)	Muhammad says that jinn informed foretellers and soothsayers.	Foretellers and soothsayers use jinn.
Bukhari	Vol. 9, book 93, no. 480	Like humans, Jinn also die.	Jinn are not immortal.
Bukhari	Vol. 5, Book 58, No. 206	Jinn can be either male or female.	Jinn have gender.
Bukhari	Vol. 6, book 60, nos. 238 and 239	Pre-Islamic Arabs worshipped jinn that later became Muslims.	Jinn existed in pre-Islamic Arabia.
Muslim	No. 2236	Muhammad acknowledged that some snakes could be Muslim jinn and thus should not be killed.	Jinn can take the form of snakes.
Muslim	No. 2814	Muhammad stated that every person has a jinni accompanying him or her, including Muhammad himself.	Everybody has a jinni.
Muslim	No. 208	Muhammad referred to jinn as "people's brother."	Do jinn have relations with humans?

APPENDIX 5

Scholars Who Have Studied or Alluded to *Ayyaana* and the Sheikh Hussein Cult

Scholar and Date	Locality of Study	Area of Focus	Methodological Approach / Methods of Study
Mario I. Aguilar, PhD dissertation (1993)	Waso Borana of Garba Tulla, Isiolo, Kenya	Practices and generational patterns	Social anthropology / ethnography
Mario I. Aguilar (1995)	Waso Borana of Garba Tulla, Kenya	Sanctifying coffee beans in Islam	Social anthropology / ethnography
Mario I. Aguilar (1996)	Waso Borana of Isiolo, Kenya	Eagle as a messenger	Social anthropology / ethnography
Tesfaye Gudeta Gerba (2015)	Oromo people in Ethiopia	Typology of Oromo personal names	Linguistic anthropology
Gudrun Dahl (1979)	Waso Borana of Isiolo Kenya	Subsistence usage of land and livestock	Socioeconomic approach
I. M. Lewis (1996, 1998)	Waso Borana and other tribal groups	Cultic tendencies in religion	Social anthropology
Terje Østebø (2012)	Oromo Muslims in Bale, Ethiopia	Localized Salafism	Narrative analysis
Setegn Eshetu (1973)	Ethiopia	Sheikh Hussein and his followers	Socio-historical approach

Scholar and Date	Locality of Study	Area of Focus	Methodological Approach / Methods of Study
B. Witalis Andrzejewski (1972)	Oromo (Galla) in Ethiopia	Diction in hymns that praise Sheikh Hussein of Bale	Linguistic / poetic approach
B. Witalis Andrzejewski (1974)	Oromo in Ethiopia	Oral traditions about Sheikh Hussein of Bale	Historical approach
Ulrich Braukamper (1989)	Ethiopia	Connection between Oromo-Somali regarding the sanctuary of Sheikh Hussein of Bale	Sociological framework
Ulrich Braukamper (2004)	Southern Ethiopia	Essays on the Sheikh Hussein cult	Historio-cultural approach
Günther Schlee & Abdullahi A. Shongolo (2012)	Sakuye people of Kenya	Brief mention of *ayyaana* among Sakuye people	Sociopolitical framework
Ton Leus & Cynthia Salvadori (2006)	Borana, Ethiopia	General customs of Borana (Dictionary of Borana traditions-*aada* Borana)	Cultural-linguistic approach
Paul Tablino (1999)	Gabra people, northern Kenya	Customs of Gabra	Sociocultural approach
Judy Wang'ombe (2007)	Munyoyaya people of Tana River in Kenya	Responding to I. M. Lewis's deprivation theory	Anthropological approach
Hassan G. W. Arero (2002)	Borana and Gabra people of northern Kenya	Peace and conflict; mentions briefly about keeping peace with *ayyaana*	Social-anthropological approach
Halkano Abdi Wario (2012)	Borana, Marsabit Kenya	Examines *tablighi ja'amat* movement	Socio-religious approach

Glossary of Non-English Words

This list includes Borana, Kiswahili, and Arabic words that appear frequently in the text and are considered to be essential in the religiocultural context.

Borana Words

Aada	Customs or rules. *Aada Borana* means "the customs of Borana people."
Abba Sera	Literally "Father / leader of laws." This is a title used for the traditional leader among Borana people. *Warra ayyaana* use this title to refer to the leader of the *Ayyaana* cult. A woman leader is called *hadha sera* (literally: "woman of laws").
Afan Borana	Literally: "mouth of Borana"; *afan Borana* means "the Borana language."
Afur	The Christian word for spirit or soul. The phrase used for the Holy Spirit is *Afur Qulqulo*.
Ayyaana	A traditional Borana spirit. It also means "fortune." Traditionally, each day has its own *ayyaana* or "auspiciousness."
Bunna	Coffee. *Bunna qala* literally means "slaughtering coffee," and it stands for a traditional ceremony that involves the roasting of coffee in ghee or oil.
Ch'iressa	Traditional Borana medicine man
Darga	Sacred place for religious ceremonies by ordinary Borana Muslims. It is also a place where sick people go for treatment.
Dhukkuba	Sickness as a noun
Dibe	Drum
Eeb	Blessings or supplications
Ekhera	Ancestral spirits

253

Garib	Ritual or prayer leaders of the Sufi groups in Marsabit County, although the word is sometimes used to refer to the adepts.
Goobana	New moon
Hadhara	Singing and clapping during the prayer or healing sessions
Jabanna	This is an Amharic word used to refer to the jug used for brewing *bunna* the Amharic way of roasting. *Warra ayyaana* in Marsabit County now use the name to refer to the ceremony and the *bunna* made by roasting on a flat pan, in contrast with *bunna qala*, where the coffee berries are boiled in oil.
Jilla	Traditional ceremonies
Maraataa	A person who behaves very oddly; an insane or mad person
Murraa	A title within the *Ayyaana* cult referring to a practitioner who feeds the *ayyaana* during the sessions. Leus and Salvadori state that the word means "a servant" within the *Ayyaana* cult circles.[1]
Nagaa	Literally means "peace," but also includes the notion of well-being, prosperity, and harmonious living with both human and supernatural beings.
Oblia	A word popularly used by participants of the *Ayyaana* cult to refer to a group of angels who are ranked higher than *ayyaana*.
Qaal	Demands made by *ayyaana*
Qaba	A verb that means "to catch"
Qallu	Spiritual leader or priest
Qileensa	Wind/air/breath. Preference, in this study, is given to "wind." *Qileesa Waaqa* means a wind/breath from/of God.
Raaga	Borana name for a prophet, or a seer, or a person of *Waaqa*
Risa	Eagle
Salawat	Communal prayers performed by *Garib*
Shibo	A chain that is used by adepts and practitioners in the *Ayyaana* cult.
Ule	A stick carried by *Ayyaana* practitioners.
Waaqa	Traditional name for the Supreme God. It is popularly used by traditional Borana and Christians.

---

1. Leus and Salvadori, *Aadaa Boraanaa*, 471.

Warra	People
Warra ayyaana	Literally "people of *ayyaana*"
Warra oblia	People of *oblia*

Kiswahili Words

Dawa	Medicine prescribed for illness
Dini	Commonly used to refer to religion
Jeshi	Army
Maombi	Prayers
Miraa	*Carta edulis*, a popular green leaf stimulant chewed for its mild intoxication effects. Also called khat.
Pepo	Spirits
Upepo	Wind

Arabic Words

Al-Ghaib	The unseen world / the realm of spirits
Ayah	Verses of the Qur'an; also means signs
Bid'ah	Unlawful religious innovations that are usually said to be heretical since they are not sanctioned by the prophet Muhammad or his companions as authentic.
Bismillah	Literally: "In the name of Allah"
Dhikr	Remembrance of Allah by repeating his names and reciting the Qur'an
Din	Creed or religion
Dua	Informal Islamic prayers
Hadith	Islamic texts containing the deeds, sayings, and actions of Prophet Muhammad
Hajj	One of the five pillars of Islam. It is the Muslim pilgrimage to Mecca during the Islamic month of Ramadhan. A Muslim is expected to perform *hajj* at least once in a lifetime. The title *Hajji* is appended to men who have made the pilgrimage.
Jahiliyyah	Literally: "ignorance." It refers to the pre-Islamic period.
Jamaat	A congregation or group of people performing religious acts together.

Madrassa	Islamic schools
Salawat	Salutation or greetings; popularly used to refer to the prayers offered during *hadhara* session by *warra oblia / warra ayyaana*.
Salat	Daily ritual prayers performed five times by Muslims. It is one of the pillars of Islam.
Shirk	Associating Allah with a partner. This is the most abominable sin in Islam.
Sufism	Mystical arm of Islam. The word is derived from *Sufi*, which means "wool." Sufis are Muslims who engage in mystical practices as they seek for a personal experience with God.
Tariqa	A brotherhood, an organization, or an order of members devoted to the mystical dimension of Islam. For instance, the *Alawiyya* movement is a Sufi *tariqa* (order).
Ziyara	Pilgrimage or journey

Bibliography

Abd-Allah, Umar, F. "The Perceptible and the Unseen: The Qur'anic Conception of Man's Relationship to God and Realities beyond Human Perception." In *Mormons and Muslims: Spiritual Foundations and Modern Manifestations*, edited by Spencer J. Palmer, Arnold H. Green, and Daniel C. Peterson, 209–64. Provo, UT: Brigham Young University, 2002.

Adho, G. Interviewed by the author's research assistants. Saku Subcounty, April 13, 2016. Code: A4-2016.

Adibah, S., Mohd M. Z. Azmir, M. N. Paimah, and Hisham M. T. Kandil. "Creativity and Innovation in Islam: It's Necessity in Islamic Education." *Social Sciences* 10, no. 1 (2015): 61–66.

Aguilar, Mario I. *Being Oromo in Kenya*. Trenton: Africa World, 1998.

———. "Current Religious Practices and Generational Patterns among the Waso Boorana of Garba Tulla, Kenya." PhD diss., University of London, 1993.

———. "The Eagle as Messenger, Pilgrim and Voice: Divinatory Processes among the Waso Boorana of Kenya." *Journal of Religion in Africa* 26, no. 1 (February 1996): 56–72. https://doi.org/10.2307/1581894

———. "The 'God of the Oromo': A Religious Paradigm in the Work of Lambert Bartels." *Journal of Oromo Studies* 12, nos. 1 & 2 (July 2005): 52–67.

———. "*Nagaa*: The Forgotten Quest for Peace in Modern Kenya." *The Month* 26, no. 5 (1993): 183–287.

———. "Recreating a Religious Past in a Muslim Setting: 'Sacrificing' Coffee-Beans among the Waso Boorana of Garba Tulla, Kenya." *Ethnos* 60, no. 1–2 (1995): 41–58.

———. "Religion as Culture or Culture as Religion? The Status Quaestionis of Ritual and Performance." *Culture and Religion* 1, no. 2 (2000): 233–45. https://doi.org/10.1080/01438300008567153

———. Ako-Garqasa. Interviewed by the author. Saku Subcounty, March 11, 2017. Code: A32-2017.

Ahmed, Akbar. Discovering Islam: Making Sense of Muslim History and Society. New York: Routledge & Kegan Paul Ltd., 1988.

Akrong, Abraham A., and John Azumah. "Hermeneutical and Theological Resources in African Traditional Religions for Christian-Muslim Relations in Africa." In *The African Christian and Islam*, edited by John Azumah and Lamin Sanneh, 65–84. Carlisle: Langham Monographs, 2013.

Al-Ajeen, Ali bin Ibrahim Saud, and Mohammed Abdul Hameed Al-Khateeb. "Islamic Legislation for Creativity and an Analysis of the Era of the Prophet (Pbuh) in the Light of Creativity." *Dirasat, Shari'a and Law Sciences* 41, no. 3 (September 2014): 1159–72.

Al-Ashqar, Umar Sulaiman. *The World of the Jinn and Devils*. Boulder, CO: Al-Basheer Company for Publications and Translations, 1998.

Al-Bukhari, Imam Muhammad. *The Translation of the Meaning of Sahih Al-Bukhari*. "The Book of the Stories of the Prophet," Book 60, translated by Muhammad Muhsin Khan. Riyadh, Saudi Arabia: Darussalam Publishers & Distributors, 1997.

Ali, A. Yusuf. *The Holy Qur'an: Text, Translation and Commentary*. 2nd ed. Beltsville: Amana Publications, 1983.

Al-karasneh, Samih Mahmoud, and Ali Mohammad Jubran Saleh. "Islamic Perspective of Creativity: A Model for Teachers of Social Studies as Leaders." *Procedia* 2, no. 2 (2010): 412–26. https://doi.org/10.1016/j.sbspro.2010.03.036

Aluke, M. Interviewed by the author. Moyale Subcounty, March 13, 2017. Code: A27-2017.

Ameen, Abu'l-Mundhir Khaleel ibn Ibraaheem. *The Jinn and Human Sickness*. Riyadh, Saudi Arabia: Darussalam, 2005.

Andrzejewsi, B. Witalis. "Allusive Diction in Galla Hymns in Praise of Sheikh Hussein of Bale." *African Language Studies* 13 (1972): 1–31.

———. "Sheikh Hussein of Bali in Galla Oral Traditions." *Accademia Nazionale Dei Lincei* 191 (1974): 463–64.

Arero, Hassan G. W. "Keeping the Peace of Borana: Aspects of Peace and Conflict in Shifting 'Indigenous' Systems of Northern Kenya." PhD diss., University of East Anglia, 2002.

Asad, Talal. "The Idea of an Anthropology of Islam." *Qui Parle* 17, no. 2 (2009): 1–30.

Ashaka, M. Interviewed by the author. Moyale Subcounty, March 4, 2017. Code: A22-2017.

Atran, Scott. *In Gods We Trust*. Oxford: Oxford University Press, 2002.

Barrett, Justin L. "Coding and Quantifying Counterintuitiveness in Religious Concepts: Theoretical and Methodological Reflections." *Method and Theory in the Study of Religion* 20, no. 4 (November 1, 2008): 308–38. https://doi.org/10.1163/157006808X371806.

———."Cognitive Science of Religion: What Is It and Why Is It?" *Religion Compass* 1, no. 6 (November 2007): 768–86. https://doi.org/10.1111/j.1749-8171.2007.00042.x

———. *Cognitive Science, Religion, and Theology: From Human Minds to Divine Minds*. West Conshohocken: Templeton Press, 2011.

Barrett, Justin L., and Melanie A. Nyhof. "Spreading Non-natural Concepts: The Role of Intuitive Conceptual Structures in Memory and Transmission of Cultural Materials." *Journal of Cognition and Culture* 1, no. 1 (February 1, 2001): 69–100. https://doi.org/10.1163/156853701300063589.

Baxter, P. T. W. "Acceptance and Rejection of Islam among the Boran of the Northern Frontier District of Kenya." In *Islam in Tropical Africa*, edited by I. M. Lewis, 233–40. Oxford: Oxford University Press, 1966.

———. "The Social Organization of the Galla of Northern Kenya." PhD diss., University of Oxford, 1954.

Bearup, Colin. *Clues to Africa, Islam, and the Gospel: Insights for New Workers*. Pasadena: William Carey Library Publishers, 2019.

Becker, Judith. *Deep Listeners: Music, Emotion, and Trancing*. Bloomington: Indiana University Press, 2004.

Bennardo, Giovanni, and Victor de Munck. *Cultural Models: Genesis, Methods, and Experiences*. New York: Oxford University Press, 2014.

Bennett, Clinton. *Studying Islam: The Critical Issues*. London: Bloomsbury Publishing/Continuum, 2010.

Bernard, H. Russell. *Research Methods in Anthropology: Qualitative and Quantitative Approaches*. 5th ed. New York: AltaMira, 2011.

Blount, Benjamin. "Situating Cultural Models in History and Cognition." In *Approaches to Language, Culture and Cognition: The Intersection of Cognitive Linguistics and Linguistic Anthropology*, edited by Masataka Yamaguchi, Dennis Tay, and Benjamin Blount, 271–298. Hampshire: Palgrave Macmillan, 2014.

Boddy, Janice. "Spirits and Selves in Northern Sudan: The Cultural Therapeutics of Possession and Trance." In *A Reader in the Anthropology of Religion*, edited by Michael Lambek, 369–74. Malden: Blackwell Publishing, 2002.

———. *Wombs and Alien Spirits: Women, Men, and the Zar Cult in Northern Sudan*. New Directions in Anthropological Writing. Madison: University of Wisconsin Press, 1989.

Boru, P. Interviewed by the author. Saku Subcounty, January 8, 2016. Code: A3-2016.

Boster, James. "Data, Method, and Interpretation in Cognitive Anthropology." Chap. 8 in *A Companion to Cognitive Anthropology*, edited by David B. Kronenfeld, Giovanni Bennardo, Victor C. de Munck, and Michael D. Fischer. Malden: Blackwell Publishing, 2011. Kindle.

Bourguignon, Erika. "Suffering and Healing, Subordination and Power: Women and Possession Trance." *Ethos* 32, no. 4 (2004): 557–74. https://doi.org/10.1525/eth.2004.32.4.557

Boyer, Pascal. *Religion Explained: The Evolutionary Origins of Religious Thought.* New York: Basic Books, 2001.

Boyer, Paul. *The Naturalness of Religious Ideas: A Cognitive Theory of Religion.* Berkeley: University of California Press, 1994.

Braukamper, Ulrich. *Islamic History and Culture in Southern Ethiopia: Collected Essays.* New Brunswick and London: Transaction Publishers, 2004.

———. "The Sanctuary of Shaykh Husayn and the Oromo-Somali Connections in Bale (Ethiopia)." *Frankfurter Africanistische Blätter*, no. 1 (1989): 108–34.

Bulbulia, T., and S. Laher "Exploring the Role of Islam in Perceptions of Mental Illness in a Sample of Muslim Psychiatrists Based in Johannesburg." *South Africa Journal of Psychology* 19, no. 2 (June 2013): 52–54.

Bultmann, Rudolf. *New Testament and Mythology and Other Basic Writings.* Edited by Schubert M. Ogden. Philadelphia: Fortress, 1984.

Chittick, William C. *Sufism: A Short Introduction.* Oxford: Oneworld, 2000.

Christelow, Allan. *Muslim Law Courts and the French Colonial State in Algeria.* Princeton University Press, 2014.

Christensen, Bo T. "Creative Cognition: Analogy and Incubation." PhD diss., University of Aarhus, 2005.

Chuqule. Interviewed by the author. Moyale Subcounty, August 24, 2016. Code: A29-2016.

Cohen, Emma. *The Mind Possessed: The Cognition of Spirit Possession in an Afro-Brazilian Religious Tradition.* New York: Oxford University Press, 2007.

Cohen, Emma, and Justin L. Barrett. "Conceptualizing Spirit Possession: Ethnographic and Experimental Evidence." *Ethos* 36, no. 2 (June 2008): 246–67.

———. "When Minds Migrate: Conceptualizing Spirit Possession." *Journal of Cognition and Culture* 8, nos. 1–2 (2008): 23–48. https://doi.org/10.1163/156770908X289198.

Colleyn, Jean-Paul. "Horse, Hunter and Messenger: The Possessed Men of the Nya Cult in Mali." In *Spirit Possession: Modernity and Power in Africa*, edited by Heike Behrend and Ute Luig, 68–78. Madison: University of Wisconsin Press, 1999.

Constantinides, P. M. "Sickness and the Spirits: A Study of the Zaar Spirit-Possession Cult in the Northern Sudan." PhD diss., University of London, 1972.

———. "Women Heal Women: Spirit Possession and Sexual Segregation in a Muslim Society," *Social Science & Medicine* 21, no. 6 (1985): 685–692.

———. "The History of the Zaar in the Sudan: Theories of Origin, Recorded Observation and Oral Tradition." In *Women's Medicine: The Zar-Bori Cult in Africa and Beyond*, edited by I. M. Lewis, Sayed Hamid. Edinburgh: Edinburgh University Press, 1991.

Cooley, Dana Robert. "Cultural Models and Fishing Knowledge: A Case Study of Commercial Blue Crab Fishermen in Georgia, USA." PhD diss., University of Georgia, 2003.

Creswell, John W. *Qualitative Inquiry and Design: Choosing among Five Traditions*. London: Sage Publications, 1998.

Dabasso, B. Interviewed by the author. Saku Subcounty, August 1, 2016. Code: A20-2016.

Dahl, Gudrun. "Possession as Cure: The Ayaana Cult Among Waso Borana." In *Culture, Experience and Pluralism: Essays on African Ideas of Illness and Healing*, edited by Anita Jacobson-Widding and David Westerlund, 151–65. Vol. 13 of *Uppsala Studies in Cultural Anthropology*. Uppsala: University of Uppsala, 1989.

———. *Suffering Grass: Subsistence and Society of Waso Borana*. Stockholm: University of Stockholm, 1979.

D'Andrade, Roy G. *The Development of Cognitive Anthropology*. Cambridge, NY: Cambridge University Press, 1995.

D'Andrade, Roy G., and Claudia Strauss, eds. *Human Motives and Cultural Models*. Cambridge: Cambridge University Press, 1992.

de Heusch, Luc. *Sacrifice in Africa: A Structuralist Approach*. Manchester: Manchester University Press, 1985.

Dein, Simon, Malcolm Alexander, and A. David Napier. "Jinn, Psychiatry and Contested Notions of Misfortune among East London Bangladeshis." *Transcultural Psychiatry* 45, no. 1 (2008): 31–55. https://doi.org/10.1177/1363461507087997

Desjarlais, Robert, and C. Jason Throop. "Phenomenological Approaches in Anthropology." *Annual Review of Anthropology* 40 (2011): 87–102. https://doi.org/10.1146/annurev-anthro-092010-153345

Diid, K. Interviewed by the author. Saku Subcounty, March 9, 2017. Code: A26-2017.

Drieskens, Barbara. *Living with Djinns: Understanding and Dealing with the Invisible in Cairo*. London: Saqi Books, 2006.

Drury, Abdullah. Review of *The Anthropology of Islam Reader*, edited by Jens Kreinath.. In *Islam and Christian-Muslim Relation*, 24, no. 2 (2013): 265–67. https://doi.org/10.1080/09596410.2012.761411

Eickelman, Dale F. *The Middle East: An Anthropological Approach*. 2nd ed. Englewood Cliffs: Prentice Hall College Div, 1989.

Elliston, Edgar J. *Introduction to Missiological Research Design*. Pasadena: William Carey Library, 2011.

———.El-Zein, Abdul Hamid. "Beyond Ideology and Theology: The Search for the Anthropology of Islam." *Annual Reviews Anthropology* 6 (1977): 227–54. https://doi.org/10.1146/annurev.an.06.100177.001303

El-Zein, Amira. "The Evolution of the Concept of the Jinn from Pre-Islam to Islam." PhD diss., Georgetown University, 1995.

———.*Islam, Arabs, and the Intelligent World of the Jinn*. Syracuse, New York: Syracuse University Press, 2009.

Epley, Nicholas, Adam Waytz, and John Cacioppo. "On Seeing Human: A Three-Factor Theory of Anthropomorphism." *Psychological Review* 114, no. 4 (2007): 864–86. https://doi.org/10.1037/0033-295X.114.4.864

Eshetu, Setegn. "Sheikh Hussayn of Bale and His Followers." BA thesis, University of Addis Ababa, 1973.

Fadil, Nadia, and Mayanthi Fernando. "Rediscovering the 'Everyday' Muslim: Notes on an Anthropological Divide." *Journal of Ethnographic Theory* 5, no. 2 (Autumn 2015): 59–88. https://doi.org/10.14318/hau5.2.005

Faki, Esha, E. M. Kasiera, and O. M. J. Nandi. "The Belief and Practice of Divination among the Swahili Muslims in Mombasa District, Kenya." *International Journal of Sociology and Anthropology* 2, no. 9 (November 2010): 213–23.

Fatuma, Mernissi. *Beyond the Veil: Male-Female Dynamics in Modern Muslim Society*. Massachusetts: Schenkman Publishing Company, 1975.

Fatuma, W. Interviewed by the author. Saku Subcounty, July 21, 2016. Code: A16-2016.

Faulkner, Mark R. J. *Overtly Muslim, Covertly Boni: Competing Calls of Religious Allegiance on the Kenyan Coast*. Vol. 29 of *Studies of Religion in Africa*, edited by J. Kwabena Asamoah-Gyadu, Mary A. Nyangweso, and Hassan Juna Ndzovu. Leiden: Brill, 1970.

Ferdinando, Keith. *The Battle Is God's: Reflecting on Spiritual Warfare for African Believers*. Plateau State: Africa Christian Textbooks, 2012.

———. *The Triumph of Christ in African Perspective: A Study of Demonology and Redemption in the African Context*. Carlisle: Paternoster, 1999.

Feriali, Kamal. "Music-Induced Spirit Possession Trance in Morocco: Implications for Anthropology and Allied Disciplines." PhD diss., University of Florida, 2009.

Frankfurter, David. "Where the Spirits Dwell: Possession, Christianization, and Saints' Shrines in Late Antiquity." *Harvard Theological Review* 103, no. 1 (January 2010): 27–46.

Fugich, Wako. "Tradition, Memory, Creativity and the Self in the Personal Narratives among the Borana of Kenya: Conformity and Conflict." *Fabula* 43, no. 1 (July 2002): 18–34. https://doi.org/10.1515/fabl.2002.019

Galgallo, A. Interviewed by the author. Saku Subcounty, April 14, 2017. Code: A7-2017.

Galma, D. Interviewed by the author. Saku Subcounty, August 18, 2016. Code: A37-2016.

Gearhart, Rebecca Kathleen. "Ngoma Memories: A History of Competitive Music and Dance Performance on the Kenyan Coast." PhD diss., University of Florida, 1998.

Geertz, Clifford. "'From the Native's Point of View': On the Nature of Anthropological Understanding." *Bulletin of the American Academy of Arts and Sciences* 28, no. 1 (October 1974): 26–45. https://doi.org/10.2307/3822971

———. *Islam Observed: Religious Development in Morocco and Indonesia*. New Haven and London: Yale University Press, 1968.

Gellner, Ernest. *Muslim Society*. Cambridge Studies in Social Anthropology 32. Cambridge: Cambridge University Press, 1981.

Gerba, Tesfaye Gudeta. "Typology of Oromo Personal Names." *International Journal of Sciences: Basic and Applied Research* 19, no. 2 (2015): 17–34.

Gilbert, Pierre. "Further Reflections on Paul Hiebert's 'The Flaw of the Excluded Middle.'" *Direction* 36, no. 2 (Fall 2007): 206–18.

Giles, Linda L. "Possession Cults on the Swahili Coast: A Re-examination of Theories of Marginality." *Africa: Journal of the International African Institute* 57, no. 2 (1987): 234–58. https://doi.org/10.2307/1159823.

———. "The Dialectic of Spirit Possession: A Cross-cultural Dialogue." *Mankind Quarterly* 39, no. 3 (1989): 243–265.

———. "Spirit Possession and the Symbolic Construction of Swahili Society." In *Spirit Possession: Modernity and Power in Africa*, edited by Heike Behrend and Ute Luig, 142–64. Madison: University of Wisconsin Press, 1999.

Gilsenan, Michael. *Recognizing Islam: Religion and Society in the Moodern Middle East*. London: I. B. Tauris, 1982.

Godana, Mzee. Interviewed by the author's research assistants. Saku Subcounty, July 27, 2016. Code: A42-2016.

Goodenough, Ward H. "In Pursuit of Culture." *Annual Review of Anthropology* 32 (October 2003): 1–12. https://doi.org/10.1146/annurev.anthro.32.061002.093257.

Guyoh, G. Interviewed by the author. Moyale Subcounty, March 11, 2017. Code: A49-2017.

Hale, Lindsay. Review of *The Mind Possessed: The Cognition of Spirit Possession in an Afro-Brazilian Religious Tradition*, by Emma Cohen. *American Anthropologist* 112, no. 3 (September 2010): 479–80.

Halkano, D. Interviewed by the author. Moyale Subcounty, August 24, 2016. Code: A46-2016.

Handwerker, W. Penn. "How to Collect Data That Warrant Analysis." In *A Companion to Cognitive Anthropology*, edited by David B. Kronenfeld, Giovanni Bennardo, Victor C. de Munck, and Michael D. Fischer. West Sussex: Blackwell Publishing / Wiley-Blackwell, 2011. https://doi.org/10.1002/9781444394931.ch7

Hanley, Jane, and Amy Brown. "Cultural Variations in Interpretation of Postnatal Illness: Jinn Possession amongst Muslim Communities." *Community Mental Health Journal* 50, no. 3 (2014): 348–53. https://doi.org/10.1007/s10597-013-9640-4

Hiebert, Paul G. "The Flaw of the Excluded Middle." *Missiology: An International Review* 10, no. 1 (January 1982): 35–47. https://doi.org/10.1177/009182968201000103

Hiebert, Paul G., R. Daniel Shaw, and Tite Tienou. *Understanding Folk Religion: A Christian Response to Popular Beliefs and Practices*. Grand Rapids: Baker Books, 1999.

Holland, Dorothy, and Naomi Quinn, eds. *Cultural Models in Language and Thought*. Cambridge: Cambridge University Press, 1987.

Hussein, T. Interviewed by the author. Saku Subcounty, July 19, 2016. Code: A17-2016.

Ibn Taymiyah. *Ibn Taymiyah's Essay on the Jinn (Demons)*. Abridged and translated by Abu Ameenah Bilal Philips. Cape Town: Shahid Esau, 1989.

Ibn Taymiyah. *Ibn Taymiyah's Essay on the Jinn (Demons)*. 2nd ed. Abridged, annotated, and translated by Abu Ameenah Bilal Philips. United Arab Emirates: International Islamic Publishing House, 2007.

Imtiyaz, Yusuf S. "Islam and African Socialism: A Study of the Interactions Between Islam and Ujamaa Socialism in Tanzania." PhD diss., Temple University, 1990.

Jankowsky, Richard C. "Music, Spirit Possession and the In-between: Ethnomusicological Inquiry and the Challenge of Trance." *Ethnomusicology Forum* 16, no. 2 (November 2007): 185–208. https://www.jstor.org/stable/20184594.

———. *Stambeli: Music, Trance, and Alterity in Tunisia*. Chicago: University of Chicago Press, 2010.

Jeldtoft, Nadia. "Lived Islam: Religious Identity with 'Non-organized' Muslim Minorities." *Ethnic and Racial Studies* 34, no. 7 (July 2011): 1134–51. https://doi.org/10.1080/01419870.2010.528441

Jennings, Anne M. "A Nubian Zikr: An Example of African/Islamic Syncretism in Southern Egypt." *Anthropos* 86, no. 4/6 (1991): 545–52. https://www.jstor.org/stable/40463676

Jillo, G. Interviewed by the author. Moyale Subcounty, March 11, 2017. Code: A25-2017.

Jimoh, Shaykh Luqman. "The Yoruba Concept of Spirit Husband and the Islamic Belief in Intermarriage Between *Jinn* and Man: A Comparative Discourse." Paper presented at the International Conference on Humanities, Literature and Management, Dubai, United Arab Emirates, January 2015, 93–98.

Kaniki, M. H. Y. "The Impact of Islam on African Societies." Paper presented at the Seminar of Department of History, University of Dar-es-Salaam, November 1974.

Keener, Craig S. "Spirit Possession as a Cross-Cultural Experience." *Bulletin for Biblical Research* 20, no. 2 (2010): 215–36.

Kelly, Hilarie Ann. "From Gada to Islam: The Moral Authority of Gender Relations among the Pastoral Orma of Kenya." PhD diss., University of California, 1992.

Kenyon, Susan M. "The Case of the Butcher's Wife: Illness, Possession and Power in Central Sudan." In *Spirit Possession: Modernity and Power in Africa*, edited by Heike Behrend and Ute Luig, 89–108. Madison: University of Wisconsin Press, 1999.

———. "'Movable Feast of Signs': Gender in Zar in Central Sudan." *Material Religion: The Journal of Objects, Art and Belief* 3, no. 1 (2007): 62–75. https://doi.org/10.2752/174322007780095672

Khalifa, Najat, Tim Hardie, and Mohammad S. I. Mullick. "Jinn and Psychiatry: Comparison of Beliefs among Muslims in Dhaka and Leicester." Royal College of Psychiatrists, 2012. http://www.rpsych.ac.uk/workinpsychiatry/specialinterestgropus/spirituality/publicationsarchive.aspxk.

Kim, Caleb Chul-Soo. "Considering 'Ordinariness' in Studying Muslim Cultures and Discipleship." In *Discipleship in the 21st Century Mission*, edited by Timothy K. Park and Steve K. Eom, 177–92. Korea: East-West Center, 2014.

———. *Islam among the Swahili in East Africa*. 2nd ed. Nairobi: Acton Publishers, 2016.

———. "Supernaturalism in Swahili Islam: With Special Reference to the Therapeutic Cults of Jinn Possession." PhD diss., Fuller Graduate School, 2001.

Kim, Caleb Chul-Soo, John Travis, and Anna Travis. "Relevant Responses to Folk Muslims." In *From Seed to Fruit: Global Trends, Fruitful Practices, and Emerging Issues among Muslims*, edited by J. Dudley Woodberry, 265–78. Pasadena: William Carey Library, 2008.

Kirkegaard, Annemette. "Music and Transcendence: Sufi Popular Performances in East Africa." *Temenos* 48, no. 1 (June 2012): 29–48.

Kitaab Waaqa: Ka Kitaaba Deutarokanonikol/Apokrifa Qabu. Bible Society of Kenya, Nairobi. 1994.

Knibbe, Kim, and Peter Versteeg. "Assessing Phenomenology in Anthropology: Lessons from the Study of Religion and Experience." *Critique of Anthropology* 28, no. 1 (2008): 47–62. https://doi.org/10.1177/0308275X07086557

Knutsson, Karl Eric. *Authority and Change: A Study of the Kallu Institution among the Macha Galla of Ethiopia*. Goteborg: Etnografiska Museet, 1967.

Konso, A. Interviewed by the author. Moyale Subcounty, August 26, 2016. Code: A28-2016.

Kövecses, Zoltán. *Metaphor in Culture: The Universality and Variation*. Cambridge: Cambridge University Press, 2005.

Kraft, Charles H. *Defeating Dark Angels: Breaking Demonic Oppression in the Believer's Life*. Ann Arbor: Servant Publications / Vine Books, 1992.

Kreinath, Jens, ed. *The Anthropology of Islam Reader*. London: Routledge, 2011.

Krings, Matthias. "On History and Language of the 'European' Bori Spirits: Kano, Nigeria." In *Spirit Possession: Modernity and Power in Africa*, edited by Heike Behrend and Ute Luig, 53–67. Madison: University of Wisconsin Press, 1999.

Lakoff, George. *Women, Fire, and Dangerous Things: What Categories Reveal about the Mind*. Chicago: University of Chicago Press, 1987.

Lakoff, George, and Mark Johnson. *Metaphors We Live By*. Chicago: University of Chicago Press, 2008.

Lambek, Michael. *Human Spirits: A Cultural Account of Trance in Mayotte*. Cambridge: Cambridge University Press, 1981.

Langer, Robert, and Udo Simon. "The Dynamics of Orthodoxy and Heterodoxy: Dealing with Divergence in Muslim Discourses and Islamic Studies." *Die Welt Des Islams* 48, nos. 3/4 (2008): 273–88.

Larsen, Kjersti. *Where Humans and Spirits Meet: The Politics of Rituals and Identified Spirits in Zanzibar*. Vol. 5 of *Social Identities*. New York: Bergahn Books, 2008. https://www.jstor.org/stable/j.ctt9qd455

Laughlin, Vivian A. "A Brief Overview of al Jinn within Islamic Cosmology and Religiosity." *Journal of Adventist Mission Studies* 11, no. 1 (2015): 67–78. https://dx.doi.org/10.32597/jams/vol11/iss1/9/

Lebling, Robert. *Legends of the Fire Spirits: Jinn and Genies from Arabia to Zanzibar*. London: I. B. Tauris, 2010.

LeCompte, Margaret Diane., and Jean J. Schensul. *Analyzing and Interpreting Ethnographic Data*. Vol. 5 of *Ethnographer's Toolkit*. Walnut Creek: AltaMira, 1999.

———. *Designing and Conducting Ethnographic Research: An Introduction*. Vol. 1 of *Ethnographer's Toolkit*. Lanham: AltaMira, 2010.

Leistle, Bernhard. "From the Alien to the Other: Steps toward a Phenomenological Theory of Spirit Possession." *Anthropology of Consciousness* 25, no. 1 (2014): 53–90. https://doi.org/10.1111/anoc.12019

Leus, Ton, and Cynthia Salvadori. *Aadaa Boraanaa: A Dictionary of Borana Culture*. Addis Ababa: Shama Books, 2006.

Lewis, I. M. *Ecstatic Religion: A Study of Shamanism and Spirit Possession*. 2nd ed. London: Routledge, 1989.

———. "Exorcism and Male Control of Religious Experience." *Ethnos: Journal of Anthropology* 55, nos. 1–2 (1990): 26–40. https://doi.org/10.1080/00141844.1990.9981400.

———. *Religion in Context: Cults and Charisma*. 2nd ed. Cambridge: Cambridge University Press, 1996.

Lewis, I. M., and P. A. Jewell. "The Peoples and Cultures of Ethiopia." *Proceedings of the Royal Society of London. Series B, Biological Sciences* 194, no. 1114 (1976): 7–16.

Lim, Anastasia, Hans W. Hoek, and Jan Dirk Blom. "The Attribution of Psychotic Symptoms to Jinn in Islamic Patients." *Transcultural Psychiatry* 52, no. 1 (2014): 1–15. https://doi.org/10.1177/13634615145431

Love, Rick. *Muslims, Magic and the Kingdom of God: Church Planting among Folk Muslims*. Pasadena: William Carey Library, 2000.

Lukens-Bull, Ronald A. "Between Text and Practice: Considerations in the Anthropological Study of Islam." *Marburg Journal of Religion* 4, no. 2 (December 1999): 1–21. https://doi.org/10.17192/mjr.1999.4.3763

Ma, Wonsuk. "A 'First Waver' Looks at the 'Third Wave': A Pentecostal Reflection on Charles Kraft's Power Encounter Terminology." *Pneuma: The Journal of the Society for Pentecostal Studies* 19, no. 2 (1997): 189–206. https://doi.org/10.1163/157007497X00127.

Maalim Haro. Interviewed by the author. Saku Subcounty, July 20, 2016. Code: A11-2016.

Maarouf, Mohammed. *Jinn Eviction as a Discourse of Power: A Multidisciplinary Approach to Moroccan Magical Beliefs and Practices*. Leiden, The Netherlands: Brill, 2007.

Mackenrodt, Lisa. *Swahili Spirit Possession and Islamic Healing in Contemporary Tanzania: The Jinn Fly on Friday*. Hamburg: Verlag Dr. Kovac, 2011.

Makris, Gerasimos P. *Islam in the Middle East: A Living Tradition*. Oxford: Blackwell Publishing / Wiley-Blackwell, 2007.

Maranz, David. E. *Peace Is Everything: The World View of Muslims and Traditionalists in the Senegambia*. Dallas: International Museums of Cultures, 1993.

Marranci, Gabriele. *The Anthropology of Islam*. Oxford: Berg, 2008.

Masquelier, Adeline. "The Invention of Anti-Tradition: Dodo Spirits in Southern Niger," In *Spirit Possession in Africa*, eds. Heike Behrend & Ute Luig, Oxford: James Currey Ltd., 1999.

———. "The Bloodstain: Spirit Possession, Menstruation, and Transgression in Niger." *Ethnos: Journal of Anthropology* 76, no. 2 (June 2011): 157–82. https://doi.org/10.1080/00141844.2010.546867.

———. "Lightning, Death and the Avenging Spirits: Bori Values in a Muslim World." *Journal of Religion in Africa* 24, no. 1 (1994): 2–51. https://doi.org/10.1163/157006694X00020.

———. *Prayer Has Spoiled Everything: Possession, Power, and Identity in an Islamic Town of Niger*. Durham and London: Duke University Press, 2001.

Matory, Lorand J. "Rival Empires: Islam and the Religions of Spirit Possession among the Ọyọ́-Yorùbá." *American Ethnologist* 21, no. 3 (1994): 495–515. https://doi.org/10.1525/ae.1994.21.3.02a00030

McCauley, Robert N., and Emma Cohen. "Cognitive Science and the Naturalness of Religion." *Philosophy Compass* 5, no. 9 (2010): 779–92. https://doi.org/10.1111/j.1747-9991.2010.00326.x.

McIntosh, Janet. "The Edge of Islam: Religion, Language, and Essentialism on the Kenyan Coast." PhD diss., University of Michigan, 2002.

———. "Reluctant Muslims: Embodied Hegemony and Moral Resistance in a Giriama Spirit Possession Complex." *Royal Anthropological Institute* 10, no. 1 (2004): 91–112. https://www.jstor.org/stable/3804099.

———. *The Edge of Islam: Power, Personhood, and Ethno-Religious Boundaries on the Kenya Coast*. Durham: Duke University Press, 2009.

———. McKinney, Carol, V. *Globe-Trotting in Sandals: A Field Guide to Cultural Research*. Dallas: SIL International, 2000.

Megerssa, Gemetchu. "The Oromo World-View." *Journal of Oromo Studies* 12, nos. 1 & 2 (2005): 68–79.

Merga, Seyoum. "An Archaeological Survey of Islamic Shrines in Jimma Zone, South Western Ethiopia." Master's thesis, Addis Ababa University, 2012.

Mohamed, Abdisalam Yassin. "Sufi Poetry in Somali: Its Themes and Imagery." PhD diss., University of London, 1977.

Mohamed-Salih, El Tigani Mustafa. "Islam, Traditional Beliefs and Ritual Practices among the Zaghawa of Sudan." PhD diss., University of St. Andrews, 1991.

Mohammad, Worku H. M. "Folk Islam in Wallo: An Examination of Folk Islam Beliefs and Practices in Comparison to Charismatic Evangelicals." Master's thesis, Ethiopian Graduate School of Theology, 2008.

Moreau, Scott A., *The World of Spirits: A Biblical Study in the African Context*. Nairobi: Evangel Publishing House, 1990

Moreno, Rosa, E. Vega. *Creativity and Convention: The Pragmatics of Everyday Figurative Speech*. Amsterdam: John Benjamins Publishing Company, 2007.

Morton, Alice Louise. "Some Aspects of Spirit Possession in Ethiopia." PhD diss., University of London, 1973.

Mullick, Mohammad, Khalifa Najat, Nahar Jhunu, and Walker Dawn-Marie. "Beliefs about Jinn, Black Magic and Evil Eye in Bangladeshi: The Effects of Gender and Level of Education." *Mental Health, Religion, and Culture* 16, no. 7 (2013): 719–29.

Musk, Bill A. *The Unseen Face of Islam: Sharing the Gospel with Ordinary Muslims.* Sussex: MARC Evangelical Missionary Alliance, 1989.

Muslim, Imam. *Sahih Muslim*. Translated by 'Abdul Hamid Siddiqi. Book 1, no. 903–4. Beirut: Dar Al Arabia, (n.d.)

Natvig, Richard. "Oromos, Slaves, and the Zar Spirits: A Contribution to the History of the Zar Cult." *International Journal of African Historical Studies* 20, no. 4 (1987): 669–89. https://doi.org/10.2307/219657.

Nizah, Mohd Azmir bin Mohd, Anita Ismail, Muhammad Mustaqim Mohd Zarif, Adibah Sulaiman Mohamad, Hisham Muhammad Taky Eldin Kandil, and Paimah Atoma. "A Preliminary Study on the Islamic Creativity Practices." *Mediterranean Journal of Social Sciences* 6, no. 4 (July 2015): 517–22. http://dx.doi.org/10.5901/mjss.2015.v6n4s1p517

Nurea, Ma. Inteviewed by the author. Saku Subcounty, July 16, 2016. Code: A9-2016.

Nureah, H. Interviewed by the author. Saku Subcounty, July 18, 2016. Code: A8-2016.

O'Brien, Susan Marie. "Power and Paradox in Hausa *Bori*: Discourses of Gender, Healing and Islamic Tradition in Northern Nigeria." PhD Diss., University of Wisconsin, 2000.

Olali, Tom. "Alawiyya Sufism and the Sufi: Diffusion and Counter-Diffusion of Swahili Islamic Mysticism in the Lamu Archipelago, Kenya." *International Journal of Humanities, Social Sciences and Education* 1, no. 12 (2014): 1–11.

'Omar, 'Abdul Mannan. *Dictionary of the Holy Qur'an (Arabic-English)*. 2nd ed. USA: Noor Foundation International, 2003.

Osindo, Oscar. "An Examination of the Garre Space: The Concept of Fulla." PhD Diss., Oxford Centre for Mission Studies, 2018.

———."'Righteousness by Faith' in the Qur'an?" Chap. 10 in *A Man of Passionate Reflection: A Festschrift Honoring Jerald Whitehouse*, edited by Bruce L. Bauer. Berrien Springs: Andrews University Press, 2011.

Østebø, Terje. *Localising Salafism: Religious Change among Oromo Muslims in Bale, Ethiopia.* Vol. 12 of *Islam in Africa*, edited by Mauro Nobili, Rüdiger Seesemann, and Knut Vikør. Leiden: Brill, 2012.

Patton, Michael Quinn. *Qualitative Research and Evaluation Methods.* Thousand Oaks: Sage Publications, 2002.

Philips, Abu Ameenah Bilal. "Exorcism in Islam." PhD diss., University of Wales, 1993.

———. *The Exorcist Tradition in Islam*. Sharjah: Dar Al Fatah / Al Hidaayah Publishing, 1997.

Purzycki, Benjamin Grant, and Aiyana K. Willard. "MCI Theory: A Critical Discussion." *Religion, Brain and Behavior* 6, no. 3 (2015): 207–48. https://doi.org/10.1080/2153599X.2015.1024915.

Quinn, Naomi. "'Commitment' in American Marriage: A Cultural Analysis." Chap. 13 in *Directions in Cognitive Anthropology*, edited by Janet W. D. Dougherty. Chicago: University of Illinois Press, 1985.

Quinn, Naomi, and Dorothy Holland. "Culture and Cognition." Chap. 1 in *Cultural Models in Language and Thought*. New York: Cambridge University Press, 1987. https://doi.org/10.1017/CBO9780511607660.

Qumbo, M. Interviewed by the author. Moyale Subcounty, March 10, 2017. Code: A24-2017.

Qur'an Arabic Corpus. 2019. "*Jinn*" http://alim.org/quran/syntax/.

Rasmussen, Susan. "An Ambiguous Spirit Dream and Tuareg-Kunta Relationships in Rural Northern Mali." *Anthropological Quarterly* 88, no. 3 (Summer 2015): 635–63. https://www.jstor.org/stable/43652755.

Redfield, Robert. *Peasant Society and Culture*. Chicago: University of Chicago Press, 1956.

Rosander, Eva Evers. "The Islamization of 'Tradition' and 'Modernity.'" In *African Islam and Islam in Africa: Encounters between Sufis and Islamists*, edited by David Westerland and Eva Evers Rosander, 1–27. London: Hurst, 1997.

Rouget, Gilbert. *Music and Trance: A Theory of the Relations between Music and Possession*. Chicago: University of Chicago Press, 1985.

Ruto, Paul. "Qualitative Data Analysis Using Nvivo." Seminar Presentation at the Anthropological Research Methods Seminar at Africa International University, Nairobi Kenya, 2014.

Safari, J. F. *Making of Islam in East Africa*. Tanzania: Benedictine Publications Ndanda, 1994.

Samuel, Geoffrey. "Possession and Self-Possession: Towards an Integrated Mind-Body Perspective." In *Spirit Possession and Trance: New Interdisciplinary Perspectives*, 35–52. London: Bloomsbury Publishing/ Continuum, 2010.

Santo, Diana Espirito, Arnaud Halloy, Pierre Liénard, and Emma Cohen. "An Author Meets Her Critics: Around 'The Mind Possessed: The Cognition of Spirit Possession in an Afro-Brazilian Religious Tradition' by Emma Cohen." *Religion and Society: Advances in Research* 1 (2010): 164–76.

Saukko, Paula. *Doing Research in Cultural Studies: An Introduction to Classical and New Methodological Approaches*. London: Sage Publications, 2003.

Schensul, Stephen L., Jean J. Schensul, and Margaret Diane LeCompte. *Essential Ethnographic Methods: Observations, Interviews, and Questionnaires*. Vol. 2 of *Ethnographer's Toolkit*. Walnut Creek: AltaMira, 1999.

Schielke, Samuli, and Liza Debevec, eds. "Introduction." In *Ordinary Lives and Grand Schemes: An Anthropology of Everyday Religion*. New York: Berghahn Books, 2012.

Schlee, Günther. *Identities on the Move: Clanship and Pastoralism in Northern Kenya*. Manchester: Manchester University Press, 1989.

Schlee, Günther, and Abdullahi A. Shongolo. *Islam and Ethnicity in Northern Kenya and Southern Ethiopia*. Suffolk: James Currey, 2012.

Schmidt, Bettina E. "Varieties of Non-ordinary Experiences in Brazil: A Critical Review of the Contribution of Studies of 'Religious Experience' to the Study of Religion." *International Journal of Latin American Religion*, no. 1 (2017): 104–15.

Schmidt, Bettina E., and Lucy Huskinson. *Spirit Possession and Trance: New Interdisciplinary Perspectives*. London: Bloomsbury Publishing/ Continuum International Publishing, 2010. Available from http://site.ebrary.com.

———, eds. "Introduction." In *Spirit Possession and Trance: New Interdisciplinary Perspectives*, 1–15. Vol. 6 of *Continuum Advances in Religious Studies*. London: Bloomsbury Publishing/ Continuum, 2010.

Sesi, Josephine Katile Mutuku. "Social Change among Digo Muslim Women: Implications for Mission." PhD diss., Fuller Theological Seminary, 2007.

Sesi, Stephen Mutuku. "Prayer among the Digo Muslims of Kenya and Its Implications for Christian Witness." PhD diss., Fuller Theological Seminary, 2003.

Sharp, Lesley A. "Possessed and Dispossessed Youth: Spirit Possession of School Children in Northwest Madagascar." *Culture, Medicine and Psychiatry* 14, no. 3 (September 1990): 339–64. https://doi.org/10.1007/bf00117560

———. "The Possessed and the Dispossessed: Spirits, Identity, and Power in a Madagascar Migrant Town." PhD Dissertation, University of California, 1990.

Sheikh Abdi. Interviewed by the author. Moyale Subcounty, August 27, 2016. Code: B02-2016.

Sheikh Alisa. Interviewed by the author. Saku Subcounty, May 16, 2017. Code: B03-2017.

Sheikh Amr. Interviewed by the author. Saku Subcounty, May 17, 2017. Code: B06-2017.

Sheikh Gayo. Interviewed by the author. Saku Subcounty, May 16, 2017. Code: B05-2017.

Sheikh Ibra. Interviewed by the author. Moyale Subcounty, August 27, 2016. Code: B01-2016.

Sheikh Khadi Interviewed by the author. Moyale Subcounty, August 30, 2016. Code: B04-2016.

Sheikh Munur. Interviewed by the author. Saku Subcounty, May 18, 2017. Code: B07-2017.

Sheikh Umar. Personal interview by author. Saku Sub-County, May 16, 2017. Code: B08-2017. 16th May 2017.

Shenk, David W. "The African Christian and Islamic Mysticism: Folk Islam." Chap. 11 in *The African Christian and Islam*, edited by John Azumah and Lamin Sanneh. Carlisle: Langham Monographs, 2013.

Shore, Bradd. *Culture in Mind: Cognition, Culture, and the Problem of Meaning.* Oxford: Oxford University Press, 1996.

Smith, Jonathan A., Paul Flowers, and Michael Larkin. *Interpretative Phenomenological Analysis: Theory, Method and Research.* London: Sage Publications, 2009.

Smith, Stephen, Thomas B. Ward, and Ronald A. Finke (eds.). *The Creative Cognition Approach.* Massachussetss: Massachusetts Institute of Technology, 1995.

Spradley, James P. *The Ethnographic Interview.* New York: Holt, Rinehart and Winston, 1979.

———. *Participant Observation.* New York: Holt, Rinehart and Winston, 1980.

Stoller, Paul. *Fusion of the Worlds: An Ethnography of Possession among the Songhay of Niger.* London: University of Chicago Press, 1989.

Stroomer, Harry. *A Comparative Study of Three Southern Oromo Dialects in Kenya: Phonology, Morphology and Vocabulary.* Vol. 6 of *Cushitic Language Studies*, edited by Hans-Jürgen Sasse. Hamburg, Germany: Helmut Buske, 1987.

———. *A Grammar of Boraana Oromo (Kenya): Phonology, Morphology, Vocabularies.* Vol. 11 of *Cushitic Language Studies*, edited by Hans-Jürgen Sasse. Köln: Rüdiger Köppe Verlag, 1995.

Susare, C. Interviewed by the author. Saku Subcounty, July 18, 2016. Code: A48-2016.

Tablino, Paul. *The Gabra: Camel Nomads of Northern Kenya.* Nairobi, Kenya: Paulines Publications Africa, 1999.

Tarimo, F. Interviewed by the author. Moyale Subcounty, March 10, 2017. Code: A33-2017.

Tiilikainen, Marja. "Somali Saar in the Era of Social and Religious Change." Chap. 6 in *Spirit Possession and Trance: New Interdisciplinary Perspectives*, edited by Bettina E. Schmidt and Lucy Huskinson. London: Bloomsbury Publishing/Continuum, 2010.

Tola, Sintayehu. "The Conservation of Dirre Sheikh Hussein Heritage Site." Oromia Culture and Tourism Bureau, Ethiopia, 2000. https://www.hdm.lth.se/fileadmin/hdm/alumni/papers/CMHB_2008b/10_ETH_Sintayehu_Tola-Kenea_Sheikh_Hussein_Heritage_Site.pdf

Trimingham, Spencer, J. *Islam in Ethiopia.* London: Frank Cass, 1965.

Turunesh. Interviewed by the author. Saku Subcounty, July 29, 2016. Code: A36-2016.

Umashankar, Rachana Rao. "Defending Sufism, Defining Islam: Asserting Islamic Identity in India." PhD Diss., University of North Carolina at Chapel Hill, 2012. https://doi.org/10.17615/wfxk-zb34.

Varisco, Daniel Martin. *Islam Observed: The Rhetoric of Anthropological Representations*. New York: Palgrave Macmillan, 2005.

Walker, Sheila S. *Ceremonial Spirit Possession in Africa and Afro-America: Forms, Meaning, and Functional Significance for Individual Social Group*. Leiden: Brill, 1972.

Wang'ombe, Judy Wanjiru. *A Missiological Study of the Phenomenon of Spirit Possession among the Munyoyaya Women in the Madogo Location, Tana River District in Kenya: A Response to I.M. Lewis' Theory of Deprivation*. Master's thesis, Nairobi Evangelical Graduate School of Theology, 2007.

Waqo, W. Interviewed by the author. Saku Subcounty, May 19, 2017. Code: A45-2017.

Wario, Halkano Abdi. "Networking the Nomads: A Study of Tablighi Jama'at among the Borana of Northern Kenya." PhD diss., University of Bayreuth, 2012.

Watson, Elizabeth, and Hassan Hussein Kochore. "Religion and Climate Change in Northern Kenya: New Moral Frameworks for New Environmental Challenges?" *Journal for the Study of Religion, Nature and Climate* 6, no. 3 (2012): 319–43.

Whitehouse, Harvey. *Arguments and Icons: Divergent Modes of Religiosity*. New York: Oxford University Press, 2000.

———. *Modes of Religiosity: A Cognitive Theory of Religious Transmission*. Oxford: AltaMira, 2004.

———. "Modes of Religiosity." *CSSR Bulletin* 37, no. 4 (2008): 108–12.

Wood, John Colman. *When Men Are Women: Manhood among Gabra Nomads of East Africa*. Wisconsin: University of Wisconsin Press, 1999. https://books.google.ca/books?id=WuU3tcQS-asC

———. "When Men Are Women: Opposition and Ambivalence among Gabra Nomads of East Africa." PhD diss., Emory University, 1997.

Yaatani, D. Interviewed by the author. Saku Subcounty, December 26, 2015. Code: A1-2015.

Yarmolinsky, Benjamin Levi. "The Music of Jillala: A Repertoire of Spirits." PhD diss., City University of New York, 1991.

Yousif, Wahida. "Creativity in Islamic Thought: A Comparative Analysis." Master's thesis, International Islamic University, Malaysia, 1999.

Zafir, Muhammad Mustaqim Mohd, Mohd Azmir Mohd Nizah, Anita Ismail, and Adibah Mohamad. "Creating Creative and Innovative Muslim Society: Bid'ah as an Approach." *Asian Social Science* 9, no. 11 (2013): 121–27.

Zitelmann, Thomas. "Oromo Religion, Ayyaana and the Possibility of a Sufi Legacy." *Journal of Oromo Studies* 12, nos. 1 & 2 (July 2005): 80–99. [[bookmark: 2526]]

Langham Literature, with its publishing work, is a ministry of Langham Partnership.

Langham Partnership is a global fellowship working in pursuit of the vision God entrusted to its founder John Stott –

> *to facilitate the growth of the church in maturity and Christ-likeness through raising the standards of biblical preaching and teaching.*

Our vision is to see churches in the Majority World equipped for mission and growing to maturity in Christ through the ministry of pastors and leaders who believe, teach and live by the word of God.

Our mission is to strengthen the ministry of the word of God through:
- nurturing national movements for biblical preaching
- fostering the creation and distribution of evangelical literature
- enhancing evangelical theological education

especially in countries where churches are under-resourced.

Our ministry

Langham Preaching partners with national leaders to nurture indigenous biblical preaching movements for pastors and lay preachers all around the world. With the support of a team of trainers from many countries, a multi-level programme of seminars provides practical training, and is followed by a programme for training local facilitators. Local preachers' groups and national and regional networks ensure continuity and ongoing development, seeking to build vigorous movements committed to Bible exposition.

Langham Literature provides Majority World preachers, scholars and seminary libraries with evangelical books and electronic resources through publishing and distribution, grants and discounts. The programme also fosters the creation of indigenous evangelical books in many languages, through writer's grants, strengthening local evangelical publishing houses, and investment in major regional literature projects, such as one volume Bible commentaries like the *Africa Bible Commentary* and the *South Asia Bible Commentary*.

Langham Scholars provides financial support for evangelical doctoral students from the Majority World so that, when they return home, they may train pastors and other Christian leaders with sound, biblical and theological teaching. This programme equips those who equip others. Langham Scholars also works in partnership with Majority World seminaries in strengthening evangelical theological education. A growing number of Langham Scholars study in high quality doctoral programmes in the Majority World itself. As well as teaching the next generation of pastors, graduated Langham Scholars exercise significant influence through their writing and leadership.

To learn more about Langham Partnership and the work we do visit **langham.org**

www.ingramcontent.com/pod-product-compliance
Lightning Source LLC
Chambersburg PA
CBHW070235240426
43673CB00044B/1803